The Social Construction of Rationality

There are many different forms of rationality. In current economic discourse the main focus is on instrumental rationality and optimizing, while organization scholars, behavioural economists and policy scientists focus more on bounded rationality and satisficing. The interplay with value rationality or expressive rationality is mainly discussed in philosophy and sociology, but never in an empirical way. This book shows that not one, but three different forms of rationality (subjective, social and instrumental) determine the final outcomes of strategic decisions executed by major organizations.

Based on an argumentation analysis of six high-profile public debates, this book adds nuance to the concept of bounded rationality. The chapters show how it is socially constructed, and thus dependent on shared beliefs or knowledge, institutional context and personal interests. Three double case studies investigating the three rationalities illustrate how decision makers and stakeholders discuss the appropriateness of these rationalities for making decisions in different practice contexts. The first touches more on personal concerns, like wearing a niqab or looking at obscene art exposed in a public environment; the second investigates debates on improving the rights and position of specific minorities; and the third is based on the agreement on instrumental reasons for two kinds of investments, but the cost arguments are regarded less relevant when social norms or personal interests are violated.

The Social Construction of Rationality is for those who study political economy, economic psychology and public policy, as well as economic theory and philosophy.

Onno Bouwmeester is Associate Professor in Management and Consulting at Vrije Universiteit Amsterdam, the Netherlands, and responsible for a Masters specialization in Management Consulting as part of business administration.

Routledge Frontiers of Political Economy

The Social Construction of Rationality

Policy Debates and the Power of Good Reasons

Onno Bouwmeester

LONDON AND NEW YORK

First published 2017 by Routledge

2 Park Square, Milton Park, Abingdon, Oxfordshire OX14 4RN
52 Vanderbilt Avenue, New York, NY 10017

Routledge is an imprint of the Taylor & Francis Group, an Informa business

First issued in paperback 2018

British Library Cataloguing in Publication Data
A catalogue record for this book is available from the British Library

Library of Congress Cataloging in Publication Data
Names: Bouwmeester, Onno, 1966- author.
Title: The social construction of rationality: policy debates and the power of good reasons / Onno Bouwmeester.
Description: Abingdon, Oxon; New York, NY: Routledge, 2017. | Includes index.
Identifiers: LCCN 2016046615 | ISBN 9781138851085 (hardback) | ISBN 9781315724379 (ebook)
Subjects: LCSH: Rational choice theory. | Rational expectations (Economic theory)
Classification: LCC HM495.B68 2017 | DDC 302/.13–dc23
LC record available at https://lccn.loc.gov/2016046615

ISBN: 978-1-138-85108-5 (hbk)
ISBN: 978-0-367-03117-6 (pbk)

Typeset in Times New Roman
by Sunrise Setting Ltd., Brixham, UK

To all who experience the effects of human decisions

Contents

Illustrations

Figures

Tables

Preface

In our lives, we make many private and professional decisions. Some decisions relate to our subjectivity, like writing a book, deciding where to live or whom we trust. Next there are decisions with a social grounding that relate more to others and less to ourselves. This is when, for example, we support Fairtrade products on idealistic grounds, decide on rules in an organization or family, or participate in a demonstration to challenge rules or policies on social grounds. While these first two orientations for decision-making consider questions about what to do, we also want to be rational in how we realize effects. Do we travel by bus, bike or car to reach our destination? Do we buy or rent an apartment to live in? Do we, as management, try to realize employee satisfaction by investing in flexible work or in a more traditional work setting? Instrumental motivations inform the latter type of decisions. They are studied by economists, the social motives by the sociologist. But the relevance of the first one is overlooked in traditional debates on rationality, and so are the interactions between these three different rationalities. When studying economics and social philosophy, I was always wondering why in particular economists take rationality so narrowly.

The idea to write a book on these questions was born in 2008, when I went to a conference in Rome. Before I went, I got an email from Routledge editor Thomas Sutton to discuss a paper I had submitted and any ideas I would have regarding book projects. At that moment I had started my study of rationality based on the reasons expressed in public debates on controversial strategic decisions. Gijs van Houwelingen joined the project and first wrote a bachelor and later a Masters thesis on the subject. We had just published on the subject in a Dutch journal when I asked if this project would fit Routledge. Interest was evidenced by the emails I received from Routledge every year, to hear me out on the book project. Although Gijs stepped out of the project when he finished his studies at my university, his input was quite substantial when starting the project.

After having published a second article on the subject in 2013, I felt ready to send in a book proposal. I discussed the proposal with Andy Humphries and some friendly reviewers – Gjalt de Graaf, Ard-Pieter de Man and Brian Tjemkes – who gave great feedback and support. Saar Frieling helped me to better present the key ideas in the proposal. Receiving enthusiastic anonymous reviews from Routledge, and then also a contract in August 2014, was a great encouragement.

The book had to be written next to other research projects, PhD and Masters thesis supervision, teaching and management tasks, including being deputy head of my department in 2015. My main project was managing the transition from a traditional to a flexible work environment. It offered a great opportunity to observe how different rationalities interacted during this project, enriching my understanding of the last debate studied for the book. Towards the end of the writing process, several university colleagues and friends were willing to comment on all book chapters, which helped me a lot in improving clarity and readability. Some had a practitioner background as consultant, policy adviser or manager, while others were more academic. For reading one or two chapters and sharing their thoughts I would like to thank Koen van Bommel, Floor van den Born, Derek Harmon, Anne-Mette Jørgensen, Julia Mühlhaus, Diederik Ogilvie, Geert Smid, Ruben van Werven and Rogier Zelle. I further discussed some of my book ideas during a research seminar at the department of Management and Organization in May 2016, and at the 12th Biannual Conference on Organizational Discourse in July 2016. Both were held at Vrije Universiteit Amsterdam.

Substantial support for the book project also came from home. Phoebe, Tibor and Frank let me go for a few writing leaves: two weeks in Berlin in May 2015, two weeks in early spring 2016, two weeks in Hamburg in May 2016 and two weeks in Amsterdam in August 2016. I am really grateful for this opportunity to focus for the entire day on the book, and for creating the required mental space. Given the size and complexity of writing a monograph, it is the most challenging academic task I am aware of. What I also really enjoyed were the open questions I got from Frank and Tibor about the book, what it was about, and to explain to them what guides us in our decisions. I hope the effort pays off in making the rationality behind complex decisions more transparent to those who read the book. The book proves what many might forget, due to the growing dominance of economic conceptions of rationality, that we do not decide with our heads only, but also with our hearts.

Acknowledgements

Parts of this book and earlier versions of such parts have been published before (see below for the list of publications).

Bouwmeester, O. (2013) Field dependency of argumentation rationality in decision-making debates. *Journal of Management Inquiry*, 22(4), 415–33.

Bouwmeester, O. (2016) Expressive rationality and its contribution to complex decision making, in Reed, C., Sabelis, I., Ybema, S., Sims, D., Izak, M., Beech, N., Hardy, C., Keenoy, T., Oswick, C. and Thomas, R. (eds), *Organizational Discourse: Silence, Significance and White Space*. Amsterdam: Vrije Universiteit Amsterdam, pp. 24–6.

Houwelingen, G. van and Bouwmeester, O. (2008) Situationele rationaliteit in publieke besluitvorming. *Filosofie in Bedrijf*, 18(2), 26–40.

1   What is rational?

Introducing practical challenges for rational decision-making

At certain moments we have to make decisions with great future implications. Degrees of uncertainty can be high. Our decisions can also affect the interests of others, without being neatly aligned with our interests. The impact of other decisions may change over time: in the short run their impact is what we want, but in the long run their effects can become problematic. Usually we do not decide easily in such cases, as our deliberations are not immediately conclusive. Still, we intend to decide in a rational way. We want to be able to explain our decisions to ourselves and to others. We want to act on good reasons. But it is not always easy to determine what the rational thing to do is in such cases, or what the better reasons are in that moment.

Some difficult decisions we make once in a lifetime, whereas other complex decisions are more regular ones. How to celebrate a birthday is a returning difficult decision for many of us. Some decide not to celebrate it at all, due to the social complexities of who should be invited: do we want to please them, help them, not offend them? Usually, such reasons do not make the best combination of guests for a party. Since it is your birthday, not celebrating can be the best option for you, as it is an easy way to avoid a party you do not like. However, some ignore the possibility of disappointment for others and invite the friends they like the most, thus deciding on subjective instead of social motives. Other party dilemmas can be that a party for everyone you like becomes too expensive, is too much work to enjoy or includes too many nice people, which makes it impossible to socialize with them all. These issues question not *if* but *how* to celebrate. Making the right decision for yourself and for others when celebrating your birthday can be a challenge, as the social-rational perspective (what is important for others) and the expressive-rational perspective (what is important for me) can point in different directions.

A more strategic and long-term personal decision is the question of what profession we choose after graduating from secondary school. This is a time for deep deliberation, and the outcomes can have a lifelong impact. We might think of what interests us, what talents we have, what society might demand, what reputation our future occupation might have, the salaries that are paid, etc. Since you intend to choose a profession for the rest of your lifetime, or at least for a long time, job coaches advise to take your abilities and talents quite seriously from the start: for example, are you able to perform the job? This is a question based on instrumental means–end logic. Also, the question of whether you could do the job repeatedly without getting bored is important, which is more an expressive-rational consideration. To mind this subjective perspective seems good advice, but it is not the entire picture, as you are also choosing a job for the purposes of making a living. Those who opt for studies like philosophy or the arts should be aware that these choices might be fun for them during their studies, but not the best means to make a living after graduation. Expressive rationality (the fun aspect) and instrumental rationality (best means for making a living) might contradict each other.

Other difficult decisions have to be made as part of our professional lives. In many organizations, there are rules for promotion. Managers make them as simple as possible. For instance, in academia, publishing articles in top journals is more and more seen as an entry ticket to the profession. As journals have impact factors, the quality of the journal articles can be derived from how often they are cited. For managers, article acceptance by high-impact journals makes a good approximation of article quality, and a good approximation of academic performance. And even better, managers do not need to read or understand such articles while being able to assess their quality. Measuring academic performance based on monographs is more difficult, so they appear less in the lists for requirements of making a next career step. For an academic it thus seems rational to focus on writing high-impact articles, as it is the most effective way to get promoted or tenured. This reasoning is instrumental rational. However, was the profession you wanted to enter that of 'academic article writer' or 'academic' in a broader sense? And who should define and develop the professional standards – the manager, with his easy performance indicators, or the entrepreneurial professional, who develops the field with new ideas that might not get published in high-impact journals immediately? How rational is it from the perspective of the manager to impose such simple standards in a field that is grounded in more complex and differentiated professional values? And how rational is it to follow management guidance if you have to compromise your professional intuitions? Or do we need to balance these different perspectives that are instrumental rational (increasing the output of high-impact articles), social rational (enacting professional values) and expressive rational (following your professional intuitions)?

Some professionals make the courageous decision to become an entrepreneur, which creates a new challenging field for making decisions. Their rationality needs to be more instrumental and economic to make a living and to run a business. Thus, entrepreneurs need a sound business plan to convince investors. They should address the necessary costs and investments and estimate revenues they want to realize. However, for entrepreneurs this will not be the whole story. The motives for becoming an entrepreneur could also be that they dislike bosses or have a desire to be more autonomous in making their own decisions, which are expressive-rational grounds for starting a business. When we speak about a social entrepreneur, there might even be social-rational motives involved, which would explain why, for example, they started their enterprise in green energy, slow food or fair trade. These social motives explain why it is not only a matter of making the right choice for a social entrepreneur in person, but also for society more broadly. When convincing green or socially engaged investors, these arguments might also be persuasive, as for them it is rational to invest in such a social enterprise, as it meets the values they want to support.

What we consider good reasons to act on stems from different domains of rationality. These rationalities can be more aligned, as in the discussed case of the social entrepreneur, where expressive and social rationality are aligned. However, what is rational from a perspective of professional values is not necessarily the same from a management perspective, as in the example from academia. And what is rational from a personal perspective (the fun aspect of a study or job) is not necessarily so in economic terms (as fun jobs might pay less). Also, what is rational from a social perspective (keeping your friends happy) is not necessarily so from a subjective point of view (keeping yourself happy), as illustrated with the birthday party. What is rational depends on the perspective we choose for evaluation.

Within each rationality perspective we can also find variation or disagreement. Social rationality can relate to smaller or larger circles, or different social perspectives, such as organizational, professional, political, legal or higher-class versus lower-class values (MacIntyre 1988); they only partly overlap. Expressive rationality refers to subjective motives, which makes them as diverse as subjectivity is (Engelen 2006; Scherer 2011). Also, instrumental or economic rationality, which is widely acknowledged as very dominant in current understandings of rationality (Diesing 1976; Elster 2009; Gigerenzer and Sturm 2012; Kahneman 2011), shows a huge variety in suggested good reasons, as our rationality is fundamentally bounded (Gigerenzer and Selten 2001; March and Simon 1958). Given this variety in motives and understandings, rational decision-making is, in practice, the result of much debate and deliberation, before calculation or optimization would even be possible. Decision-making debates that exchange good reasons to act on will be analysed in this book. They are the best context to further explore rationality in its instrumental, social and expressive appearances, and how the three rationalities interact.

Open questions in theorizing on rationality

Instrumental rationality is limited by our boundedness

Instrumental rationality has been central to economists' understanding of rationality for a long time (Elster 1989; Stewart 1995; Tomer 2008; Weber 1972). Economists seek the most efficient or effective goal realization by aiming at optimization (Klamer 1987; McCloskey 2016; Weirich 2004). Gigerenzer and Sturm (2012: 245) characterize it as the 'default notion' regarding rationality. Economic goals are usually set to optimize utility, profit or welfare, and the effort goes into selecting the right means to reach the predefined goal as efficiently as possible. Instrumental rationality is, thus, effect- or goal-oriented (Habermas 1988: 127), as in the case of an entrepreneur trying to attract investors with a sound business plan that links investments to expected revenues.

What matters most for instrumental rationality is a good understanding of the relevant causalities. The selected means should serve as causes to realize the intended effects regarding set goals like utility or profit maximization. Criteria to be rational relate to consistency, calculability and well-supported beliefs regarding causalities (Henderson 2010: 35). Less rational would be not choosing the most effective or efficient means, or not fully realizing the intended effects, especially if their realization is possible against acceptable efforts. When we can assume feasibility when aiming at optimizing effectiveness or efficiency, this provides additional good reasons to act on (Majone 1992; Tinbergen 1956). And indeed, not only economists consider it more rational to reach one's objectives without using ineffective or superfluous means.

However, we can ask ourselves how often we behave truly rational in this way when making decisions. For instance, do we really maximize utility when deciding on a holiday as a consumer? Do we investigate all holiday options? Can we compare these options based on costs and expected utilities? Mostly, our information is incomplete, our search strategy quite random and our willingness to compare options rather limited. Planning a holiday is a buying decision that we spend a relatively large amount of time on; however, it is hardly the goal of optimization that is at play here. Consequently, optimization calculus as the ultimate way of being rational is criticized for being a theoretical illusion (Gigerenzer and Selten 2001; Klamer 1987; Klein 2001; McCloskey 2016).

The first scholars to criticize this mathematical optimization conception of rationality were March and Simon (1958). They argued that the rationality assumptions of economists are flawed. Human beings are, at best, bounded rational, and, thus, not able to optimize efficiency and effectiveness to the maximum. Their brains do not work like computers, and if they were to try to optimize, it would take them too much time before a decision could be made. Elster (2009: 64) follows up on this critique by arguing that less is more. He criticizes the implied suggestion of 'hyperrationality'. The costs for optimization are so high that they outweigh the possible benefits of being fully rational. Gigerenzer and Selten (2001) argue likewise by suggesting that using heuristics in making decisions often produces better results than optimization. Paradoxically, satisficing, as argued by March and Simon (1958), is, therefore, the more rational procedure, given our mental limitations regarding optimization. Optimization calculus is the exceptional case, and might occur when computers are programmed to make buying and selling decisions on how stocks should be traded, or perhaps when logistics can be optimized to increase efficiency in the transport sector. However, these are the more extreme cases in decision-making. Satisficing is more the standard in human decision-making, which makes bounded rationality a concept with more external validity than rationality as conceptualized by economists.

Still, bounded rationality is also limited by its focus on satisficing objectives. The underlying means–end orientation cannot cover all the kinds of good reasons we are willing to accept when evaluating or preparing for a decision. The reasons available when arguing based on bounded rationality are still instrumental and refer to causalities that can be proved and have a status of being objective and fact-based

(Sandberg and Tsoukas 2011). The focus of instrumental rationality is on *how* we can do things better, not on the goals people want to achieve. It excludes the question of why we think certain objectives or values are worth aiming at. Instrumental rationality thus ignores many good reasons to act on; for instance, the motives for action that Weber (1972: 12) calls value rational. Such reasons can also be socially constructed and accepted as good reasons to act on, next to instrumental-rational arguments. This is the case when socially engaged investors want to invest their money in a social enterprise. Instrumental reasons still remain important by selecting a sufficiently profitable social enterprise as a means to realize their social objective, but profitability is not the main ground for deciding in that case. The main ground is a value consideration.

Beyond instrumental rationality: good reasons to act on grounded in norms and values

Instrumental rationality offers a narrow version of human rationality, by its focus on means–end logics and on how to realize objectives effectively or efficiently. In practice, we rarely express good reasons for action by only referring to expected profits, efficiency or utility maximums. Often we explain our decisions differently when investing in green start-ups for instance (Bergset 2015). Weber (1972), therefore, distinguishes between instrumental rationality and value rationality. Value rationality helps with setting and discussing standards, norms and principles for evaluating what we do. Values can be to fight poverty, to protect the weak, to consider the interests of future generations and to encourage freedom of expression. These values need to have intersubjective validity in order to get social presence (Habermas 1988). Diesing (1976) is another sociologist who shares the criticism that instrumental rationality offers too narrow a definition of the concept of rationality. He adds social, legal and political forms of rationality to what he labels, in contrast, as technical and economic rationality. He demonstrates how many good reasons for action can stem from disciplines and logics other than only technical or economic means–end argumentations. Political rationality (Diesing 1976; Eisenhardt and Zbaracki 1992; Harrison 1993) aims, for instance, at getting sufficient stakeholder support to establish the power needed for securing the sufficient protection of shared interests, thus demonstrating intersubjective or social logics. In the example of writing monographs, as some academics still do, the academic's own professional values appear to counteract instrumental logics as increasingly imposed by academic management, which reward writing high-impact articles for making an academic career, as they contribute most to the ranking of a university.

Intersubjective reasoning in support of social rationality depends on support by shared interests, values, norms or principles (Elster 1989, 2006; Satow 1975; Weber 1972). As these are shared, they can legitimize what we do in a social context. Still, the groups that share them can differ, and so do the values they share, as is the case with different political parties, or between city and countryside. Such differences can be acknowledged by the concept of 'social rationality' (Churchman 1962; Dahms 1997; Diesing 1976; Sen 1993). Social rationality has validity for specific groups of people (Diesing 1976; MacIntyre 1988), or times and places when social values are grounded in fashions, traditions or local customs (Abrahamson 1996; Esposito 2011; Kilduff and Mehra 1997). Social rationality is, thus, bound to context and depends on the shared social nature of such good reasons to act on.

Value rationality as defined by Weber (1972) and Habermas (1988) articulates a universal extreme within the possibilities of social rationality. The ambition is being valid for mankind as a whole, and preferably permanently so. Still, critiques on the universalistic pretence of these more deontological ways of social reasoning abound as well (ten Bos and Willmott 2001; Diesing 1976; Fisher and Freshwater 2014; Gigerenzer 2010; MacIntyre 1988), as more local social and moral values also inspire principles, norms or national laws. Weber (1972: 12) was aware of these more traditional motives for action, but he considers them not as rational as value rationality, or instrumental rationality, but more a borderline case. Still, we can accept them as good reasons to act on when others legitimize their decisions, or try to prepare them. By saying we did follow the law, or by aiming at giving men and women equal career opportunities, we adhere, for instance, to traditional values shared in a liberal and Western higher-class culture, which is a specific social context. The context of Chinese entrepreneurship demands its own social rationality (Zhu 2015). In addition, actors will be bounded by their social rationality (Gigerenzer 2010; Taylor 2016), as they are when applying instrumental-rational arguments to prepare for their actions. They cannot know every law, norm, social principle or value applicable to the relevant context and, thus, often act motivated by social heuristics. Thus, social rationality as defined here includes both Weber's value rationality and traditional rationality. They are the general and local extremes in a more inclusive concept of good reasons that we share, and that have inter-subjective validity for particular social groups that can be smaller or bigger, and more or less subject to time boundaries.

Still, when combining instrumental rationality and social rationality, we miss out on one more rationality perspective; we do not relate to a social perspective when decisions mainly have relevance for the decision maker when, for example, making a career decision. Sometimes, instrumental considerations are hardly relevant because realization of the decision is quite simple. For instance, when you decide to take a nap and give room to your fatigue, instrumental- and social-rational considerations are far less relevant than your personal desire. Only if the situation does not allow you to fall asleep can social consideration become more important than your subjective needs, but there are numerous situations where this social perspective is not relevant. What matters most, then, is the subjectivity of the decision maker, or, alternatively, of important stakeholders affected by a decision. This subjective or affective perspective is rarely explored, and usually played down as irrational in debates on rationality by those who discuss instrumental- and social-rational points of view, like Bergset (2015), Colic-Peisker (2016), Diesing (1976), Gigerenzer (2010), Habermas (1988), Harrison (1993), MacIntyre (1988), March and Simon (1958) or Weber (1972). Still, in practice this subjective perspective offers important orientation to what we consider the right thing to do.

Beyond social rationality: good reasons to act on grounded in our subjectivity

Usually, emotions, desires and personal impulses are seen as undermining rationality. When calculating optimal decisions, emotions can negatively interfere. With the use of many experiments, Kahneman (2011) shows how our feelings can lead to severe mistakes in our judgments; for instance, due to over-optimism or over-confidence. Moods or an illness like depression or euphoria can also disturb balanced emotional assessment (Li *et al*. 2014; Scherer 2011). Weber (1972: 12) also considers affective judgments mostly beyond rationality; even though he considers affective and emotional judgments important in explaining what we do, they are not generally based upon a rational impulse. However, he does argue that sometimes they *can* be based upon a rational impulse when feelings become conscious, or supportive towards values. Habermas is slightly more positive than Weber, but still overly sceptical. He considers expressive reasoning based on affects, feelings and emotions weaker than instrumental or moral reasoning. That is because a general consensus based on what he calls universal 'discourse' is not possible (Habermas 1988: 41–5). Still, aesthetic judgments by art critics or therapeutic criticism by a therapist can help us to reflect on the authenticity and truthfulness of artistic and personal expressions. Such critiques can help prevent self-deception. Subjective grounds for our actions, such as taste as ground for deciding what to eat, or sympathy as motive for engaging in friendship, benefit from such authenticity (Habermas 1988: 42). Scherer (2011: 341) is positive towards the rationality of emotions and argues that the rationality of our feelings can be assessed by their 'reasonableness'. He contends that it can even be irrational not to feel anger in certain situations, or not to feel anything at all. Our social environment mostly considers that inappropriate. Withholding emotions is, thus, no entry ticket to being more rational.

Expressive arguments that give good reasons for individual action can refer to someone's enthusiasm, commitments, desires, feelings of sympathy or to opposite emotions such as fear, dislike, anger, etc. (Greenspan 2004; Li *et al*. 2014; Scherer 2011). Engelen (2006) labels reasoning based on expressive or subjective motives, therefore, expressive rational (see also Hargreaves Heap 2001). Expressive rationality helps us make decisions that have personal relevance, such as celebrating a birthday or choosing a profession, or professional questions which have great personal impacts. It also helps us to explain to others why we are going to do what we do, and to legitimate why we did what we did. Such feelings help to assess what is relevant to us (Scherer 2011). Most of us can understand that we try to avoid what scares us, unless we think it is quite important for us to ignore our fears in certain situations, like when accepting surgery, dental treatment or accepting a great challenge that might help us to develop ourselves.

Ignoring the subjective and affective aspects of rationality gets more and more contested by authors who see the benefits of including expressive rationality in a more comprehensive idea of rationality (Bouwmeester 2013; Calabretta *et al*. 2016; Engelen 2006; Fisher and Freshwater 2014; Gigerenzer and Selten 2001; Haidt 2001). The difficult decisions discussed at the start of this introduction hardly required instrumental-rational deliberation, as realization was mostly not very complex for these cases. They did require some social-rational deliberation, as with the birthday party, the career decisions and the decision to become a social entrepreneur. Still, all these decisions required expressive rationality: what birthday party suits me? What profession inspires me? What motivates me to write a monograph or become a social entrepreneur? These types of decisions are mainly supported by subjective motives, and their character can be more or less hedonic in the sense of pleasure seeking (Cabanac and Bonniot-Cabanac 2007), aesthetic in the sense of creating a good and emotionally fulfilling life (Fisher and Freshwater 2014) or authentic in seeking truthful expressions (Habermas 1988).

Expressive rationality offers motives somewhat similar to social-rational ones. The main difference with social rationality is not so much in the content; we can feel anger when something is against moral principles, which then makes the social and expressive motives quite aligned in pushing towards a conclusion. However, expressive rationality is not grounded in intersubjective agreement, but in personal motives underlying these agreements. The main difference is, thus, in the source for evaluation: social values, norms or principles versus our own subjective feelings, impulses, desires or intuitions. Expressive rationality refers to what we value subjectively or as a single person. Expressive arguments can, for instance, explain the rationality of what we do during a holiday, how we dress, what music we listen to, etc. Acting on personal impulses, interests or motives can make our actions rational from a subjective perspective (Bouwmeester 2013; Engelen 2006; Greenspan 2004; Li *et al.* 2014; Scherer 2011). However, as we share our subjective nature with other humans, we mostly understand each other's subjectivity quite well, even if our feelings about an event differ from those of others; we are able to empathize with someone who has different tastes, passions or interests. This empathy makes expressive rationality more convincing for giving reasons to act on, more so than usually assumed in the rationality debate, where it is rather overlooked (Townley 2008: 157). Expressive rationality is a third complementary perspective, next to social and instrumental rationality.

Three complementary rationalities

The discussed theoretical studies indicate three types of rationality. The first and most often presupposed rationality is instrumental. Still, we are quite bounded in the way we are able to use it when legitimating and preparing for decisions. Second, there is social rationality, where value rationality is the more universal extreme next to legal rationalities with a national scope or political rationality, which is even more local. The local forms of social rationality can depend on community, class, time, etc. Such social rationalities are much more referred to in practice than Weber's value rationality, despite his theoretical authority. Third, there is expressive rationality, which is the least discussed in theory, but covers a whole range of reasons that have a strong presence in practice when preparing for many kinds of key decisions. Table 1.1 summarizes the key differences between the three rationalities as discussed up until now.

As the marriage example shows, the three rationalities can all help to convince us that our actions are based on good reasons. These good reasons cannot convince

Table 1.1 Core differences of instrumental, social and expressive rationality

Rationalities	Instrumental	Social	Expressive
Rational motives socially constructed as:	*Objective*, grounded in fact-based reasons	*Intersubjective*, grounded in shared social values, norms or principles	*Subjective*, grounded in a personal interest or impulse
Good reasons based on:	Cause–effect or means–end arguments	Deductive arguments that apply socially shared norms, principles, values, ideals, etc.	Motivational arguments based on personal desires, interests, sympathies, moral intuitions, etc.
Assessment based on:	Maximizing or satisficing effectiveness, efficiency, feasibility	Social acceptability	Alignment with personal motives, interests
Fit with Weber's four types of social action	1. Effect- or goal-oriented, and based on calculation	2. Based on values 3. Based on traditions	4. Based on affective motives
Example:	I want to marry you because it will raise my standard of living	I want to marry you as this is what society expects me to do, now you are pregnant	I want to marry you because it is my own and deepest desire

everyone always or in all situations. In Western liberal societies, expressive rationality will be quite convincing as grounds for marriage and, equally, for divorce. However, in many religious communities, marriage is far more acceptable than living together without being married. And in societies where social security is low, marriage can have an important instrumental value. Romantic love is a luxury only available to so many people in Western societies in recent times (De Botton 2016). Today, we can hardly imagine loving differently. Still, in the case of divorce, social and instrumental considerations can offer strong counterarguments, especially when there are children involved. Thus, all rationalities seem to matter, and a truly rational decision might be a balanced one.

Reviewing theories on rationality leads to the conclusion there might be three general types that provide good reasons to act on in practice. However, rationality scholars have hardly explored how we *do* legitimate decisions by giving good reasons, and which reasons we consider good, when making real-life decisions. Rationality based on the actual reasons put forward publicly when preparing, making or challenging decisions is rarely studied. Some exceptions are Cabantous *et al.* (2010), Calabretta *et al.* (2016), Fisher and Freshwater (2014) and Townley (1999, 2002, 2008), but still these scholars do not systematically study argumentations. This is a missed opportunity, since many controversial decisions are discussed in newspapers when people disagree, want to change proposed decisions or want to defend what they do. Decision-making takes time in such controversial cases and the underlying reasoning develops stepwise, so studying them requires 'longitudinal case analysis', as earlier suggested by Townley (2002: 177). Not everyone will say everything in such debates, but since many stakeholders are involved, all positions can potentially be articulated if there is freedom of expression and stakeholders are sufficiently able to express themselves.

Researching multiple rationalities

Rationality defined as having good reasons to act on (Davidson 2004: 169; Elbanna 2006: 3; Elbanna and Child 2007: 433; Elster 2009: 2; Engelen 2006: 427; Gigerenzer and Sturm 2012: 243–5; Green 2004: 655; Henderson 2010: 32) can cover good reasons based on instrumental rationality, social rationality and expressive rationality. Expressive reasons to act on are the least discussed due to the focus in economics on utility calculations or on universal and uncontested values and principles that are assumed to guide our decisions inspired by Weber's ideas. Local social rationalities get more attention (MacIntyre 1988), but they are also under-explored. That most studies on rationality are quite theoretical until now might explain this current focus. Studies argue, at best, based on stylized illustrations, that there are some flaws in predominant rationality understandings (Davidson 2004; Henderson 2010; MacIntyre 1988). Rationality studies are rarely based on a more grounded theory approach, starting inductively by analysing the given reasons in cases where complex decisions are legitimized, as in Bouwmeester (2013) versus van Houwelingen and Bouwmeester (2008) or versus von Werder (1999). The most discussed empirical studies on rationality are limited to experimental research designs, as reported by Kahneman (2011). These designs illustrate how little rational we are, due to our boundedness and due to the existence of shortcuts that often work out fine, but not in the experimental settings designed to unmask them. However, these exceptional designs are also the biggest weakness of such studies. This is the reason that Gigerenzer (2010: 548) and Cabantous *et al.* (2010) argue that rationality should be studied in its natural environment.

When studying rationality, a grounded and exploratory research approach is quite possible, as we discuss our decisions a lot, sometimes among friends and partners, sometimes in public and also in written form. Newspapers report the pros and cons of many contested decisions. The only thing we need to do is to study the given reasons and interpret their rationality. Are the reasons instrumental and cause–effect-based? Are they based on rules and principles, as in social rationality, by applying deductive reasoning in arguments from classification? Or are the arguments motivational, based on personal impulses, as in expressive rationality? We could ask in what situations the different rationalities appear, and for what kind of decisions. We could wonder if expressive rationality appears in public decision-making at all, questioning the relevance of such decisions for our own personal lives. This book seeks to answer such questions by studying public debates on major strategic decisions by asking: *how are different publicly debated decisions supported and challenged by arguments, and what kind of rationality or irrationality do these arguments express?* The book will answer that question based on argumentation analysis inspired by Toulmin's (1994) ideas, studying the rationality behind micro arguments in the context of debates. Within this context, rationality is socially constructed but also challenged. The social construction of rationality and its performativity in shaping decisions is, thus, not limited beforehand to forms of instrumental rationality only, as in Cabantous *et al.* (2010) or Racko (2011). Considering debates in our research context implies the analysis of all rationalities expressed in complex argumentations, based on micro arguments that are connected in such debates. Next to the debates, which can be seen as discourses, there is a wider research context. It is the history of events as reflected in these debates, and influenced by them. Stakeholders and decision makers create events, they realize projects, change institutions or decide not to do so, due to the support or resistance they experience in the debates. Here, the analysis reaches the level of behaviours, and thus enables a comparison of the rationality of words and deeds, as called for by Gigerenzer (2010).

The book chapters will all be introduced shortly in the next sections, including their main findings. First, methodology will be explained (Chapter two), then three double case studies are discussed, each with the main focus on another rationality (Chapters three, four and five). An overall cross-case analysis follows in Chapter six, and the book concludes with implications for practice in Chapter seven.

Argumentation analysis to explore rationalities

Rationality is usually explored by means of theoretical studies or experimental studies. Still, rationality defined as 'having good reasons to act on' could also be studied with the help of argumentation analysis, as such good reasons are usually expressed as arguments that legitimize a decision in a public context. Chapter two presents a method to explore rationality with the help of argumentation analytical tools, as initiated by Toulmin (1994). These tools allow for exploring different types of arguments that prepare for or legitimate action by explicating their warrants. Based on the warrant, the rationality of these arguments can be identified as expressive, social or instrumental. By studying the relations between arguments pro and con, critical and supportive interactions between different rationalities can be identified. The data used are arguments presented in articles from newspapers and magazines retrieved from LexisNexis. They report about six different publicly debated decisions; cases that are theoretically sampled to study each of the three rationalities in two countries. The main contribution of Chapter two is the presentation of the method of analysis used in the remainder of the book. It is a new means to study how expressive, social and instrumental rationality interact and develop over time, when guiding practical and complex decisions.

Expressive rationality and complex public decisions

Chapter three explores expressive rationality first, as it is the most under-explored aspect of rationality. In academic debates on rationality, emotions are commonly said to disturb our rationality, like making a decision for the short term instead of the long term, or being over-optimistic. However, in many situations we are served best by an emotional orientation to guide our decisions. Expressive rationality can help being rational in deciding when to go to bed, whom to marry or what job to choose. Some of these decisions are quite important for us and have a long-term impact. The question posed in Chapter three is: how can expressive rationality help improve decision-making when decisions are strategic and public? In the debate on McCarthy's somewhat obscene sculpture of Santa Claus in the Netherlands, and in the veil-ban debate in the UK, expressive rationality dominates the debates due to the strong subjective relevance of the debated questions. Expressive rationality appears to be quite powerful in rebutting suggestions of irrationality based on social- and instrumental-rational evaluations that assess wishes as unacceptable or unrealistic. Thus, expressive rationality deserves a more central position in academic debates on rationality, where our subjectivity has been downplayed for too long (cf. Kahneman 2011). In the end, it is us who are the ones who decide what is rational or not, and ignoring our expressive rationality proves to be little helpful in reaching good decisions.

Social rationality and complex public decisions

Chapter four explores the social rationality behind publicly debated decisions, where decision makers and their critics refer mainly to socially shared norms, principles and values as sources for legitimation. Current conceptions of social rationality range from generally shared values or principles with universal character to those that are more temporal, local and community-based. Local values, principles and norms can guide action by explicating what is expected from a decision maker in a more limited social context. Between these local contexts, values can differ or even contradict each other. However, values, norms or principles can also be contested due to a mismatch with expressive rationality when people get angry at the rules, or by a mismatch with instrumental-rational logics when value realization becomes utopian or infeasible. The analysis of two public debates, one on the failures of multicultural integration policies in the Netherlands and the other on the extension of Gurkha rights in the UK, both illustrate these tensions. Such irrationalities can be corrected by better aligning social rationality with the two other rationalities. Social rationality can solve value conflicts internally by defining a hierarchy of values. The identified rationality interactions challenge Weber's (1972) traditional view of values as the highest form of rationality, as well as the opposite position of value relativism (MacIntyre 1988).

Instrumental rationality and complex public decisions

The third double case study discussed in Chapter five is on instrumental rationality. Instrumental rationality is widely acknowledged as fundamental for legitimizing how we execute our decisions, as long as we acknowledge that we are bounded rational. It aims at realizing feasible effects in the outside world effectively and efficiently. Thus, instrumental rationality helps to find good reasons to act on. However, efficient acts based on instrumental rationality can still feel irrational sometimes, if at odds with social or expressive rationality. This chapter explores how decisions that are mainly based on instrumental-rational considerations can be challenged or supported by social- and expressive-rational arguments. In the debate on Heathrow's extension, the challenges are merely social rational. The debate frames the narrow focus on the instrumental reasons for extension as irrational due to unacceptable social and environmental damage by 'unintended' consequences. In the Dutch debate on flex work, which means working when and where you want, the counterarguments are mainly expressive rational. They criticize flex work for being presented as a one-size-fits-all solution. This is irrational due to an unacceptable mismatch with the likings and abilities of substantial groups of people that are forced into flex-work settings. The mismatch between instrumental-rational logics and expressive or social rationality creates irrationalities in practice when realized effects are evaluated as upsetting or even immoral. These irrationalities have been ignored in academic debates, which usually frame emotional or social impulses as irrational against the standards of instrumental rationality (cf. Kahneman 2011).

Observed interactions between expressive, social and instrumental rationality

The question posed in Chapter six is: how can expressive, social and instrumental rationality influence each other? A cross-case analysis of six public debates shows many interplays, ranging from supportive to very critical and challenging. Critical rationality interactions based on expressive rationality are grounded in motivational arguments combined with arguments from analogy or generalization. Expressive rationality can indicate self-deception in internal evaluation. In evaluating social and instrumental rationality, tensions appear, such as frustrating norms or upsetting effects. Social-rationality evaluation indicates an internal value conflict, and in evaluating expressive or instrumental rationality, tensions such as unacceptable desires or immoral effects are highlighted. Social evaluations are mainly based on arguments from classification. Instrumental rationality provides a reality check for expressive- and social-rational arguments by evaluating the efficiency, effectiveness and feasibility of personal impulses or social values, using arguments from cause. It can indicate internal means–end inconsistencies based on analogical reasoning; for instance, when comparing intended consequences with realized consequences. All critical rationality evaluations help to determine or correct forms of irrationality, whereas positive cross-rationality evaluations can result in mutual support.

How to check for irrationalities when preparing complex strategic decisions

Decision makers and consultants aim towards rational decision-making, especially when the stakes are high and decisions complex. Possible irrationalities need to be avoided, and are, thus, the first to be acknowledged. Based on the study of six public debates on strategic decisions, different kinds of irrationality are found that affect five inductively identified key elements found in decision preparation: the decision's purpose, pros, cons, conditions and policies for execution. The first three key elements refer predominantly to expressive and social rationality in establishing good reasons to act on. The last two are more grounded in instrumental rationality. Three forms of internal inconsistency and six forms of cross-rationality contradictions can undermine the rationality of these key elements. By using standards of expressive rationality, irrationalities appear as emotional misfits (like self-deception), frustrating norms or upsetting effects. When using standards of social rationality, irrationalities indicate value conflicts or wrong application, intolerable desires or immoral effects. Standards of instrumental rationality indicate means–end inconsistencies (like unintended effects), unrealistic desires or utopian values or ideals as forms of irrationality. Chapter seven proposes questions that help to identify these irrationalities, in order to support decision makers and their advisers in better addressing them.

References

Abrahamson, E. (1996) Management fashion. *Academy of Management Review*, 21(1), 254–85.

Bergset, L. (2015) The rationality and irrationality of financing green start-ups. *Administrative Sciences*, 5(4), 260–85.

Bos, R. ten and Willmott, H. (2001) Towards a post-dualistic business ethics: Interweaving reason and emotion in working life. *Journal of Management Studies*, 38(6), 769–93.

Bouwmeester, O. (2013) Field dependency of argumentation rationality in decision-making debates. *Journal of Management Inquiry*, 22(4), 415–33.

Cabanac, M. and Bonniot-Cabanac, M.-C. (2007) Decision making: Rational or hedonic? *Behavioral and Brain Functions*, 3(1), 1–8.

Cabantous, L., Gond, J. P. and Johnson-Cramer, M. (2010) Decision theory as practice: Crafting rationality in organizations. *Organization Studies*, 31(11), 1531–66.

Calabretta, G., Gemser, G. and Wijnberg, N. M. (2016) The interplay between intuition and rationality in strategic decision making: A paradox perspective. *Organization Studies*. DOI: 10.1177/0170840616655483.

Churchman, C. W. (1962) On rational decision making. *Management Technology*, 2(2), 71–6.

Colic-Peisker, V. (2016) Ideology and utopia: Historic crisis of economic rationality and the role of public sociology. *Journal of Sociology*. DOI: 10.1177/1440783316630114.

Dahms, H. F. (1997) Theory in Weberian Marxism: Patterns of critical social theory in Lukács and Habermas. *Sociological theory*, 15(3), 181–214.

Davidson, D. (2004) *Problems of Rationality*. Vol. 4. Oxford: Oxford University Press.

De Botton, A. (2016) *The Course of Love*. London: Hamish Hamilton.

Diesing, P. (1976) *Reason in Society: Five Types of Decisions and Their Social Conditions*. Westport, CT: Greenwood Press.

Eisenhardt, K. M. and Zbaracki, M. J. (1992) Strategic decision making. *Strategic Management Journal*, 13(S2), 17–37.

Elbanna, S. (2006) Strategic decision-making: Process perspectives. *International Journal of Management Reviews*, 8(1), 1–20.

Elbanna, S. and Child, J. (2007) Influences on strategic decision effectiveness: Development and test of an integrative model. *Strategic Management Journal*, 28(4), 431–53.

Elster, J. (1989) Social norms and economic theory. *The Journal of Economic Perspectives*, 3(4), 99–117.

Elster, J. (2006) Fairness and norms. *Social Research: An International Quarterly*, 73(2), 365–76.

Elster, J. (2009) *Reason and Rationality*. Princeton, NJ: Princeton University Press.

Engelen, B. (2006) Solving the paradox: The expressive rationality of the decision to vote. *Rationality and Society*, 18(4), 419–41.

Esposito, E. (2011) Originality through imitation: The rationality of fashion. *Organization Studies*, 32(5), 603–13.

Fisher, P. and Freshwater, D. (2014) Towards compassionate care through aesthetic rationality. *Scandinavian Journal of Caring Sciences*, 28(4), 767–74.

Gigerenzer, G. (2010) Moral satisficing: Rethinking moral behavior as bounded rationality. *Topics in Cognitive Science*, 2(3), 528–54.

Gigerenzer, G. and Selten, R. (2001) Rethinking rationality, in Gigerenzer, G. and Selten, R. (eds), *Bounded Rationality: The Adaptive Toolbox*. Cambridge, MA: MIT Press, pp. 1–12.

Gigerenzer, G. and Sturm, T. (2012) How (far) can rationality be naturalized? *Synthese*, 187(1), 243–68.

Green Jr, S. E. (2004) A rhetorical theory of diffusion. *The Academy of Management Review*, 29(4), 653–69.

Greenspan, P. (2004) Practical reasoning and emotion, in Mele, A. R. and Rawling, P. (eds), *The Oxford Handbook of Rationality*. New York: Oxford University Press, pp. 206–21.

Habermas, J. (1988) *Theorie des Kommunikativen Handelns, Band 1, 2*. Frankfurt: Suhrkamp.

Haidt, J. (2001) The emotional dog and its rational tail: A social intuitionist approach to moral judgment. *Psychological Review*, 108(4), 814–34.

Hargreaves Heap, S. (2001) Expressive rationality: Is self-worth just another kind of preference?, in Mäki, U. (ed), *The Economic World View: Studies in the Ontology of Economics*. Cambridge: Cambridge University Press, pp. 98–113.

Harrison, E. F. (1993) Interdisciplinary models of decision making. *Management Decision*, 31(8), 27–33.

Henderson, D. (2010) Explanation and rationality naturalized. *Philosophy of the Social Sciences*, 40(1), 30–58.

Houwelingen, G. van and Bouwmeester, O. (2008) Situationele rationaliteit in publieke besluitvorming. *Filosofie in Bedrijf*, 18(2), 26–40.

Kahneman, D. (2011) *Thinking, Fast and Slow*. New York: FSG.

Kilduff, M. and Mehra, A. (1997) Postmodernism and organizational research. *Academy of Management Review*, 22(2), 453–81.

Klamer, A. (1987) As if economists and their subjects were rational, in Nelson, J. S., Megill, A. and McCloskey, D. (eds), *The Rhetoric of the Human Sciences*. Madison, WI: The University of Wisconsin Press, pp. 163–83.

Klein, G. (2001) The fiction of optimization, in Gigerenzer, G. and Selten, R. (eds), *Bounded Rationality: The Adaptive Toolbox*. Cambridge, MA: MIT Press, pp. 103–14.

Li, Y., Ashkanasy, N. M. and Ahlstrom, D. (2014) The rationality of emotions: A hybrid process model of decision-making under uncertainty. *Asia Pacific Journal of Management*, 31(1), 293–308.

McCloskey, D. N. (2016) Max U versus Humanomics: A critique of neo-institutionalism. *Journal of Institutional Economics*, 12(01), 1–27.

MacIntyre, A. C. (1988) *Whose Justice? Which Rationality?* London: Duckworth.

Majone, G. (1992) *Evidence, Argument and Persuasion in the Policy Process*. New Haven, CT: Yale University Press.

March, J. G. and Simon, H. A. (1958) *Organizations*. New York: John Wiley.

Racko, G. (2011) On the normative consequences of economic rationality: A case study of a Swedish economics school in Latvia. *European Sociological Review*, 27(6), 772–89.

Sandberg, J. and Tsoukas, H. (2011) Grasping the logic of practice: Theorizing through practical rationality. *Academy of Management Review*, 36(2), 338–60.

Satow, R. L. (1975) Value-rational authority and professional organizations: Weber's missing type. *Administrative Science Quarterly*, 20(4), 526–31.

Scherer, K. R. (2011) On the rationality of emotions: Or, when are emotions rational? *Social Science Information*, 50(3–4), 330–50.

Sen, A. (1993) Internal consistency of choice. *Econometrica*, 61(3), 495–521.

Stewart, H. (1995) A critique of instrumental reason in economics. *Economics and Philosophy*, 11(01), 57–83.

Taylor, B. J. (2016) Heuristics in professional judgement: A psycho-social rationality model. *British Journal of Social Work*. DOI: 10.1093/bjsw/bcw084.

Tinbergen, J. (1956) *Economic Policy: Principles and Design*. Amsterdam: Noord Hollandsche Uitgeversmaatschappij.

Tomer, J. (2008) Beyond the rationality of economic man, toward the true rationality of human man. *Journal of Socio-Economics*, 37(5), 1703–12.

Toulmin, S. E. (1994) *The Uses of Argument*. Cambridge: Cambridge University Press.

Townley, B. (1999) Practical reason and performance appraisal. *Journal of Management Studies*, 36(3), 287–306.

Townley, B. (2002) The role of competing rationalities in institutional change. *Academy of Management Journal*, 45(1), 163–79.

Townley, B. (2008) *Reason's Neglect: Rationality and Organizing*. Oxford: Oxford University Press.

Weber, M. (1972) *Wirtschaft und Gesellschaft: Grundriß der Verstehenden Soziologie*. 5th ed. Tubingen, Germany: JCB Mohr (Paul Siebeck).

Weirich, P. (2004) Economic rationality, in Mele, A. R. and Rawling, P. (eds), *The Oxford Handbook of Rationality*. Oxford: Oxford University Press, pp. 380–98.

Werder, A. von (1999) Argumentation rationality of management decisions. *Organization Science*, 10(5), 672–90.

Zhu, Y. (2015) The role of Qing (positive emotions) and Li 1 (rationality) in Chinese entrepreneurial decision making: A Confucian Ren-Yi wisdom perspective. *Journal of Business Ethics*, 126(4), 613–30.

2 How argumentation analysis reveals different rationalities

Introducing a method to study rationality

The importance of better understanding rationality stems from the assumption that rationality is associated with decision-making. Elbanna and Child (2007) find a positive relation between rationality, understood as having good reasons to act on, and decision effectiveness in strategic decision-making. Fredrickson and Iaquinto (1989) find a positive relation between the rationality of a decision-making process and firm performance in stable environments. Furthermore, psychological and rhetorical management research has shown that in ambiguous situations, people tend to rely on reasoning to guide choice (Mellers *et al.* 1998; Shafir *et al.* 1993; Sillince *et al.* 2011).

Over the years, management scholars have developed diverse understandings of rationality, including instrumental rationality, political rationality, economic rationality, organizational rationality, value rationality and forms of bounded rationality (Churchman 1962; Hendry 2000; Lagueux 2010; March and Simon 1958; Schipper 1996; Townley 2002; Vaara 2002; Weber 1972). All these rationalities might help to prepare and legitimize a decision by giving good reasons to act on. Still, they all have limitations. For instance, economic rationality gives maximizing profits or utility as motive for action, but is criticized for being a too-narrow set of reasons, given how humans legitimize their actions in practice (Bergset 2015; Eisenhardt and Zbaracki 1992; Fisher and Freshwater 2014; Townley 1999, 2002). Value rationality or political rationality add relevant perspectives, but cannot be made operational as easily as economic rationality. Mueller *et al.* (2007: 857), therefore, argue that there is a need for 'empirical research which operationalizes the construct of rationality in a more fine-grained manner, including [. . .] socio-political elements'.

The need to explore the concept of rationality in more detail increases when stakeholders challenge the decision makers' rationality by arguing, for example, that it is not efficiency or lower costs that should motivate their decision, but rather value-rational or moral considerations about justice or environmental care (Barraquier 2011; Clegg *et al.* 2007; Freeman 2010). In contrast, others could claim that high moral standards are not sufficient to legitimize the decision, because there is not enough political support. Controversial decisions tend to be plagued by dilemmas that stem from conflicting rationalities (Diesing 1976; Healy *et al.* 2010; MacIntyre 1988), leading to different types of legitimacy (Suchman 1995).

What these different rationalities have in common is that they all support decisions 'based on considerations which [are] reasons worth acting on' (Engelen 2006: 427; see also Davidson 2004: 169; Elbanna 2006: 3; Elbanna and Child 2007: 433; Elster 2009: 2; Gigerenzer and Sturm 2012: 243–5; Green 2004: 655; Henderson 2010: 32). Rationality seen more broadly can, thus, be defined as having good reasons to act on. And being rational then also implies the ability of expressing your reasons as arguments. As the concept of rationality includes the notion of having good reasons to act on, it is surprising that so few scholars have explored rationality based on analysis of the actual reasons given for making decisions in practice. Argumentation analysis seems to be a quite suitable method to analyse rationality. Especially as it is a way to study rationality in its natural environment, as Gigerenzer (2010: 548) argues for. However, today rationality is little explored along these lines. Instead, theoretical studies (Davidson 2004; MacIntyre 1988; March and Simon 1958; Weber 1972) by philosophers, economists and sociologists, and experimental studies by psychologists (see Kahneman 2011) dominate the field.

This chapter seeks to develop an analytical method for exploring rationality in real-life cases in which decisions are made and discussed, based on argumentation analysis. The data for this analysis are six major decisions with strategic impact that are publicly debated in newspapers and magazines. Three decisions are debated in the UK, three in the Netherlands. Articles about these decisions in which the relevant stakeholders voice their views are retrieved from LexisNexis.

The chapter starts with a categorization of three general types of rationality and explores the types of arguments that relate to these rationalities, based on those who discuss these different rationalities. Next, the analytical approach inspired by Brockriede and Ehninger (1960) and Toulmin (1994) is outlined to explain how Toulmin analysis is used to study the different rationalities visible in the six debated decisions explored in this book. Then the case study design is discussed, as the cases are theoretically sampled. It is important to note that the debated decisions offer the research context to explore rationality as it is socially constructed in these debates. This implies an open approach towards the rationality construct, and no limitations beforehand, as if rationality is only constructed as instrumental and defined by a focus on realizing ends by appropriate means; a focus illustrated in Cabantous *et al.* (2010) and Racko (2011). The chapter concludes with a discussion that outlines contributions and limitations related to this analytical method for studying rationality.

The method contributes to the study of the three main types of rationality without any preference for expressive, social or instrumental rationality. The method builds on the studies by Bouwmeester (2013), van Houwelingen and Bouwmeester (2008) and von Werder (1999). What is new is the focus on rationality interactions, and the social construction of irrationality next to rationality. Studying the relations between arguments pro and con helps to reveal irrationalities. They are constructed when pro and con arguments express a different form of rationality.

Rationality and reasoning

Although there are sufficient references to the definition of rationality as having good reasons to act on, exploration of the kind of reasons related to different rationalities is still rare. Also, indications of differences between the kinds of arguments needed for being instrumental rational or social rational remain rather implicit, as the project of differentiating kinds of rationality is still nascent. However, Diesing (1976) has some useful reflections on the reasoning related to instrumental and social forms of rationality. For expressive rationality, such indications are more difficult to find in the literature on rationality. What the rationalities have in common is that they all suggest what to do or why to do something. They all give orientation to our actions (Weber 1972).

Argumentation behind instrumental rationality

Instrumental rationality assumes we know our objectives. Here, rationality is about how we can achieve our objectives in a rational way. That is, not spending resources without need, but acting efficiently. It also assumes we choose the right means for being able to achieve our objectives, thus acting effectively. In order to do so, we need to know the means–end logic behind our rational actions. If we know this logic, we can select the means with the right effects, and we can explain why we did so by referring to this means–end logic and the underlying causalities. Such instrumental thinking is what economists proclaim (Diesing 1976; Majone 1992; Peacock 1992; Tinbergen 1956; Weirich 2004): that they help policymakers improve their policies by making them more effective and efficient, without discussing or influencing the objectives. What economists add to technical rationality is trying to maximize outcomes by achieving the best combination of several related lower-level ends (Diesing 1976: 44), which together make higher utility, welfare or profit, which become the higher-level ends. So, the reasoning remains instrumental or goal-oriented, and economic rationality applies to the use of means.

Diesing (1976: 244) recognizes this form of economic reasoning in one of the conceptions of practical reason in social philosophy: 'reason appears [. . .] as calculation in Hobbes, Bentham and the utilitarians'. For these classical authors, reason is seen as the slave of passions, where passions define the goals (Diesing 1976: 246; Sedlacek 2011). The same applies to self-interest: it might inform your goals, but if your preferences or passions are social you can also calculate which means suggest the best outcomes for such preferences. Instrumental rationality is indifferent towards these goals. Still, emotions or desires are expected not to interfere with the calculation process themselves.

The link between instrumental rationality and argumentation that supports instrumental reasoning is quite obvious. When analysing the reasoning behind instrumental-rational arguments from a rhetorical point of view (Brockriede and Ehninger 1960), the argumentation used is clearly means–end, or cause-based. As goals or values are given, the reasons to act on only come from economizing, or saving on effort, costs or pains as the means. They make goal realization feasible.

Instrumental rationality has a focus on how to act rationally, or how one can best achieve predefined goals. Cause-based argumentation supports feasibility analysis and evaluations of efficiency and effectiveness (Majone 1992). The more efficient, effective or feasible, the more rational a course of action is, evaluated against standards of instrumental rationality.

However, when means achieve unintended consequences, inconsistencies appear between means and ends, which tend towards irrationality from an instrumental perspective; especially when based on 'wishful thinking' (Davidson 2004: 170), by more or less consciously ignoring the possibility of the unintended consequences implied in the means that are used as cause. It is a form of irrationality that Davidson (2004: 170) labels as 'believing something that one holds to be discredited by the weight of the evidence'. Elster (2009: 40) would characterize such influences as the 'hot sources of irrationality'. Weakness of will, for instance, can lead to the dominance of single desires or a temporal inversion of preferences that invalidate maximization calculations. Kahneman (2011) gives similar examples of how emotions can disturb calculations behind instrumental rationality.

Argumentation behind social rationality

Social rationality, with variations like value rationality, legal rationality or political rationality, is based on socially shared interests, moral values, norms or principles (Elster 1989, 2006; Satow 1975; Weber 1972). As they are shared, they are grounded in intersubjective agreements that can legitimize what we do. Social norms are rational within groups or communities. From this social perspective it is good to follow such norms. If we do so, these norms legitimate our actions as national laws do, or community values we adhere to. By acting socially rational we act in accordance with what our community considers acceptable, appropriate or even admirable behaviour. Social forms of rationality have their foundations in social philosophy; most clearly so regarding legal and moral reasoning (Habermas 1988; Hegel 1986; Kant 1990; Weber 1972). Diesing (1976: 244) recognizes this form of rule-based reasoning in the legal–moral conception of practical reason. It is the 'application of rules to cases [. . .] in the natural law theorists, such as Aquinas, Locke and Kant'.

The argumentation mentioned here is deductive. A case or situation is connected to a rule, a principle, a norm, a value, etc., as in deontological ethics. Brockriede and Ehninger (1960) characterize such deductive reasoning as based on arguments from classification. The rule or norm applies to a class of situations, but not to all situations. The norm needs to be properly applicable to the case. That is part of the argument. Not any rule will have the force to convince that actions need to be organized accordingly. It is rational to pay your taxes, to clean/sweep the snow in front of your door, to follow the traffic rules and to respect your neighbour's desire for a peaceful and quiet environment. Such rules contribute to good citizenship and apply to us as adults, but less to our children. For adults, it is rational to follow them, as they support our living together; we accept more noise from children. So, there are different rules and values that are specific for the group and apply to friendship, being a family member or being part of a specific culture. Irrationality in applying this logic starts when you relate your behaviour to the wrong social rules, or even ignore them, like a ghost driver, with the risks involved for everyone. This implies acting 'contrary to one's own best judgment' (Davidson 2004: 170).

Argumentation behind expressive rationality

Whereas social rationality finds reason in norms, values and principles shared by many, expressive rationality finds reasons for action in how we feel about something. Weber (1972: 12) categorizes this as affective reasons to act on, which can have some rationality in his view, but often not. Such feelings or passions are direct grounds for acting: our taste helps us to decide what to eat, sympathy is a motive for engaging in friendship and fear warns us of dangers. These feelings can provide good reasons for individual action and they benefit from authenticity (Habermas 1988: 42). Other expressive reasons might refer to someone's identity, commitments and desires or to dislike and anger (Greenspan 2004; Li *et al.* 2014; Scherer 2011). They are different from social-rational consideration because it is a subjective reality, not a social reality, that generates the motives we act on; it is about what is important to me, irrespective of social desirability, and, for many decisions, these reasons suffice.

Expressive rationality is not well articulated yet, but attention is growing (Engelen 2006; Greenspan 2004; Hargreaves Heap 2001; Li *et al.* 2014; Scherer 2011). Expressive rationality is quite nascent in its conceptualization, and relating this rationality to its underlying argumentations is also under-explored. The subjectivity of expressive-rational arguments has the best fit with motivational arguments (Brockriede and Ehninger 1960). The motivation for action does not stem from norms or principles that need to be followed in a certain situation, but they originate directly from affective impulses, desires, fears, commitments, ambitions, intuitions and inspirations without a need for being mediated by social principles. Rhetoricians consider affects in themselves sufficient to explain why we do something. People can also understand what we do and why, when we refer to such expressive motives, as long as they believe our feelings are authentic (Habermas 1988). Irrationality starts when we misunderstand ourselves or our interests due to 'self-deception' (Davidson 2004: 170), when we cannot balance our feelings (Elster 2009) or when we are not authentic in expressing them.

Conceptual tensions

In current discussions on social and expressive rationality (Diesing 1976; Engelen 2006) there is some confusion in distinguishing the two. Diesing (1976), for instance, adds two somewhat subjective forms of rationality to what he considers legal–moral rationality. In his wording, these are forms of social rationality on the informal group level, and political rationality as a process of creating meanings and rules for making decisions. Diesing (1976: 244) relates these two more subjective forms of social rationality to a third philosophical stream next to utilitarian, instrumental reasoning and deontological, rule-based reasoning. This third stream stresses creativity in its reasoning, which gives it a subjective twist: 'reason appears as creativity in the work of Plato, Hegel and Whitehead, among others'. Diesing is quite concerned about this third approach and concludes his book with a mission: 'Social and political rationality are the most neglected of the forms of rationality today, and their study is most important, both in theoretical terms and in relation to the principal world problems of today' (Diesing 1976: 247). It is difficult to say if Diesing would have applauded a pure subjective grounding of rationality as a third form in line with this third philosophical tradition. Given his focus on creativity, it seems he could have been open to this differentiation, as creativity has a subjective origin. It makes social rationality at least more local and temporal than in Weber's (1972) version of value rationality.

A similar conceptual overlap between social and subjective motives applies to the characterization of expressive rationality made by Engelen (2006: 431). He points to a subjective grounding of expressive rationality when he sets it apart from instrumental rationality: 'expressive acts also imply a certain level of psychological and emotional involvement'. However, he connects such expressions (in the example, it is care) to norms, principles and traditions when setting it apart from instrumental rationality: 'Insofar as one cares about some social norm, principle, tradition [...], it is expressively rational to act in accordance with these'. The social and the subjective element are both acknowledged, but not yet treated as fundamentally different origins that organize the motives informing our actions.

Weber (1972) and Habermas (1988) make this clear conceptual distinction, but they are somewhat reluctant to attribute full rationality to affective motives, as they can easily turn into irrationality. However, more and more scholars have started to differentiate expressive rationality as being an independent and autonomous form of rationality in guiding our actions and decisions (Bouwmeester 2013; Fisher and Freshwater 2014; Scherer 2011). Expressive rationality is able to criticize social and instrumental rationality as being irrational against expressive standards. Jogging can be useful for staying healthy, but if we do not like it, we can do something else that is just as healthy.

Reasoning and rationality interactions

The three rationalities – expressive, social and instrumental rationality – are conceptually distinct by their orientation towards subjectivity, intersubjectivity and objectivity. These three perspectives give guidance to our actions in different ways and are reinforced by the kinds of arguments we use when giving good reasons to act on. Technical and economic rationality, as variations of instrumental rationality, are based on means–end arguments. Value, moral, legal or political rationality are variations of social rationality building on deductive reasoning, often by means of arguments from classification. Expressive rationality could also be differentiated into more hedonic, therapeutic or aesthetic directions, supported by motivational arguments for establishing well-balanced, affective reasons to act on.

Given these differences, one might ask how these rationalities can influence each other. Kahneman (2011: 323) argues that there is an undermining relationship between emotions and rationality, as emotions disturb calculations and estimations, thus explaining the success of lotteries by our emotional irrationality and inability to understand our self-interest well. He sets instrumental rationality as the norm. However, in classical conceptions of rationality passions and desires tell us what we want, and instrumental rationality only tells us how to achieve what we want. This view is argued by classical authors like Adam Smith in his theory of moral sentiments (1982: 320) and, more recently, again, by Haidt (2001) and Sedlacek (2011). Expressive rationality would, thus, set the norm for instrumental rationality. A third view is put forward by Weber (1972). He does not start from passions as being leading, but from value rationality. Like Habermas (1988), he assumes the possibility of rational discourse about social values, principles and moral goals. When the importance of social values and goals is determined, instrumental rationality is secondary in finding ways to realize these values and goals.

Diesing considers the relationship between different rationalities as more lateral. There is no one-way hierarchy. Diesing (1976: 247) concludes about calculation (technical-economic rationality), rule application (moral-legal rationality) and creativity (social-political rationality): 'The three conceptions of rationality are not basically incompatible, but differ primarily in emphasis. Each approach must eventually include the other within itself in some fashion.' It is also interesting to note Diesing's more general division into three streams of rationality here, instead of five. Engelen (2006: 435) develops similar lateral thoughts for his two rationalities, where expressive rationality includes elements of social rationality: 'Instrumental and expressive motivations, as I have analysed them, are two opposing ends of a single scale.' The relational views on rationality held by Diesing (1976) and Engelen (2006) imply that different rationalities do interact with each other more equally. An example of this is individual taste, which can be influenced by fashions, which are social, while these fashions start with some inspired individuals, indicating that influences between expressive and social rationality can be mutual.

A great deal seems to be possible in the domain of rationality, but when and why such different relationships appear is not yet clear. Moreover, the more lateral ideas suggested by Diesing and Engelen have not changed the dominance of more hierarchical sociological views on rationality as inspired by Weber, nor the dominance of instrumental views on rationality as prevailing in economics and reinforced by Kahneman's experiments. Mutual influences between different rationalities have, thus, never been explored in sufficient detail. Rich descriptions of practical argumentations aimed at undermining or supporting other rationalities might add new and much required insights into these research questions.

Analytical approach

For studying the questions raised above, some clarifications are needed of what distinctions between different kinds of arguments are possible (Brockriede and Ehninger 1960) and how they might construct rationality. Some basic arguments have already been mentioned in discussing different rationalities, like means–end arguments, arguments from classification and motivational arguments, but there are some more arguments at work when rationalities interact. Next, the analysis of micro arguments will be discussed and ways to map the connectedness of arguments and their interactions. Finally, the relation between arguments' argumentation fields is addressed, mainly inspired by Toulmin (1994).

Kinds of arguments

When we consider what to do, and discuss internally or with others why we want to do something, we use arguments. Often, it is intuitively clear that these arguments support what we want to do, or why we should think twice before acting. For that reason, we hardly ever explain an argument by explicating the warrant (Toulmin 1994: 100). A warrant builds the bridge between grounds and claims. If grounds and conclusion are given, the assumed warrants can always be made explicit. And even a conclusion we leave implicit sometimes, as enthymemes (incomplete arguments) often make sufficiently clear what we want to argue, or want to suggest; although they leave some more room for interpretation. With the help of Toulmin's categorizations we can make such missing parts explicit (Brockriede and Ehninger 1960: 47).

There are different kinds of arguments, linked to different kinds of warrants (Brockriede and Ehninger 1960; Perelman 1982; Toulmin 1994; Toulmin *et al.* 1984). Basic variations are discussed in Brockriede and Ehninger (1960). They could all be used when explaining what is rational to do, but some connect better to one kind of rationality than others. Decision makers could make use of substantive arguments by using a causal warrant to explain an effect related to a means or cause, as prevails in instrumental-rational reasoning. Other substantive arguments that also fit to instrumental rationality use a warrant that signals a deeper phenomenon, for instance a cause, by interpreting some sign as a symptom or effect of the indicated cause. Another possibility is a warrant that generalizes towards patterns, rules or causalities based on inductive reasoning, and, finally, warrants based on analogical reasoning; they can project a known regularity into an unknown context. Warrants that relate well to social rationality often use arguments from classification which are based on deductive reasoning. Arguments from classification can apply moral rules, principles or value to a case, which is common when making a social-rational argument that something is not fair or needs to be improved to meet a social standard. Analogies could also be used by projecting our norms onto other social contexts. Next to substantive arguments, Brockriede and Ehninger (1960) distinguish authoritative warrants referring to an author's or speaker's ethos, and motivational warrants using pathos by referring to what an audience and relevant stakeholders consider important or feel attached to. Motivational arguments fit well to expressive rationality, as they can refer to affects, passions, desires, etc., to give good reasons for action. All of the above-mentioned arguments are defined in Table 2.1.

Substantive arguments relate to what Aristotle considers logos and they provide information about the subject of investigation. They are quite relevant in explicating instrumental and social rationality by referring to causal or moral rules or principles. Ethos is different. It does not add content to the arguments, which makes the connection with any form of rationality unlikely. Ethos can add persuasive power by

Table 2.1 Kinds of arguments

	Explanation of the kind of argument based on its warrant
Substantive arguments	
• Cause	'In an argument from cause the data [grounds] consist of one or more accepted facts about a person, object, event, or condition. The warrant attributes to these facts a creative or generative power and specifies the nature of the effect they will produce. The claim relates these results to the person, object, event, or condition named in the data'. (p. 48)
• Sign	'In an argument from sign the data [grounds] consist of clues or symptoms. The warrant interprets the meaning or significance of these symptoms. The claim affirms that some person, object, event, or condition possesses the attributes of which the clues have been declared symptomatic'. (p. 49)
• Generalization	'In an argument from generalization the data [grounds] consist of information about number of persons, objects, events, or conditions, taken as constituting a representative and adequate sample of a given class of phenomena. The warrant assumes that what is true of the items constituting the sample will also be true of additional members of the class not represented in the sample. The claim makes explicit the assumption embodied in the warrant'. (p. 49)
• Parallel case [or analogy]	'In an argument from parallel case or analogy the data [grounds] consist of one or more statements about a single object, event, condition [or relationship]. The warrant asserts that the instance reported in the data bears an essential similarity to a second instance in the same category. The claim affirms about the new instance what has already been accepted concerning the first'. (pp. 49–50)
• Classification	'In an argument from classification the statement about the data [grounds] is a generalized conclusion about known members of a class of persons, objects, events, or conditions. The warrant assumes that what is true of the items reported in the data will also be true of a hitherto unexamined item which is known (or thought) to fall within the class there described. The claim then transfers the general statement which has been made in the data to the particular item under consideration'. (p. 50)

(Continued)

Table 2.1. (continued)

	Explanation of the kind of argument based on its warrant
Authoritative arguments	'In authoritative arguments the data [grounds] consist of one or more factual reports or statements of opinion. The warrant affirms the reliability of the source from which these are derived. The claim reiterates the statement which appeared in the data, as now certified by the warrant'. (p. 51)
Motivational arguments	'In motivational arguments the data [grounds] consist of one or more statements which may have been established as claims in a previous argument or series of arguments. The warrant provides a motive for accepting the claim by associating it with some inner drive, value, desire, emotion, or aspiration, or with a combination of such forces. The claim as so warranted is that the person, object, event, or condition referred to in the data should be accepted as valuable or rejected as worthless, or that the policy described should or should not be adopted, or the action there named should or should not be performed'. (p. 51)

Source: adapted from Brockriede and Ehninger 1960: 48–51.

stressing who makes the argument: the more authority a person has, the more convincing the arguments he or she puts forward. Pathos based on motivational warrants can increase persuasiveness by tailoring the argument to the perceptions and preferences of a reader or listener. When someone feels sympathy for specific ideas, arguments and claims, appealing to these sympathies becomes quite persuasive. This is what motivational arguments aim for and they relate quite well to expressive rationality, with their reference to sympathy, affect, desire or the opposite (Brockriede and Ehninger 1960).

Logos, ethos and pathos arguments can build on each other. Without authority, good logos arguments have little chance of being convincing. Without some initial sympathy from an audience, persuasion will be difficult as well. Even if logos arguments are most important to many social and instrumental-rational questions, minimum levels of ethos and pathos are always required. The reverse is true as well: authority without content has no power, nor can we feel anything about nothing. By explicating authority or motivational aspects in our arguments, the persuasiveness of a logos argument can be amplified. This leads Aristotle to conclude that there are three means of persuasion that work together (Aristotle 1991: 1356a), and not exclusively logos arguments. Pathos (motivational) and logos (substantive) arguments are most central to the current analysis.

Micro arguments and complex arguments

Argumentation analysis is used to study the quality of complex strategic decisions in Bronn (1998), Mitroff and Mason (1980) and Mitroff *et al.* (1982). They have applied Toulmin's analytical framework to explore micro argumentations. Others have also focused on the interrelatedness and hierarchy of multiple arguments (Bouwmeester 2010, 2013; van Houwelingen and Bouwmeester 2008; von Werder 1999) in decision-making debates. Both analytical perspectives help to study rationality. The micro perspective helps to explicate warrants; a more general perspective helps to trace the different positions defended by decision makers or stakeholders, to explore clusters of reasons they give and the interrelatedness of arguments expressing different rationalities.

For studying micro arguments, Toulmin (1994) distinguishes six elements: an asserted claim; grounds supporting the claim; warrants that justify the inference between grounds and claim; backings that prove the warrants; qualifiers addressing the modality or likelihood of a claim; and rebuttals that (partly) counter the claim by stating conditions for its validity, or exceptions. Figure 2.1 illustrates for each form of rationality (expressive, social and instrumental) a main ground with implied warrant, leading to the same claim. The illustrative arguments are selected from the first case. The given claim is a main argument in the debate, which supports the final conclusion of the debate (which is added to the main argument in brackets). The rebuttal (also in brackets) works against the debate's conclusion.

Four out of the six elements identified by Toulmin are quite relevant for exploring rationality: (sub)grounds, warrants, (sub)rebuttals and main claim. Modal qualifiers and backings tell little about the kind of rationality. They only influence the force of

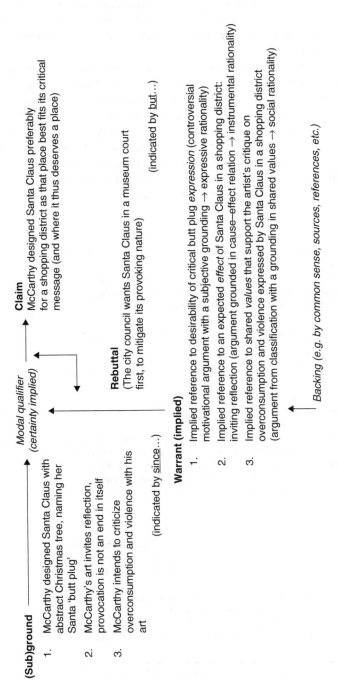

(Sub)ground

1. McCarthy designed Santa Claus with abstract Christmas tree, naming her Santa 'butt plug'

2. McCarthy's art invites reflection, provocation is not an end in itself

3. McCarthy intends to criticize overconsumption and violence with his art

(indicated by <u>since</u>...)

Modal qualifier
(certainty implied)

Claim
McCarthy designed Santa Claus preferably for a shopping district as that place best fits its critical message (and where it thus deserves a place)

(indicated by <u>but</u>...)

Rebuttal
(The city council wants Santa Claus in a museum court first, to mitigate its provoking nature)

Warrant (implied)

1. Implied reference to desirability of critical butt plug *expression* (controversial motivational argument with a subjective grounding → expressive rationality)

2. Implied reference to an expected *effect* of Santa Claus in a shopping district: inviting reflection (argument grounded in cause–effect relation → instrumental rationality)

3. Implied reference to shared *values* that support the artist's critique on overconsumption and violence expressed by Santa Claus in a shopping district (argument from classification with a grounding in shared values → social rationality)

Backing (e.g. by common sense, sources, references, etc.)

Figure 2.1 Implied warrants related to kinds of rationality.

an argument (likelihood and validity). Moreover, the implied modal qualifiers mainly suggest certainty in the cases, without much variation. The warrant, when explicated, tells most specifically about the implied rationalities behind the three arguments. Figure 2.1 gives three sub-grounds supporting one main argument in the debate, thus presenting only three micro arguments, but there are many more that have been put forward.

To analyse complex argumentation, a tabular representation offers better possibilities to include and relate all sub-arguments, as exhibited, for instance, in von Werder (1999). Von Werder's presentation is superior to a pyramid presentation, as in Minto (1995), as it also presents rebuttals, whereas Minto ignores them. In addition, the kind of rationality can be added as a label to every argument (here, IR for instrumental rationality, SR for social rationality and ER for expressive rationality). It describes the kind of connection (based on warrant) to the next higher hierarchical level (mostly main ground or claim). Table 2.2 shows how to analyse complex argumentation based on the first and last main argument in the debate on

Table 2.2 Example of presenting complex argumentation

Claim, grounds and rebuttals		IR	SR	ER
Claim	Santa Claus (*Santa with butt plug*) deserves a visible place in a public environment in Rotterdam city centre			
Since	McCarthy designed Santa Claus for a shopping district as that place best fits its critical message			X
	Since McCarthy designed Santa Claus holding a bell and a Christmas tree, naming the work 'Santa with butt plug'			X
	Since McCarthy's art invites reflection among consumers. Provocation is not an end in itself	X		
	Since McCarthy intends to criticize unlimited consumerism, capitalism and violence in his art		X	
	Since McCarthy reframes meaning: with Santa Claus (response to Coca-Cola), Pinocchio (Disney) and other works			X
	Since McCarthy developed the idea for his first public artwork in 2000 as an assignment by the city of Rotterdam	X		
[…]				
But	The city wanted Santa Claus, first, in the court of the Museum Boijmans van Beuningen in 2003, to mitigate its provoking nature	X		
	But Before Santa Claus was unveiled in the museum it was stored in a secure location to keep it secret	X		
	But Proponents suggested alternative public locations as they considered the museum not a right fit for Santa Claus			X
	But Before going public in 2008 Santa Claus had to stay briefly in front of the museum due to a renovation of the court	X		

Note: IR: instrumental rationality; SR: social rationality; ER: expressive rationality.

Santa Claus (a ground and a rebuttal), including their sub-grounds and sub-rebuttals. The first four arguments were also presented in Figure 2.1.

The table format allows the representation of all the necessary information required for a rationality analysis: the claims, grounds, rebuttals and rationality connected to the explicated warrants. It is also possible to present the opponents' arguments in italics. Table 2.2 only shows the arguments given by the proponents (in normal case). As the rationality of each argument is labelled, it is possible to see how lower-level instrumental or social arguments can support or rebut a higher-level expressive one, and vice versa. The exploration of interactions between rationalities is of particular interest to the current study, which makes rationality more concrete, practical and empirical.

Rationality and argumentation fields

Following Toulmin (1994), practical argumentation in public debates on major strategic decisions is always bound to context, and is thus field dependent. As rationality is based on good reasons to act on, these arguments and their rationality must be field dependent as well. Toulmin (1994) and Toulmin *et al.* (1984) explain, for instance, how the legal field requires types of arguments that do not convince in the context of art criticism, or for making a business case. What is legal does not necessarily follow taste, nor does it have to be profitable. Therefore, arguments that are considered regular differ between fields. Argumentation fields can be distinguished in different ways, through their procedures; for example, required degrees of formality (law court proceedings vs. art criticism), required degrees of precision (physics vs. strategic planning), used modes of resolution (consensus seeking or adversary) and goals of argumentation (like to agree on a diagnosis or argue for a decision with lifelong implications).

Toulmin (1994: 15) stresses that argumentation is always 'contextually field dependent'. Argumentation does follow formal, near-universal patterns, but it follows these patterns in such a way that it will always be 'local rationalities that determine if a given argument is relevant' (Corvellec 2007: 134). Similar awareness for context can be recognized in pragmatist theory (Austin 2003; Rorty 1992). Dewey (2008: 353) stresses the need to link reasoning with experience, which also implies contextualization. Relevance of context is also acknowledged as the 'situatedness' of discursive practices (e.g. Cornelissen *et al.* 2008: 11; Harre and Gillett 1994: 28–9, 33; Hendry 2000: 968; Phillips *et al.* 2008: 774; Schildt *et al.* 2011). In addition, fields can be different, but not always indifferent. Sometimes they are able to support or undermine each other (Harmon *et al.* 2015) when, for example, cultures clash or institutional norms and values are conflicting and push for transition.

When relating argumentation fields to the different rationalities that have been discussed, like instrumental (i.e. technical, economical), social (i.e. legal, political, informal, organizational) and expressive forms of rationality (i.e. hedonic, aesthetic, therapeutic), we can thus expect field dependency related to rationality. The cases relating to public art or modes of dressing belong more to the humanities; the integration and rights of minorities are more sociological and political; and airport planning and workplace designs are more economical in their reasoning. When analysing rationality based on public debates, the choice of debates and the questions discussed will influence what rationality is most appropriate, given the field dependence of practical argumentation. However, it is unlikely that only one rationality perspective related to one field can solve the entire problem in complex cases, and we might, therefore, expect rationality conflicts (Goodnight 2010). Still, the study selects such debated questions that predominantly require one rationality. If the expected rationality is dominant, it is further proof for the proposition that rationalities, or good reasons to act on, are as field dependent as other forms of practical argumentation.

Multiple case study design

Case selection based on expected rationality

Rationality is explored in six public debates; three in the UK and three in the Netherlands. The cases are theoretically sampled so that each predominantly fits one type of rationality best, due to the debated question and its most related argumentation field (humanities, sociology, economics). The longitudinal cases are about controversial strategic decisions, based on reasoning grounded in subjective, intersubjective or more objective fields. This creates maximum variation in rationality by covering exemplary instances of expressive, social and instrumental rationality.

The selected cases present debates about controversial strategic decisions that are all publicly debated in newspapers. In controversial public debates the reasons to act on can also be communicated in magazines, on TV and on the Internet. Thus, the reasons are ubiquitous in our everyday life (Weick and Browning 1986) and relatively easy to observe (Phillips *et al.* 2008; Tans 2006). This is in line with Eisenhardt's (1989) recommendation of choosing cases where the phenomenon of interest is relatively straightforward to observe (see also Eisenhardt and Graebner 2007; Yin 2003).

The first double case study is about a sculpture designed by McCarthy for Rotterdam city centre, which is criticized for being obscene (the Santa Claus debate) followed by a debate about the permissibility of religious symbolism in modern-day British society (the veil-ban debate). The debates belong to the argumentation field concerned with the question of subjective relevance related to the humanities. They focus on artist expression, taste and religious identity, leading to an expected dominance of expressive rationality. The second double case study is about minority integration in the Netherlands (integration debate) and the extension of settlement and pension rights of Gurkha veterans in the UK (Gurkha debate). Both belong to the argumentation field based on intersubjective reasoning as studied by sociologists or political scientists, and dominance of social rationality is expected. The third double case study is about the extension of Heathrow airport in London, and flex-work implementation in the Netherlands. Both questions affect the objective world 'out there' by extending a runway and by changing workplace design and ways of working as predominantly physical means for improvement. These debates, therefore, belong to the argumentation field of economics, and dominance of instrumental rationality is expected.

Research context: debates, actors and events

The studied debates provide a natural research context for asking the question which rationality dominates, and what reasons are perceived as most convincing given the discussed question. For the study of rationality, seen as acting on good reasons, public debates provide the place to find the given reasons for performed public acts. They are about large world problems, and thus meet the context requirements suggested by Gigerenzer (2010: 548). Moreover, the public debates do not only touch on the more general public aspects of instrumental and social rationality, but also touch on the expressive rational motivations, as it is always humans who make public decisions and who are affected by them.

However, next to these debates, which can be studied as discourses, there is a wider research context. It is not only the debates that matter, with their socially constructed and accepted or contested rationality. As a consequence of the debates decisions are made. And as a consequence of intended decisions debates get sparked. Therefore, the case studies consider the case history, based on the most relevant events that unfold during these debates. It helps to relate the expressed words and arguments with the actual historical decisions when studying rationality, as suggested by Cabantous *et al.* (2010), Gigerenzer (2010: 548) and Townley (2002: 177).

While the rationality is socially constructed in the debates, Heathrow's third runway also gets physically constructed and becomes part of history. Settlement and pension rights of Gurkhas are granted and become part of history as well. Santa Claus is a statue that appears physically as well, and then moves around. These events, and the actors performing them, constitute the wider research context, which is reflected on in the cases as 'case history' and as 'stakeholders and decision makers', before moving to the argumentation analysis.

Sources for studying the debates

The data sources are articles published in newspapers and magazines that report how decision makers and stakeholders debate complex decisions with major impact. The analysis investigates arguments in the newspaper articles presented by opponents and proponents. The articles were collected from the LexisNexis database by searching the indicated UK newspapers for articles about 'Muslim' or 'Islam' and 'veil', about 'Gurkha' and 'pension', and about 'Heathrow', 'third runway' and 'new runway'. The Dutch newspapers and magazines were searched using a combination of the words 'Santa Claus', 'McCarthy' and 'butt plug', and a combination of 'integration' (integratie), 'minorities' (minderheden) and 'debate' (debat). Articles about the flex-work debate were searched with the words 'new ways of working' (het nieuwe werken); in the Dutch context, this is the most common label for flex work. Table 2.3 shows when and where the articles were published and how many were included in each debate.

Table 2.3 Sources used

Debate	Period	Articles (N)	Newspapers (all debates) and Magazines (integration, flex work)
UK debates			Newspapers: *The Daily Express* and *The*
• Veil ban	2005–2009	335	*Sunday Express, The Financial Times,*
			The Guardian, The Herald and *The*
• Gurkhas	2009	88	*Sunday Herald, The Independent* and *The*
			Independent on Sunday, The Daily Mirror
• Heathrow	2003–2009	309	and *The Sunday Mirror, The Sun, The*
			Daily Telegraph and *The Sunday Tele-*
			graph, The Times and *The Sunday Times.*
Dutch debates			Newspapers: *AD Amersfoortse Krant, AD de*
• Santa Claus	2003–2014	34	*Dordtenaar, AD Rivierenland, Algemeen*
			Dagblad, ANP, Dagblad de Pers, Finan-
• Integration	2005–2014	65	*cieele Dagblad, Metro, Nederlands*
			Dagblad, NRC, NRC Next, Parool,
• Flex work	2007–2014	79	*Provinciaalse Zeeuwse Courant, Refor-*
			matorisch Dagblad, Rotterdams Dagblad,
			Telegraaf, Trouw, Volkskrant.
			Magazines: *De Groene Amsterdammer,*
			Elsevier, Fem Business & Finance,
			Forum, Opzij, Vrij Nederland.

It is important to note that not all debates are closed at the end of the study period, which is 2009 for the UK debates and 2014 for the Dutch debates. Heathrow's extension is an ongoing story in which only one episode is discussed – the third runway. The Dutch integration debate started decades ago and is still ongoing. Again, this is an episode of criticizing multicultural policies and trying to develop better ones. Likewise, the flex-work debate is ongoing. The other three debates are getting more closure: the veil ban has been rejected, settlement rights of Gurkhas have been granted and the Santa Claus sculpture has its final placement in a shopping area.

Analytical steps in case analysis

The analysis of newspaper articles starts at the level of single arguments expressed in text quotes, explores the connectedness of the arguments and moves up to the entire debate by relating all arguments to the most central claim in the debate, as in Bouwmeester (2010) or von Werder (1999). This coding process thus required several steps (see Corbin and Strauss 1990; Gioia *et al.* 2013) and was done using ATLAS.ti.

First, the grounds and rebuttals were identified in the newspaper articles by looking for relevant quotes and summarizing each one (open coding). Second, similar formulations were grouped under one code per ground or rebuttal (first-order codes). Third, all (sub)grounds and (sub)rebuttals were related to the final conclusion of the debate or what seemed to be the most widely shared conclusion at the moment of coding in the ongoing debates discussing Dutch integration policies,

Heathrow's extension and flex work. The hierarchy of arguments is established based on axial coding and presented in argumentation maps as Tables 3.1 and 3.2 (Chapter three), 4.1 and 4.2 (Chapter four) and 5.1 and 5.2 (Chapter five). All grounds in these tables follow 'since' and all rebuttals follow 'but'. This process of open coding and axial coding took several rounds to refine the formulation of the arguments as based on the summary of the underlying quotes. The tables representing the six debates also include a quantitative element, which is the groundedness of the codes. It is the number of quotes summarized by a primary code (ground or rebuttal). I included only those grounds and rebuttals in the debates that are grounded in at least two different articles to assure their relevance to the debated question.

As a last step, the coding process continued with second-order coding (Gioia *et al.* 2013) by identifying implied warrants that connect main grounds with grounds or grounds with sub-grounds, using Brockriede and Ehninger's (1960) categorization of warrants. Based on the warrant, the rationality was coded as instrumental when it referred to cause–effect or means–end relations often indicated by addressing causes (like expansion, measures, policies or barriers) and effects (like burnt fuel, costs, savings, burnouts or drawing attention). The rationality was coded as social rational in the case of arguments that referred to applicable social values, norms, rights or principles that served as grounds for action, such as bravery that needs to be rewarded, an expectation to adapt to Western society or a reference to labour laws that should protect workers. The rationality was coded as expressive when motivational arguments referred to individual emotions or desires as motives to act on, such as negative feelings of suppression, dislike or anger and positive feelings like sympathy or desire. Figure 2.1 gives examples of three such different types of arguments, indicated by implied warrants: 1 (individual motive), 2 (cause) and 3 (social value) referred to in the Santa Claus debate. Because rebuttals are counterarguments, their rationality could also be assessed.

Because a warrant is somewhat fluid (Tans 2006), and language somewhat ambiguous, arguments can imply more than one kind of rationality, like an effect and a feeling or value attached to the effect. For the sake of clarity, warrants are coded according to the rationality that is most dominant. Consider, for instance, a decision that might damage the reputation of a decision maker. If the original formulations in the newspaper articles stress that a bad reputation is unacceptable according to standards of key stakeholders, the warrant was coded as social rational (SR). However, if the argument stresses that the decision causes a bad reputation, the warrant was coded instrumental rational (IR). A formulation like 'we are unhappy with this reputation' would be coded as expressive rational (ER), as its focus is on personal emotions. Given the inclusive scope of the three rationalities together, all warrants expressed one of the three rationalities most clearly.

The last step also coded if the grounds or rebuttals were supportive (pro) or undermining towards the main claim (con) by using italics for the 'con' case. Each double case study in the following three chapters concludes with a cross-case analysis, which is further synthesized and deepened in Chapter six. By comparing the Dutch and English cases on the dominance of the expected rationality, and by analysing ways this dominant rationality gets undermined or supported by the other two rationalities, irrationalities can be coded (see the second column in Table 2.4).

Table 2.4 Critical rationality interactions

Cross-rationality evaluation	Signs indicating types of irrationality	Critical argumentation based on
Expressive by expressive	Emotional misfit/ self-deception	Motivational analogies and generalization
Social by expressive	Frustrating norms/values	Motivational amplified from generalization
Instrumental by expressive	Upsetting effects	Motivational amplified from generalization
Social by social	Value conflicts/ misapplied values	Classifications combined with analogies
Expressive by social	Intolerable wishes/desires	Classifications (deductive reasoning)
Instrumental by social	Immoral/inacceptable effects	Classifications (deductive reasoning)
Instrumental by instrumental	Means–end tensions/ unintended effects	Arguments from cause, sign and analogies
Expressive by instrumental	Impractical wishes/desires	Arguments from cause and motivation
Social by instrumental	Utopian norms/values	Arguments from cause and classification

Table 2.5 Four steps in the coding process, from left to right

Open in-vivo codes	First-order codes	Axial coding	Second-order codes
Summarizing an argument from a text quote	Same quotes together make arguments	Making argumentation map that connects all arguments	• Rationalities based on warrant • Pro and con arguments • Types of irrationality

Next the cross-case analysis explores the underlying argumentations for such irrationality criticisms or mutual support, as characterized in the last column of Table 2.4. These insights are new in the field of rationality studies. The entire coding process is summarized in Table 2.5.

The codes are inductively grounded (Corbin and Strauss 1990; Gioia *et al.* 2013) and work towards higher-order categories and relations between arguments and rationalities. These codes are linked to the literature, as far as such links can be found.

Discussion

Contribution to a method for studying rationality

The development of a method to analyse rationality based on argumentation analytical techniques began with the studies of van Houwelingen and Bouwmeester (2008)

and Bouwmeester (2013), and was inspired by the work of von Werder (1999), Toulmin (1994) and Toulmin *et al.* (1984). In the current study, the method is further developed to identify rationality interactions that lead to the discovery of different forms of cross-rationality critique, and the identification of different types of irrationality (Gaut 2012: 261). These critiques can help to improve the overall rationality of a decision. The impact of such critiques resonates with propositions developed in von Werder (1999) and Hoefer and Green (2016).

The analytical approach to explore rationality based on argumentation analysis fits the 'linguistic turn' in organization studies (Alvesson and Kärreman 2000a, 2000b, 2011). It is an interpretive method that belongs to a tradition of rhetorical analysis in management studies (Hoefer and Green 2016; Sillince and Suddaby 2008; Sillince *et al.* 2011; van Werven *et al.* 2015) and can also be seen as a form of discourse analysis (Putnam and Fairhurst 2001: 103–9). It brings back the awareness for discourse, rhetoric and dialectic in the study of rationality. It responds to calls for studying managers as rhetors (Hoefer and Green 2016), and to focus on controversies in decision-making (Goodnight 2010). As rationality is defined by having good reasons to act on, it remains surprising how little attention the rationality construct has got from discourse scholars, and how little the debate on rationality has paid attention to analytical possibilities of rhetoric and argumentation analysis.

Compared to experimental methods to study rationality as reported in Kahneman (2011), the current method contributes to developing a grounded theory approach, as it starts from the reasons given to act on in real-life situations. Earlier calls for studying rationality empirically and in real-life situations are made in Gigerenzer (2010: 548), Mueller *et al.* (2007: 857) and Townley (2002: 177). Complex real-life settings are fundamentally different from the experimental setting, which is short term, excludes learning, is focused and is simple to allow for unambiguous measurement. For our brains the experimental tasks are often too difficult to allow for quick answers, as demonstrated in the experiments discussed and co-designed by Kahneman (2011). These experiments demonstrate the limitations of our mind convincingly; however, such results do not allow for drawing conclusions about complex, real-life decision-making situations, as they are quite different. They run over time and enable debate and learning. The current study of the development of argumentation in decision-making debates meets such calls better.

Compared to philosophical and sociological studies in rationality research (Davidson 2004; Diesing 1976; MacIntyre 1988), the studied decision-making debates can add detail to the stylized examples commonly used. Such stylized examples can only replicate existing theoretical insights, but cannot build new theory as a grounded theory approach is designed for. For that reason, some types of rationality and irrationality are overlooked in earlier studies. However, they do show up in complex decision-making next to the more familiar forms of social and instrumental rationality. Moreover, the idealized versions of social and instrumental rationality, like Weber's (1972) universal value rationality or optimization calculus as suggested by economists (Weirich 2004) appear rather marginal in empirical studies (see, for instance, Cabantous *et al.* 2010). There is more evidence for localized and time-dependent rationalities in the rare empirical studies (see Bouwmeester 2013; Calabretta *et al.*

2016; Fisher and Freshwater 2014; Townley 1999, 2002, 2008). Also, compared to the studies on bounded rationality and heuristics, the rhetorical analysis allows for adding more breadth to the concept of rationality by studying all given reasons for a decision in their natural environment. It includes social- (Gigerenzer 2010) and expressive-rational considerations (Mellers *et al.* 2001), both still under-explored by scholars who focus on bounded rationality (Gigerenzer and Selten 2001: 1).

Limitations of the method

The first limitation related to the study of rationality expressed in public debates relates to how open a democracy is, where the analysed discussion takes place. Debates in the UK or the Netherlands are relatively open as newspapers can publish without censorship. The situation in Turkey is different today, and Russia or China are also more restrictive in what can be said publicly. This will influence the representation of a public debate, and thus the study of rationality, as certain reasons cannot be expressed. It might influence a debate on homosexuality as advocating gay and lesbian rights in Russia is illegal today. A debate where freedom of expression is important regarding government investments will be problematic in Turkey, as open debate implies government criticism and that is not allowed today. These positions in the debate will get repressed, and the picture we get on rationality will be disturbed. When data on rationality are gathered in public debates, researchers need to be aware of any restrictions applied to the media they use to gather their data. For the current study, such forms of silencing seem limited.

A second limitation concerns the scope of this research. When studying the rationality of major strategic decisions in a public setting, there is no single decision maker, making one well-defined decision or judgment, as in most experiments reported by Kahneman (2011). In complex and long-term strategic decisions, many stakeholders share responsibility and influence. In more small-scale real-life decisions, as reported in the introduction of this book, complexities also arise, many parties can be affected and decisions can take longer. In that sense, these more personal real-life decisions can be assumed to be analogue to the studied 'large world' real-life decisions in this book. Generalizability might be strong regarding the balance and fit of rationalities, and the evaluation of irrationalities. However, generalization to experimental settings can be doubted due to the fundamental differences between real-life and experimental settings (Gigerenzer 2010).

A third limitation is a focus on bounded rationality in this study. The approach cannot study how decision makers might maximize over different ends as economists do by aiming at a net positive effect. The arguments studied do not mention such procedures, but would also not be able to represent them in details as these calculations move beyond words. The studied arguments do report satisficing on many debated criteria (March and Simon 1958). Instrumental, social and expressive rationality allow for an independent assessment, and overall rationality increases when there is at least some rationality acknowledged for all perspectives. If one rationality assessment is negative, it makes the whole decision irrational from this perspective. However, optimization as procedure is also never referred to in the debates as being part of the decision-making processes, so this seems merely a theoretical limitation.

A last methodological limitation is that the study cannot distinguish between ex ante and post hoc rationalizations. However, as the public debates develop over time, arguments do influence debates and decisions ex ante. Decisions change based on what people bring forward. Still, participants might also legitimate behaviour ex post by not presenting the initial reasons that informed their decisions. For instance, it might be more effective for them to argue they wear a niqab based on their personal desire, thus referring to freedom of expression, instead of presenting it as a social norm or expectation in a religious community. Due to text analysis, these differences will stay out of sight, as we cannot ask probing questions or triangulate findings from different sources. Nevertheless, the cases will still allow the study of ex ante rationalizations due to their longitudinal character, as the influence of the given arguments on decisions that follow them is visible over time.

References

Alvesson, M. and Kärreman, D. (2000a) Taking the linguistic turn in organizational research: Challenges, responses, consequences. *The Journal of Applied Behavioral Science*, 36(2), 136.

Alvesson, M. and Kärreman, D. (2000b) Varieties of discourse: On the study of organizations through discourse analysis. *Human relations*, 53(9), 1125–49.

Alvesson, M. and Kärreman, D. (2011) Decolonializing discourse: Critical reflections on organizational discourse analysis. *Human Relations*, 64(9), 1121–46.

Aristotle (1991) *On Rhetoric: A Theory of Civil Discourse*. Oxford: Oxford University Press.

Austin, J. L. (2003) *How to do Things with Words: The William James Lectures Delivered in 1955*. Cambridge: Harvard University Press.

Barraquier, A. (2011) Ethical behaviour in practice: Decision outcomes and strategic implications. *British Journal of Management*, 22(s1), S28–46.

Bergset, L. (2015) The rationality and irrationality of financing green start-ups. *Administrative Sciences*, 5(4), 260–85.

Bouwmeester, O. (2010) *Economic Advice and Rhetoric: Why Do Consultants Perform Better Than Academic Advisers?* Cheltenham: Edward Elgar.

Bouwmeester, O. (2013) Field dependency of argumentation rationality in decision-making debates. *Journal of Management Inquiry*, 22(4), 415–33.

Brockriede, W. and Ehninger, D. (1960) Toulmin on argument: An interpretation and application. *Quarterly Journal of Speech*, 46(1), 44–53.

Bronn, C. (1998) Applying epistemic logic and evidential theory to strategic arguments. *Strategic Management Journal*, 19(1), 81–95.

Cabantous, L., Gond, J. P. and Johnson-Cramer, M. (2010) Decision theory as practice: Crafting rationality in organizations. *Organization Studies*, 31(11), 1531–66.

Calabretta, G., Gemser, G. and Wijnberg, N. M. (2016) The interplay between intuition and rationality in strategic decision making: A paradox perspective. *Organization Studies*. DOI: 10.1177/0170840616655483.

Churchman, C. W. (1962) On rational decision making. *Management Technology*, 2(2), 71–6.

Clegg, S., Kornberger, M. and Rhodes, C. (2007) Business ethics as practice. *British Journal of Management*, 18(2), 107–22.

Corbin, J. M. and Strauss, A. (1990) Grounded theory research: Procedures, canons, and evaluative criteria. *Qualitative Sociology*, 13(1), 3–21.

Cornelissen, J. P., Oswick, C., Thøger Christensen, L. and Phillips, N. (2008) Metaphor in organizational research: Context, modalities and implications for research—introduction. *Organization Studies*, 29(1), 7–22.

Corvellec, H. (2007) Arguing for a license to operate: The case of the Swedish wind power industry. *Corporate Communications: An International Journal*, 12(2), 129–44.

Davidson, D. (2004) *Problems of Rationality.* Vol. 4. Oxford: Oxford University Press.

Dewey, J. (2008) Democracy and education, in Boydston, J. A. (ed), *The Middle Works of John Dewey 1899–1924: Volume 9 1916.* Carbondale, IL: Southern Illinois University Press, pp. 343–55.

Diesing, P. (1976) *Reason in Society: Five Types of Decisions and Their Social Conditions.* Westport: Greenwood Press.

Eisenhardt, K. M. (1989) Building theories from case study research. *The Academy of Management Review*, 14(4), 532–50.

Eisenhardt, K. M. and Zbaracki, M. J. (1992) Strategic decision making. *Strategic Management Journal*, 13(S2), 17–37.

Eisenhardt, K. M. and Graebner, M. E. (2007) Theory building from cases: Opportunities and challenges. *The Academy of Management Journal*, 50(1), 25–32.

Elbanna, S. (2006) Strategic decision-making: Process perspectives. *International Journal of Management Reviews*, 8(1), 1–20.

Elbanna, S. and Child, J. (2007) Influences on strategic decision effectiveness: Development and test of an integrative model. *Strategic Management Journal*, 28(4), 431–53.

Elster, J. (1989) Social norms and economic theory. *The Journal of Economic Perspectives*, 3(4), 99–117.

Elster, J. (2006) Fairness and norms. *Social Research: An International Quarterly*, 73(2), 365–76.

Elster, J. (2009) *Reason and Rationality.* Princeton, NJ: Princeton University Press.

Engelen, B. (2006) Solving the paradox: The expressive rationality of the decision to vote. *Rationality and Society*, 18(4), 419–41.

Fisher, P. and Freshwater, D. (2014) Towards compassionate care through aesthetic rationality. *Scandinavian Journal of Caring Sciences*, 28(4), 767–74.

Fredrickson, J. W. and Iaquinto, A. L. (1989) Inertia and creeping rationality in strategic decision processes. *Academy of Management Journal*, 32(3), 516–42.

Freeman, R. E. (2010) *Strategic Management: A Stakeholder Approach.* Cambridge: Cambridge University Press.

Gaut, B. (2012) Creativity and rationality. *The Journal of Aesthetics and Art Criticism*, 70(3), 259–70.

Gigerenzer, G. (2010) Moral satisficing: Rethinking moral behavior as bounded rationality. *Topics in Cognitive Science*, 2(3), 528–54.

Gigerenzer, G. and Selten, R. (2001) Rethinking rationality, in Gigerenzer, G. and Selten, R. (eds), *Bounded Rationality: The Adaptive Toolbox.* Cambridge, MA: MIT Press, pp. 1–12.

Gigerenzer, G. and Sturm, T. (2012) How (far) can rationality be naturalized? *Synthese*, 187(1), 243–68.

Gioia, D. A., Corley, K. G. and Hamilton, A. L. (2013) Seeking qualitative rigor in inductive research notes on the Gioia methodology. *Organizational Research Methods*, 16(1), 15–31.

Goodnight, G. T. (2010) Complex cases and legitimation inference: Extending the Toulmin model to deliberative argument in controversy, in Hitchcock, D. and Verheij, B. (eds),

Arguing on the Toulmin Model: New Essays in Argument Analysis and Evaluation. Dordrecht: Springer, pp. 39–48.

Green Jr, S. E. (2004) A rhetorical theory of diffusion. *The Academy of Management Review*, 29(4), 653–69.

Greenspan, P. (2004) Practical reasoning and emotion, in Mele, A. R. and Rawling, P. (eds), *The Oxford Handbook of Rationality*. New York: Oxford University Press, pp. 206–21.

Habermas, J. (1988) *Theorie des Kommunikativen Handelns, Band 1, 2*. Frankfurt: Suhrkamp.

Haidt, J. (2001) The emotional dog and its rational tail: A social intuitionist approach to moral judgment. *Psychological Review*, 108(4), 814–34.

Hargreaves Heap, S. (2001) Expressive rationality: Is self-worth just another kind of preference?, in Mäki, U. (ed), *The Economic World View: Studies in the Ontology of Economics*. Cambridge: Cambridge University Press, pp. 98–113.

Harmon, D. J., Green, S. E. and Goodnight, G. T. (2015) A model of rhetorical legitimation: The structure of communication and cognition underlying institutional maintenance and change. *Academy of Management Review*, 40(1), 76–95.

Harre, R. and Gillett, G. (1994) *The Discursive Mind*. Thousand Oaks, CA: SAGE Publications.

Healy, G., Kirton, G., Özbilgin, M. and Oikelome, F. (2010) Competing rationalities in the diversity project of the UK judiciary: The politics of assessment centres. *Human Relations*, 63(6), 807–34.

Hegel, G. F. W. (1986) *Grundlinien der Philosophie des Rechts*. Frankfurt am Main: Suhrkamp.

Henderson, D. (2010) Explanation and rationality naturalized. *Philosophy of the Social Sciences*, 40(1), 30–58.

Hendry, J. (2000) Strategic decision making, discourse, and strategy as social practice. *Journal of Management Studies*, 37(7), 955–78.

Hoefer, R. L. and Green, S. E. (2016) A rhetorical model of institutional decision making: The role of rhetoric in the formation and change of legitimacy judgments. *Academy of Management Review*, 41(1), 130–50.

Houwelingen, G. van and Bouwmeester, O. (2008) Situationele rationaliteit in publieke besluitvorming. *Filosofie in Bedrijf*, 18(2), 26–40.

Kahneman, D. (2011) *Thinking, Fast and Slow*. New York: FSG.

Kant, I. (1990) *Kritik der Praktischen Vernunft*. Hamburg: Felix Meiner.

Lagueux, M. (2010) *Rationality and Explanation in Economics*. London: Routledge.

Li, Y., Ashkanasy, N. M. and Ahlstrom, D. (2014) The rationality of emotions: A hybrid process model of decision-making under uncertainty. *Asia Pacific Journal of Management*, 31(1), 293–308.

MacIntyre, A. C. (1988) *Whose Justice? Which Rationality?* London: Duckworth.

Majone, G. (1992) *Evidence, Argument and Persuasion in the Policy Process*. New Haven, CT: Yale University Press.

March, J. G. and Simon, H. A. (1958) *Organizations*. New York: John Wiley.

Mellers, B. A., Schwartz, A. and Cooke, A. D. J. (1998) Judgment and decision making. *Annual Review of Psychology*, 49(1), 447–77.

Mellers, B. A., Erev, I., Fessler, D. M., Hemelrijk, C. K., Hertwig, R., Laland, K. N., Scherer, K. R., Seeley, T. D., Selten, R. and Tetlock, P. E. (2001) Effects of emotions and social processes on bounded rationality, in Gigerenzer, G. and Selten, R. (eds), *Bounded Rationality: The Adaptive Toolbox*. Cambridge, MA: MIT Press, pp. 263–79.

Minto, B. (1995) *The Pyramid Principle: Logic in Writing and Thinking*. London: Pitman Publishing.

Mitroff, I. I. and Mason, R. O. (1980) Structuring III structured policy issues: Further explorations in a methodology for messy problems. *Strategic Management Journal*, 1(4), 331–42.

Mitroff, I. I., Mason, R. O. and Barabba, V. P. (1982) Policy as argument–a logic for ill-structured decision problems. *Management Science*, 28(12), 1391–404.

Mueller, G. C., Mone, M. A. and Barker, V. L. (2007) Formal strategic analyses and organizational performance: Decomposing the rational model. *Organization Studies*, 28(6), 853–83.

Peacock, A. (1992) The credibility of economic advice to government. *The Economic Journal*, 102(414), 1213–22.

Perelman, C. (1982) *The Realm of Rhetoric*. Notre Dame: University of Notre Dame Press.

Phillips, N., Sewell, G. and Jaynes, S. (2008) Applying critical discourse analysis in strategic management research. *Organizational Research Methods*, 11(4), 770–89.

Putnam, L. L. and Fairhurst, G. T. (2001) Discourse analysis in organizations, in Jablin, F. M. and Putnam, L. L. (eds), *The New Handbook of Organizational Communication: Advances in Theory, Research, and Methods*. Thousand Oaks, CA: SAGE Publications, pp. 78–136.

Racko, G. (2011) On the normative consequences of economic rationality: A case study of a Swedish economics school in Latvia. *European Sociological Review*, 27(6), 772–89.

Rorty, R. (1992) A pragmatist view of rationality and cultural difference. *Philosophy East and West*, 42(4), 581–96.

Satow, R. L. (1975) Value-rational authority and professional organizations: Weber's missing type. *Administrative Science Quarterly*, 20(4), 526–31.

Scherer, K. R. (2011) On the rationality of emotions: Or, when are emotions rational? *Social Science Information*, 50(3–4), 330–50.

Schildt, H. A., Mantere, S. and Vaara, E. (2011) Reasonability and the linguistic division of labor in institutional work. *Journal of Management Inquiry*, 20(1), 82–6.

Schipper, F. (1996) Rationality and the philosophy of organization. *Organization*, 3(2), 267–89.

Sedlacek, T. (2011) *Economics of Good and Evil: The Quest for Economic Meaning from Gilgamesh to Wall Street*. Oxford: Oxford University Press.

Shafir, E., Simonson, I. and Tversky, A. (1993) Reason-based choice. *Cognition*, 49(1–2), 11–36.

Sillince, J. A. A. and Suddaby, R. (2008) Organizational rhetoric. *Management Communication Quarterly*, 22(1), 5.

Sillince, J., Jarzabkowski, P. and Shaw, D. (2011) Shaping strategic action through the rhetorical construction and exploitation of ambiguity. *Organization Science*, 23(3), 630–50.

Smith, A. (1982) *The Theory of Moral Sentiments*. Indianapolis, IN: Liberty Classics.

Suchman, M. C. (1995) Managing legitimacy: Strategic and institutional approaches. *Academy of Management Review*, 20(3), 571–610.

Tans, O. (2006) The fluidity of warrants: Using the Toulmin model to analyze practical discourse, in Hitchcock, D. and Verheij, B. (eds), *Arguing on the Toulmin Model: New Essays in Argument Analysis and Evaluation*. Dordrecht: Springer, pp. 219–30.

Tinbergen, J. (1956) *Economic Policy: Principles and Design*. Amsterdam: Noord Hollandsche Uitgeversmaatschappij.

Toulmin, S. E. (1994) *The Uses of Argument*. Cambridge: Cambridge University Press.

Toulmin, S. E., Rieke, R. J. and Janik, A. (1984) *An Introduction to Reasoning*. New York: Macmillan.

Townley, B. (1999) Practical reason and performance appraisal. *Journal of Management Studies*, 36(3), 287–306.

Townley, B. (2002) The role of competing rationalities in institutional change. *Academy of Management Journal*, 45(1), 163–79.

Townley, B. (2008) *Reason's Neglect: Rationality and Organizing*. Oxford: Oxford University Press.

Vaara, E. (2002) On the discursive construction of success/failure in narratives of post-merger integration. *Organization Studies*, 23(2), 211–48.

Weber, M. (1972) *Wirtschaft und Gesellschaft: Grundriß der Verstehenden Soziologie*. 5th ed. Tubingen, Germany: JCB Mohr (Paul Siebeck).

Weick, K. E. and Browning, L. D. (1986) Argument and narration in organizational communication. *Journal of Management*, 12(2), 243–59.

Weirich, P. (2004) Economic rationality, in Mele, A. R. and Rawling, P. (eds), *The Oxford Handbook of Rationality*. Oxford: Oxford University Press, pp. 380–98.

Werder, A. von (1999) Argumentation rationality of management decisions. *Organization Science*, 10(5), 672–90.

Werven, R. van, Bouwmeester, O. and Cornelissen, J. P. (2015) The power of arguments: How entrepreneurs convince stakeholders of the legitimate distinctiveness of their ventures. *Journal of Business Venturing*, 30(4), 616–31.

Yin, R. K. (2003) *Case Study Research: Design and Methods*. Thousand Oaks, CA: SAGE Publications.

3 Expressive rationality
A human voice in the reasons we act on

Introducing expressive rationality

When we can give good reasons for what we do, we behave rationally. This definition of acting rationally by grounding what we do in good reasons, is widely shared (Davidson 2004: 169; Elbanna 2006: 3; Elbanna and Child 2007: 433; Elster 2009: 2; Engelen 2006: 427; Gigerenzer and Sturm 2012: 243–5; Green 2004: 655; Henderson 2010: 32). Private, but also rational policy or management decisions require such good reasons to act on (Majone 1992; von Werder 1999). These reasons can be based on causal arguments: do my actions realize the purpose I have set? Or, don't my actions waste resources? Such good reasons are based on conceptions of instrumental or economic rationality (Diesing 1976; Habermas 1988; Tinbergen 1956; Weber 1972). They dominate current management and policy interpretations of rationality. They aim at optimizing utility, welfare or profit. An alternative form of instrumental rationality is called bounded rationality, which aims at satisficing instead of optimizing (March and Simon 1958). Bounded rationality dominates current understandings of instrumental rationality in organization theory, as it gives a more realistic image of what decision makers do, than optimization as assumed by economists.

Academic discussions on rationality as having good reasons to act on, do consider more aspects of rationality. Value rationality, another central concept introduced and discussed by Weber (1972), includes ethical considerations. It evaluates what goals and values we want to achieve, before we start with optimizing or satisficing our ways to achieve these goals. Weber's (1972: 12) approach aims at the universal values and principles guiding our actions. He knows that traditions also offer guidance for our actions, but he doubts their rationality in many cases. Currently, many scholars do not demand values to be universal. They consider rationality as also based on more temporary and local objectives or on shared values grounded in fashions or customs (Abrahamson 1996; Esposito 2011; Kilduff and Mehra 1997; MacIntyre 1988). Reasoning based on more local and time-bound social values lets you engage in action because of others, like more universal values do. You want to orient yourself towards shared values, when making or explaining decisions. Such local reasons are grounded in intersubjective agreement, which makes them social rational (Churchman 1962; Dahms 1997; Sen 1993), like the more universal moral principles and objectives as suggested by Weber (1972) or Habermas (1988). The same applies to majority arguments based on political rationality (Diesing 1976; Eisenhardt and Zbaracki 1992).

Least discussed in the literature on rationality are subjective grounds for our actions, like our taste for deciding what to eat, or our personal sympathies as motive for engaging in friendship. Weber (1972: 12) considers it affective action, which is, for him, like traditional action close to or beyond the borders of rationality. Today, there is increasing support for the idea that affective action can be within the borders of rationality, and more often so than suggested by Weber. Engelen (2006), Hargreaves Heap (2001) and Li *et al.* (2014) label reasoning based on such affective or subjective motives, therefore, expressive rational. Others label it affective rational (Gaut 2012). Expressive rationality seeks good reasons for individual action that refer to someone's enthusiasm, desires, feelings of sympathy and opposite emotions like fear, dislike or anger as motives (Greenspan 2004; Kim 2016; Scherer 2011). Less rational from an expressive perspective would be to choose a job you do not really like, study something that does not interest you, meet people that make you unhappy or stick to a hobby that bores you. Thus, we require authenticity of such expressive grounds if we want to evaluate their validity (Habermas 1988: 42), while self-deception (Davidson 2004) or forms of 'affective irrationality' (Gaut 2012: 261) would undermine it. These are feelings that do not relate well to a situation; like, for example, a strong fear of harmless domestic spiders.

Decisions that require predominantly expressive rationality include decisions such as what career steps we want to make, how to decorate our house, to whom we want to get married, etc. Expressive rationality gives us orientation for such personal decisions, and also helps to explain to others why we made such decisions based on what was important to us. It relates to taste, well-being, emotional fulfilment and aesthetic considerations (Fisher and Freshwater 2014), but it can also include more hedonic aspects in legitimating a decision (Cabanac and Bonniot-Cabanac 2007). In contrast, social rationality finds reasons for decisions in socially shared norms and principles; thus, more in what we ought to do based on a social motive, instead of what we want to do ourselves.

In the current debates on rationality, expressive rationality has received little attention by scholars of economics, management or public administration. What seems similar on face value are subjective preferences that help consumers to maximize their utility. However, preferences as defined by economists are quite abstract and mainly invented to facilitate optimization calculus. It hardly equals the word preference as we normally use it, which is a synonym of a liking or fondness. Economic preferences must, for instance, be fixed in their weight and value (Elster 2009: 35) to enable calculations. The concept is also extremely broad, as it may range from egoistic preferences to altruistic preferences, as long as they can get a value to enable optimization calculus. Therefore, the concept is impractical as people cannot express such preferences – neither as a private person, nor when acting professionally in a business-to-business setting (Blaug 1980: 150). The theoretical world of 'Max U', a fictitious name (Max) for the homo economicus referred to by McCloskey (2016), is too different from the world of normal people, and from how they experience and legitimize decisions in their life. McCloskey actually suggests that Max is a criminal, by only giving the first letter of the surname, which should read like Utility. It is Max U's lack of compassion, focus on self-interest and his robot-like optimization behaviour (Klamer 1987) which fits the idea of criminal, or, at least, pathological, mind.

Mellers *et al.* (2001: 265–70) frame the role of emotions differently in relation to decision-making; they have an impact, but this impact is not intrinsically rational. They see three links between emotions and decision-making. First, at the time of the choice when background emotions like joy, sadness or anxiety influence a decision. They find that anxiety makes a search process for a decision more intense (you try to reduce it), while happiness makes it less intense and less critical. Anger is found to have a similar moderating effect, as it can make deliberations more intense (Kim 2016). Second, Mellers *et al.* (2001) also found that task-related emotions, like positive affect, can positively influence making a decision. The opposite of feeling uncertain, uncomfortable or even angry about a decision can lead to delay or refusal. Third, anticipated emotions related to a decision like regret or disappointment can influence our decision by not choosing this option. Mellers *et al.* (2001: 263) consider emotions influential in the decision-making process; they act as a moderator, and are sometimes quite productive, but they are not framed as rational themselves.

Weber (1972: 12) questions the rationality of affective judgments on conceptual grounds. Goal rationality, which is only instrumental in realizing a goal, and value rationality, which helps to define these goals, both meet his idea of rationality (Weber 1972), but traditional or affective motives to act on do not, as they are often not aligned with the other two. Habermas agrees, but he adds some nuance. He also considers expressive reasoning weak in drawing conclusions because a general consensus based on what he calls 'discourse' is not possible (Habermas 1988: 41–5). Such discourse can lead to general consensus, which is only possible for Weber's two types of rationality. Instrumental, goal-rational and knowledge-based questions can be evaluated by what we consider true. The right application and proper definition of shared practical norms and universal values can help to evaluate what we do based on what we consider right. For instance, driving on the left side in England is the right thing to do, and we can all agree on this. In contrast, expressive rationality, such as aesthetic judgments made by art critics or therapeutic criticisms made by a therapist, can help to reflect on the authenticity and truthfulness of such artistic and personal expressions, but they are not universally right or true. The best result that can be achieved is preventing self-deception. Habermas (1988), therefore, argues expressive rationality cannot be part of public discourse, nor does it generate good reasons to legitimate public actions as the scope is too subjective. However, the universalistic perspectives advocated by Weber and Habermas, that universal consensus should be the norm for rationality, get more and more contested (MacIntyre 1988).

Currently, a growing number of scholars suggest to consider expressive rationality a central part of rationality. They argue expressive rationality can provide a unique and additional set of good reasons for actions by relating to our subjectivity

(Engelen 2006; Gaut 2012; Greenspan 2004; Hargreaves Heap 2001; Li *et al.* 2014; Scherer 2011), even in the context of publicly debated decisions (Bouwmeester 2013) or in the context of organizations (Fisher and Freshwater 2014). As public decisions can affect the feelings of many stakeholders, thus making them more or less supportive, the influence of such feelings and emotions on motivating decisions demands further research (Gigerenzer and Selten 2001; Volz and Hertwig 2016). This research is possible, as these stakeholders express their feelings in debates on public decisions, and they refer to them as reasons to support or fight such decisions.

This chapter seeks to explore expressive rationality in the context of two public debates on questions with subjective relevance for the involved stakeholders. The aim of the discussion is to discover the impact of expressive-rational reasons on decision-making. As expressive rationality can interact with social rationality grounded in intersubjective agreements, or with instrumental rationality grounded in means-end logics, such interactions are also the subject of inquiry. By analysing the arguments that people use when defending or objecting decisions that affect them personally, we will give more insight into the subjective foundations of expressive rationality.

A double case study on two public debates mainly grounded in expressive-rational argumentation will serve to flesh out the rationality concept by analysing the kinds of arguments used. The debates are theoretically sampled by their focus on questions with subjective relevance. The first debate discussed in this chapter is about exhibiting a sculpture designed by McCarthy called 'Santa Claus'. This debate, based in the Netherlands, is about its provocative nature and its rather obscene sexual symbolism for a public artwork. It is about liking and disliking the work. The debate lasted from 2003 to 2014 and was reported in 34 articles published in local and national Dutch newspapers. The second debate is about institution-alizing a veil ban in the UK, which mainly aims at prohibiting the niqab, a face veil that covers all of the face except for the eyes. The debate is about religious expression, and, again, about taste and personal preferences. It lasted from 2005 to 2009, and was reported in 335 articles published in national newspapers in the UK. After introducing the two debates with a short case history and exposition of all the arguments, some illustrated with underlying quotes from the newspapers, a cross-case analysis follows, which further clarifies the concept of expressive rationality. This chapter concludes with a discussion, relating the findings from the argumen-tation analysis to current scholarly discussions on expressive rationality. Later, chapters will show debates where expressive rationality is less central in supporting decisions, as these debates are sampled differently. They relate more to social norms than to affects as motives for a decision (Chapter four), or to instrumental questions about how to best reach certain objectives (Chapter five).

The first contribution of the present chapter is mapping the concept of expres-sive rationality in more detail than before (Bouwmeester 2013; Engelen 2006; Greenspan 2004; Hargreaves Heap 2001). It is built up from arguments that refer to expressions such as dislike, not wanting him, wanting to get rid of him by opponents in the Santa Claus debate, and appreciation, sympathy, wanting him close and admiration by proponents. These arguments contradict or support each other. In the veil-ban debate, the reported emotions used in expressive-rational arguments include feeling uneasy, offended, rejected or frightened. Such feelings are assigned to proponents of the veil ban who dislike the consequences of less tolerant Muslim beliefs and traditions. Expressing pride, commitment and a deeply felt religious affiliation by wearing a hijab or niqab are emotions referred to by Muslims. The attributes of expressive rationality grounded in human emotions obviously matter to others, and they fuel the public debates. During the debates, we not only see how emotions are challenged, as in therapeutic criticism (Habermas 1988), or how forms of self-deception are criticized (Davidson 2004), but the process also helps to prioritize the desire of some Muslims to wear a niqab over Western aversions. Likewise, the likings of Santa Claus eventually dominate the dislikings, but this takes a period of years. The strong emotions balance out over time, and during the debates they seem to become more rational, which means more balanced, better fitting the situation and more authentic.

Mapping the interactions between social and expressive rationality is the second contribution of this chapter; this adds to the concept of irrationality. There is not only internal expressive irrationality stemming from self-deception, over-optimism, depression, moods, etc. (Davidson 2004; Li *et al.* 2014; Scherer 2011), but some feelings are also not considered reasonable by others (Scherer 2011: 334), like, initially, the desire to wear a face veil, or the sympathy for exposing obscene art in a public environment. These decisions are not seen as reasonable against standards of social rationality. However, the study also shows how expressive rationality evaluates back, suggesting the irrationality of social norms. Arguments referring to different positive emotions help to reject the Santa Claus ban and the veil ban, bottom-up, or inductively, as suggested by Adam Smith (1982: 319–20). They help to reject social-rational arguments, such as banning Santa Claus for being obscene, or banning the veil for being repressive. Social judgments can receive both sympathy and disapproval from an expressive-rational perspective. Initially, there is much expressive support for banning obscene art from a public space based on dislike and aversion. Over time, the expressive judgment becomes more positive, with more and more people expressing their sympathy for the sculpture. In the end, the Santa Claus ban, based on social-rational arguments, is seen as irrational assessed against expressive rationality, articulated by the many who feel sympathy for the statue.

Santa Claus' trip to a shopping area

History

In November 2000 IBC (Internationale Beelden Commissie [International Art Committee of the City Rotterdam]) decided to ask Paul McCarthy to design a public artwork for Rotterdam city centre. In 2001, Rotterdam would become the cultural capital and IBC was a committee to advise the city regarding public sculptures. For McCarthy, the request to design a public sculpture was new, since he had not made public art before. Until then, his works were visible in galleries and museums and they were known to be provocative. McCarthy says: 'I admit, provocation is part of my work, but I am not an artist who consciously aims at provocation' (*Rotterdams Dagblad*, June 26, 2004).

In response to the invitation of ICB McCarthy suggested two alternative artworks: first, a metal house in the water where people could spend one night, with a key to be asked for in a museum; and second, Santa Claus with a bell and a Christmas tree in his hands – the latter also looks somewhat like a butt plug. He expected the city would choose the house, but they did not. The advisory committee IBC looked at the proposals and wanted the artist to further develop Santa Claus. In 2003, the city gave McCarthy an assignment to make Santa Claus for the price of 280,000 Euros. The statue would be six metres high and made of bronze, in a dark colour instead of bright colours, so that it would not be too provocative. McCarthy's idea was to criticize unlimited consumerism as visible during Christmas, so he envisioned a shopping district as the best location for Santa Claus. After a while the idea started to raise a lot of resistance from Christian and local right-wing parties, so much so that McCarthy suggested the city drop the idea in 2004: 'Can your city live with this?' he asked. ICB expected the resistance to be temporary and not too serious. They responded to the artist: 'Yes, this is Holland' (*Rotterdams Dagblad*, June 26, 2004).

McCarthy went on to make the statue and in 2005 it was ready. Resistance had become so strong by then that the city withdrew the idea to unveil the statue in public, instead, they chose the court of a museum as the first location to show Santa Claus, and first stored it at a secret location. On September 26, 2005, Santa Claus was unveiled in the Museum Boijmans van Beuningen, and in the years to come the interest in Santa Claus grew. In 2007, the city decided to find a new public location, as originally intended by the artist. In 2008, Santa Claus arrived at Eendrachtsplein, its final destination (see Figure 3.1). There are no longer any traces of opposition. Rotterdam got used to its statue, and started to love it. Santa Claus has since attracted a lot of tourists.

Stakeholders and decision makers

Decision authority was within the municipality from the start. The mayor and aldermen made the decision to buy Santa Claus. IBC was an advisory committee, and influenced the decision on many occasions. The city council had a say as well. They were positive before 2002, but changed their mind after the elections. Parties that were in favour of Santa Claus lost dramatically and a new local party, Leefbaar Rotterdam, entered the council with 35% of the votes. They had a critical opinion about Santa Claus and argued that a Christmas tree in the hands of Santa Claus 'needs to be green' (*Volkskrant*, September 22, 2005) if it is intended to be a Christmas tree. Christian parties were critical from the start, but also the liberals changed their mind, which made opponents the majority in the council between 2002 and 2006. After the election in 2006 things changed again. In the meantime, shopkeepers saw the potential of Santa Claus for their shopping area. They became strong supporters and some shopkeepers at Nieuwe Binnenweg even made Santa Claus footprints on the street. These started from the museum court of Boijmans van

Figure 3.1 Santa Claus, Eendrachtsplein, Rotterdam.

Beuningen where Santa Claus had temporary asylum, and ended in their street. There they showed little Santa Clauses in their windows. Also, the general audience became more and more positive towards 2008, including parents with children visiting the museum.

Arguments used

Rationality in the debate on Santa Claus is mainly expressive rational (ER), referring to liking and disliking, anger, artistic expression, etc. Proponents argue based on their liking of the statue and sympathy for its provocative message inviting reflection on unlimited consumerism and shopkeepers for its contribution to the attractiveness of the shopping district. Opponents also use expressive-rational arguments by saying that the statue is awful. They mention social-rational (SR) arguments to refer to more general norms and values, and these seem to work stronger. Taste differences are not very convincing in blocking the work of a famous international artist. Instrumental-rational (IR) arguments are used the least. They refer to effects, means, ends, etc. The effect of opposition was a three-year delay of the placement of Santa Claus in an open and public environment. Table 3.1 summarizes the main arguments in the Santa Claus debate. The last column presents the groundedness of grounds and rebuttals (their frequency of appearance in the newspapers). The arguments of the opponents of Santa Claus are presented in italics, and those of the proponents in normal case.

Arguments pro are mainly expressive rational

Proponents of Santa Claus explained the value of McCarthy's work based on his critical ability to reframe the meaning of important symbols in our Western culture, but also by addressing how others have reframed their meaning as visible in the supportive sub-arguments for the first main argument in Table 3.1:

> According to McCarthy it is no coincidence that Santa Claus got his most popular appearance from Coca-Cola's marketing agency. He appears every year as a tyrant, disconnected from the peaceful Christian idea behind Christmas. Due to an aggressive marketing campaign his will is law. The message is: buy, consume and spend your money.
>
> (*Rotterdams Dagblad*, June 26, 2004)

With Santa Claus McCarthy criticizes the reframed meaning of the Coca-Cola Santa Claus, with the butt plug symbolizing consumerism aiming at unlimited pleasure seeking. Jan van Adrichem, member of the advisory committee IBC, appreciates this paradoxical expression of the sculpture. He argues that this kind of art fits a city like Rotterdam:

> The sculpture is a paraphrase on 19th century elite culture by being made of bronze and by its imposing size. At the same time the statue refers to mass culture by resembling a garden gnome and by its loose reference to a well-known sex attribute. The statue is as complex as life in a big city.
>
> (*Volkskrant*, September 22, 2005)

IBC also argued in response to critics that the sculpture is less obscene than, for instance, advertisements about breast augmentation, as were publicly promoted on large billboards in the city (*Trouw*, November 29, 2008). Shopkeepers in the city, represented by Guus van der Werff as chair of their association, supported the sculpture in a public environment with the following argument: 'We have always argued that the sculpture has to go public at a spot where it belongs: in a shopping district' (*AD/Rivierenland*, February 29, 2008). Their motive is that it makes their shopping district more attractive and that it probably will increase sales by generating more traffic. They see the humour of this sculpture that criticizes extreme Western consumerism and, at the same time, helps them to make their street more attractive, as explained by Gerard Roijakkers, chair of the shopkeepers at Nieuwe Binnenweg and Eendrachtsplein, in *Rotterdams Dagblad* (November 27, 2008).

Table 3.1 Santa Claus debate

Claim, grounds and rebuttals; con case in italics	IR	SR	ER	(N)
Claim Santa Claus (Santa with Butt Plug) deserves a visible place in a public environment in Rotterdam city centre				
Since McCarthy designed Santa Claus for a shopping district as the place that best fits its critical message			X	5
Since McCarthy designed Santa Claus holding a bell and an abstract Christmas tree, naming the work 'Santa with Butt Plug'			X	6
Since McCarthy's art invites reflection among consumers. Provocation is not an end in itself	X			5
Since McCarthy intends to criticize unlimited consumerism, capitalism and violence in his art		X		3
Since McCarthy reframes meaning: with Santa Claus (response to Coca-Cola), Pinocchio (Disney) and other works			X	3
Since McCarthy developed the idea for his first public artwork in 2000 as an assignment by the city of Rotterdam	X			2
Since The city (mayor, aldermen, council) decided to buy Santa Claus for 280,000 Euros as public artwork for the city centre	X			5
Since Advisory committee IBC advised the city to buy Santa Claus as the most attractive option		X		4
Since Advisory committee IBC suggested a shopping district near De Doelen as best suitable location		X		6
But Advisory committee IBC did not expect very much public resistance and dislike, unlike McCarthy			X	5
But *Due to its provocative appearance Santa Claus became one of the most criticized statues*		X		4
But Advisory committee IBC and aldermen can appreciate the ongoing debate		X		3
But Art supporters claim citizen participation in designing art is not good for its development		X		2

(Continued)

Table 3.1 (continued)

Claim, grounds and rebuttals; con case in italics	IR	SR	ER	(N)
Since The city finally decided to find a public location in 2007, resulting in the shopping district Eendrachtsplein in 2008	X			7
Since General audience appreciates Santa Claus more and more between 2003 and 2010			X	17
Since Shopkeepers support Santa Claus and want him in a shopping district			X	10
But Shopkeepers Binnenweg want him close, at Binnenwegplein			X	4
But *Shopkeepers Koopgoot do not want him in their shopping district*			X	2
Since Liberals wanted Santa Claus in a museum from 2003, but sympathize again with a public location after 2007			X	3
Since Proponents of Santa Claus argue McCarthy is a leading artist in the world, by reframing icons of Western culture			X	4
Since Proponents argue his work is not about sex, but ridicules unlimited consumerism			X	4
Since Children would not recognize the butt plug as such, as it also resembles an abstract Christmas tree			X	3
Since Proponents argue that critiques signal hypocrisy. City tolerates obscene advertisements and we all like sex		X		3
Since Proponents argue taste differs between (non)elite audiences, and art might be funny instead of beautiful			X	3
Since Proponents argue taste is transient. Santa Claus is an example where we take over taste of an art elite			X	2
But Some proponents suggest temporal public locations for Santa Claus might work better to express the message			X	3
But In 2014, proponents suggest a move to a new location at Stationsplein, because it needs an obstructive element			X	2
But Others consider location Stationsplein less suitable as the place needs street performance and activity			X	2

(Continued)

Table 3.1 (continued)

Claim, grounds and rebuttals; con case in italics	IR	SR	ER	(N)
But The city (mayor, aldermen, council) *did not want Santa Claus in shopping area Doelenplein in 2003 due to resistance*			X	7
Since *Christian parties consider the statue not good for children's eyes and thus better suited for a museum*		X		5
Since Local parties and liberals were critical in 2003: a Christmas tree has to be green			X	4
Since Many inhabitants of Rotterdam initially wanted to get rid of Santa Claus			X	5
Since *Opponents consider Santa Claus below standards: too obscene for children, hermetic, elitist*		X		9
Since *Opponents consider Santa Claus too expensive*	X			3
Since *Art critics consider Santa Claus empty; deceptive and the advisory committee insensitive towards public opinion*			X	3
Since *Art critics see government as being trapped in the neutral approach of Thorbecke*		X		2
But The city wants Santa Claus first in the court of the Museum Boijmans van Beuningen in 2003, to mitigate its provoking nature	X			17
But *Before Santa Claus was unveiled in the museum it was stored in a secure location to keep it secret*	X			2
But *Proponents suggested alternative public locations as they considered the museum not a right fit for Santa Claus*			X	4
But Before going public in 2008 Santa Claus had to stay in front of the museum briefly due to a renovation of the court	X			5
Groundedness (totals)	46	31	111	188
Pro (totals)	*43*	*11*	*90*	*144*
Con (totals)	*3*	*20*	*21*	*44*

Note: IR: instrumental rationality; SR: social rationality; ER: expressive rationality.

He does not like the sculpture in itself, but he likes the debates and fights around it: 'That makes it beautiful'.

Arguments con are expressive and social rational

Opponents of Santa Claus have two groups of arguments, as visible in the supporting sub-arguments of the first rebuttal in Table 3.1. First, the sculpture is not good artwork as it is obscene, elitist, hermetic and too expensive. Therefore, it is not value for money. The following quote illustrates the complaints of elitism: 'due to its butt plug it symbolizes public art that crosses too many boundaries and thus symbolizes elitist decision-making' (*Volkskrant*, September 22, 2005). Second, it is not good for children's eyes. This argument is expressed by Christian parties to address the concerns of the voters they represent, which are shared by others, like Muslims: 'They have already for centuries no sympathy for obscene objects, especially not in the hands of a children's friend [Santa Claus] and even less when located at a public place where thousands of families will pass' (*Rotterdams Dagblad*, June 26, 2004).

Policies and conditions for acceptance

Given the resistance, one important condition for public exposition is not fulfilled – sufficient support. As this resistance was initially so massive and so broadly shared, the new city council felt that they needed to take it quite seriously: 'To respond to all the commotion the city council decides to park the statue temporarily out of sight in 2005' (*Trouw*, November 29, 2008). That was a major change of plans, due to the opposition. However, it was a temporary change of plans, as time helped to soften and change the many critical feelings regarding Santa Claus. The critics had to acknowledge that Santa Claus was not explicitly obscene, and less so than many advertisements. No child would recognize the butt plug without being told so.

Veil-ban opposition

History

Nowadays, the debate on the permissibility of the niqab (a full-face veil), or other forms of traditional Islamic clothing like the hijab (covers the hair but leaves most of the face visible), and forms in between, takes place all over Europe. In Britain, the debate was most intensive throughout the years 2006–2007. The debate was sparked by the comments of Jack Straw, a prominent Labour Member of Parliament, who revealed in a newspaper column that he had asked fully veiled women that would come to his office to take off their robe, as he believed that 'the value of a meeting, [. . .], is so that you can – almost literally – see what the other person means, and not just hear what they say'. He went on by saying that 'wearing the full veil [is] bound to make better relations between the two communities more difficult. It [is] such a visible statement of separation and of difference' (*The Lancashire Telegraph*,

October 6, 2006). Later significant events comprised a number of court cases, for instance, about women who had been fired from their jobs for wearing a niqab, such as fully veiled teaching assistant, Aishah Azmi. In one case, a check-in worker for British Airways, Nadia Eweida, was prohibited from wearing a small cross on a necklace over her uniform. These events were discussed all over the country. Due to strong opposition, the ban was not adopted.

Stakeholders and decision makers

Opponents and proponents of a veil ban can be found within many traditional stakeholder groups like political parties and religious organizations. A problem for the decision makers was the question whether the government or private organizations have sufficient authority to ban a niqab. Opponents of a veil ban forcefully argued that wearing the veil is a completely personal choice, where the government has no business interfering: 'We must all be able to think, wear and say what we like, subject only to personal ethics and restrictions truly necessary for the protection of others' (*The Guardian*, November 20, 2006), thus making a strong expressive-rational argument. Also, proponents of a veil ban seemed to be unsure whether such a ban was legitimate, legally possible and effective: 'In a secular society [. . .] the only thing that works is an agreement not to bring flamboyant demonstrations of religious affiliation into everyday life' (*The Independent on Sunday*, October 22, 2006). So, the government's decision-making authority related to the veil ban was challenged in the debate, as were organizations' veil bans challenged in court cases, strongly contesting the social-rational legitimation of these bans.

Arguments used

What is peculiar about the veil-ban debate is the fact that many arguments on both sides became increasingly expressive rational, comprising proponents referring to feelings like feeling uneasy and rejected, and opponents stressing their desire for the expression of their religious identities. Only the initial grounds put forward by proponents of a veil ban were mainly social rational, referring to the social norm to respect Western culture and to foster open communication. Opponents argued based on expressive rationality, and proponents, in turn, responded in their rebuttals based on the same rationality, showing how the debate turns into an expressive rational one as this seems to be the strongest fit with the question. Instrumental-rational arguments are less dominant and mainly refer to the effects of the veil. The arguments in the veil-ban debate are summarized in Table 3.2. The last column presents the groundedness of grounds and rebuttals (their frequency of appearance in the newspapers). The arguments of the opponents of a veil ban are presented in italics and those of the proponents in normal case. Proponents of a veil ban dominate in the debate by the number of their contributions (groundedness of grounds and rebuttals); however, opponents win the debate by the appeal of their arguments.

Table 3.2 Veil-ban debate

Claim, grounds and rebuttals; con case in italics		IR	SR	ER	(N)
Claim	Some forms of Islamic clothing should not be worn in public				
Since	The British public experiences the veil as a symbol of the suppression of women in society			X	190
Since	Women have fought hard battles to be treated equally; Muslim women are going back in time			X	35
Since	An all-concealing veil is an undesirable barrier to human interaction		X		174
Since	Effective communication is important in many places, especially education	X			85
Since	Islamic clothing is a major barrier to good community relations and, thus, integration	X			81
But	*A veil is not a barrier to integration or communication*	X			35
Since	The British experience the veil as a mark of separation in society			X	171
Since	The veil makes people of other backgrounds feel uneasy or offended			X	91
Since	Many members of the general public do not appreciate seeing the veil in public			X	31
But	*Representations of faith do not hurt anybody and are, thus, in no way offensive*			X	23
Since	Veiled women are guilty of discrimination, as they treat certain groups with disfavour		X		15
But	*Because of criticism of the veil the Muslims in Britain feel more under siege than they had already felt*			X	166
Since	*It is the debate on the veil that causes major rifts within society*	X			74
Since	*The debate on the veil is overshadowed by polarization and emotion*			X	51
Since	*The veil debate offers an excuse for Islamophobes to express their irrational fears*			X	29

(Continued)

Table 3.2 (continued)

Claim, grounds and rebuttals; con case in italics	IR	SR	ER	(N)
Since Politicians criticize the veil to score easy electoral points	X			22
But The veil debate is a healthy one and mature discussion about it should be possible		X		67
But The veil debate is a non-issue; discuss people's attitudes rather than their clothing		X		49
Since A very small proportion of Muslim women in this country appear fully covered		X		29
But Some Muslims are oversensitive to criticism and unwilling to engage in public debate			X	86
But The fact that there is so much religious diversity is part of what makes it so special		X		32
Since Muslims must try better to adapt to Western society; insistence on Islamic clothing is not a part of that		X		157
But There is no conflict between having an Islamic and a British identity			X	14
Since The niqab or burqa prevents identification, which is undesirable in today's society		X		156
Since Common sense instead of concerns about respect for cultures should govern what clothing is acceptable in what circumstances		X		145
Since It is wrong for Muslims to be given special treatment		X		96
Since If Islamic symbols are allowed, then the crucifix cannot be prohibited (as tried in the case of Nadia Eweida and Fiona Bruce)		X		40
Since Religious symbolism annuls the intended effect of uniforms in schools	X			21
Since The face veil is not obligatory in Islam		X		112

(Continued)

Table 3.2 (continued)

Claim, grounds and rebuttals; con case in italics	IR	SR	ER	(N)
Since There is a great deal of discussion within the Muslim community about the status of the veil		X		29
But *Some Muslims believe that the veil is a compulsory part of their faith*		X		53
Since Many other European countries, and even some Arab countries, do not allow the full-face veil in public		X		20
But *Religious symbolism is a way to express a deeply felt affiliation with a religion, and this expression should always be allowed*			X	260
Since Religious symbols are of exceptional importance to the bearers' identity and are worn as symbols of pride and commitment to their faith			X	122
Since *If Sikhs are allowed to wear turbans and Jews their yarmulkes, then Muslims must be allowed to wear their clothes*		X		12
But The headscarf is not a religious symbol at all; it has become the symbol of political Islam to express rejection of Western values			X	179
But *The whole point of the niqab is to protect the family unit, the core of society*		X		14
But All religious symbols should be reserved to private areas		X		52
But There is an important difference between very noticeable Islamic garments and other religious symbols		X		22
But *Just like other clothing, wearing Islamic garments is all about freedom of expression and choice*			X	249
Since *The way some people dress makes them stand out in a crowd, but that is no reason to treat them differently*		X		37
But *In a country where nobody wears a niqab, wearing one draws all the more the attention*	X			31

(Continued)

Table 3.2 (continued)

Claim, grounds and rebuttals; con case in italics	IR	SR	ER	(N)
But It is misguided to defend the veil on grounds of freedom of expression; if freedom is at stake, it is the freedom to criticize the custom	X			60
But *Prohibiting religious symbols may cause costly legal challenges, like in the cases of Azaiah Azma and Shabina Begum*				*117*
But According to several court judgments, it is not discriminatory to ban Islamic clothing from some places, for example, schools		X		18
But *The best approach to religious differences is to read, discuss and understand, not to confront and ban*		*X*		*38*
Groundedness (total)	466	1427	**1697**	3590
Pro ban (total)	218	**1163**	783	2164
Con ban (total)	*248*	*264*	***914***	*1426*

Source: adapted from Bouwmeester 2013: 424.

Note: IR: instrumental rationality; SR: social rationality; ER: expressive rationality.

Arguments pro are expressive and social rational

As we saw, Jack Straw criticized the niqab for being 'a visible statement of separation', seemingly implying that women wear the veil to express their contempt for British society. A similar sentiment is expressed in the following quote from writer Yasmin Alibhai-Brown: 'It [the wearing of the niqab] breaks our hearts. After all, caged creatures often prefer to stay in their cages even after they have been freed. I don't call that a choice' (*The Independent*, October 9, 2006). This quote illustrates the first and, with 190 examples, also the best-grounded pro argument in Table 3.2. Such expressive arguments become more important in the pro case during the debate. However, most arguments of proponents arguing for a veil ban refer to norms of how to behave and how to integrate, thus expressing social rationality as illustrated by the second pro argument in Table 3.2. Only some arguments were instrumental by claiming that face veils make communication and identification less effective, as in the quote by Tony Blair, then prime minister: 'it really is a matter of plain common sense that when it is an essential part of someone's work to communicate directly with people, being able to see their face is important' (*The Mirror*, December 9, 2006).

Arguments con are mainly expressive rational

Opponents of a veil ban argued mainly based on expressive rationality, but mixed with some instrumental- and social-rational arguments. They claimed religious freedom and freedom of expression by means of clothing, as seen in the following quote about teaching:

> Integration requires people like me to be in the workplace so that people can see that we are not to be feared or mistrusted. .... I teach perfectly well with my veil on. Give it a chance – that's what I call integration.
>
> (Azmi in *The Times*, October 20, 2006)

A stronger example of expressive argumentation, which illustrates expressive rationality in the second part of the sentence by referring to a desire of religious expression, is central in the first main rebuttal in Table 3.2: 'If I took off my hijab it would stop people recognizing my faith, and I want people to know that I'm a Muslim' (*Independent Extra*, October 17, 2006). The decision to wear the hijab is warranted here by the motive to show religious identity, which is an expressive-rational motivation. The next quote illustrates the second main rebuttal in Table 3.2, stressing that what you wear belongs to who you are, your personal identity: 'I've been wearing a *hijab* for seven years now. I was about 16 when I started wearing a veil and it was my own decision. .... Now, it is part of who I am, it is part of my identity' (Muslim student, *Independent Extra*, October 17, 2006). The last two quotes refer more to religious and personal expression, and the first one, also, to the practical side of teaching with a veil on; this argument is used as a rebuttal to the pro veil-ban arguments. Wearing a hijab gets less opposition than the niqab, as it is a veil that leaves most of the face visible. Therefore, it is easier to defend wearing the hijab on expressive grounds. Most opposition is aimed at the niqab, which is mentioned twice as many times as the hijab by all participants in the debate.

Unfulfilled conditions and change of policies

While proponents of a veil ban saw the veil as oppressive and as a barrier to integration, opponents instead presented both the niqab and hijab as a means to express one's (religious) identity and argued that only the acceptance of it could lead to integration. By consistently and successfully using an expressive-rational argumentation strategy the opponents of a veil ban forced proponents to acknowledge that legal action on the veil could not be legitimized. Also, given the law, the conditions for a ban were not good, as it was in conflict with some rights and it might cause legal challenges. The social-rational arguments expressed by those with decision-making authority could not overrule the expressive-rational arguments of opponents in the UK. Therefore, politicians decided not to implement a veil ban in the end.

Cross-case analysis on expressive rationality

Expressive rationality and the force of different motivational emotions

Expressive rationality is dominant in the debates on publicly exposing Santa Claus in the Netherlands and banning the niqab in the UK. It is a relative dominance expressed by the groundedness of expressive-rational arguments in the debates, but also by the importance given to expressive-rational arguments. This is a first sign of the relation between the debated question, which has subjective relevance, and the rationality that appears in giving reasons to act on.

Expressive rationality is grounded in subjectivity. Expressive arguments should, therefore, refer to aspects of someone's own personality – like desires, enthusiasm, feelings of sympathy or dislike, and emotions like fear, anger, etc. (Engelen 2006; Hargreaves Heap 2001; Scherer 2011). Subjectivity is bounded to the individual, but similar persons can share features of their subjectivity like a specific interest, particular passions or specific aversions. The debates on Santa Claus and the veil ban both illustrate this subjective basis of many motivational arguments suggesting good reasons to act on by referring to personal taste, likings, worries, etc. That is a further sign of the dependence between expressive rationality and the subjective relevance of the decisions that are legitimated or challenged; a fit between decision context and rationality already suggested in Bouwmeester (2013).

The subjective perspective shows up in the Dutch debate about Santa Claus. The debate circles around taste and artist expression. Proponents like the sculpture, identify with the message or see benefits for themselves and their business environment. Opponents dislike the statue, think it is awful and a sign of bad taste to present a huge butt plug in a public environment and then even suggest it is art. That is not appreciated. It is also problematic that opponents consider it anything but beautiful.

Even some artists share the aversion and consider this art hermetic, elitist and not worth the attention.

Also, for opponents and proponents in the veil-ban debate in the UK, expressive rationality gives the strongest type of reasons to legitimize the decision of wearing a niqab or hijab. What you wear is a decision to be made by the individual, based on taste, personal preference and, in principle, it is not something where law or power may interfere, because decisions stay in the private sphere. Only within the context of work or school do we accept dress codes to a certain extent and it depends on national culture how dominant they can be. Then wearing a niqab can become problematic. But in most Western countries it is almost entirely up to the individual to decide on their clothing. Decisions on what to wear are, thus, strongly connected to our subjectivity. Therefore, the debate centres around subjective taste and religious expression in relation to implicit or explicit dress codes and other inter-subjectively grounded Western views. Table 3.3 summarizes the main stakeholders in the debate and the emotions referred to in motivational arguments by opponents and proponents in the two debates.

The controversies in the veil ban and Santa Claus debate are grounded in opposite emotions (dislike, sympathy, feeling uneasy, etc.), attitudes (pride, resistance) and personal commitments. These emotions, attitudes and commitments give force to

Table 3.3 Stakeholders and discussed motivational emotions backing expressive rationality

Santa Claus in public space	Veil ban
Main stakeholders: McCarthy (pro), the city of Rotterdam; mayor, aldermen, city council, advisory committee IBC (pro), Museum Boijmans van Beuningen (pro), Christian parties (con), local parties (con), liberals, art supporters, art critics, art elite, elite audience, general audience, inhabitants of Rotterdam, shopkeepers (pro), children	**Main stakeholders:** British public, general public, today's society, schools, family unit, politicians, European countries, Arab countries, (Muslim) women, British Muslims, Muslim community, political Islam, Sikhs, Jews, (all stakeholders internally divided)
Expressed emotions of proponents: appreciation, sympathy, want him close, admiration (McCarthy seen as leading artist)	**Expressed emotions of proponents:** feeling uneasy, offended, not appreciating, express rejection
	—
	Proponents of the veil ban are called Islamophobes. Their fears are criticized as being irrational
Expressed emotions of opponents: dislike, do not want him, want to get rid of him, signs of resistance	**Expressed emotions of opponents:** veil is a way of expressing identity, pride, commitment, deeply felt affiliation. Opponents feeling under siege due to veil ban
—	—
Opponents are criticized for reacting disproportionally compared to their acceptance of billboards showing more obscene images	(Muslim) opponents are criticized for being oversensitive to criticisms

the motivational arguments of proponents and opponents who feel differently about the debated questions. As a consequence, the impact goes in different directions, which makes some motivational arguments supportive towards each other, while others undermine each other. Supporting arguments create higher degrees of expressive rationality, whereas opposing or contradicting arguments can lower the degree of expressive rationality; not so much if differences are tolerated, but more so when subjective motives are challenged or prioritized, or when some are able to dominate over the other perspectives – the latter will then be perceived as less rational on expressive grounds.

In the Santa Claus debate, opposite emotions fuel the discussion. Proponents of Santa Claus feel appreciation and sympathy for the sculpture. They express that they want him close (not in a museum) and they admire the critical work of McCarthy. These positive emotions create motivational grounds for Santa Claus in a public place. However, especially when the idea of the sculpture was introduced and the first images were presented, more and more people developed an aversion and challenged the project. They expressed their dislike, said they did not want Santa Claus, and later that they wanted to get rid of him. Many stakeholders where resisting the idea of Santa Claus initially, but the intensity of such negative feelings eased out over a period of several years, and turned into more tolerance and a more positive attitude, showing a process of increasing dominance of the more positive feelings towards Santa Claus.

Maybe because the proponents respected the initially negative feelings of opponents, opponents got sufficient time to get used to Santa Claus; they learned that their more obscene interpretations were not the only way to look at the sculpture and their initial feelings appeared to be less rational from an expressive-rational perspective. For instance, when compared to their responses to quite common billboards, with much more explicit sexual appeal, their reactions seemed disproportional. Over time, ambiguities in the sculpture even became part of its attractiveness for a continuously growing number of people.

In the veil-ban debate, most feelings shared by opponents reinforce each other, like positive emotions of pride associated with wearing a veil, desire to show religious identity and commitment to one's faith. A niqab is a very clear and expressive state-ment for showing one's religious identity. The opposite of not being allowed to wear a face veil creates negative emotions, like feeling under siege. Proponents of the veil ban feel differently. They do not share the positive feelings of opponents. In contrast, the strong expressions of religious identity feel threatening, making them feel uneasy and offended. They cannot appreciate the face veil and want to challenge, criticize and reject such forms of expression, which they also consider a sign of repression.

However, that different stakeholder groups in the debate on the veil ban feel differently is, in itself, not something that undermines expressive rationality. Preferences, likings and desires may differ due to someone's character, identity and cultural background, and they can be tolerated. Undermining starts when opponents counter feelings, suggesting the fears of proponents of the ban are irrational. For that purpose, opponents characterize them as Islamophobes. We might consider fear for a real threat rational, but phobia or paranoia are irrational. Still, proponents really dislike the extreme forms of clothing and the expressions of a fundamentalist

Muslim attitude, which they cannot respect, and they want to criticize it. In turn, they challenge Muslims for being oversensitive, as Muslims are not willing to accept criticisms towards their extreme dressings, which the proponents feel should be possible in a Western society. If true, oversensitivity would undermine the expressive rationality of Muslims. However, in the end, priority is given to accepting Muslim expressions over one's own feelings of anger and aversion.

As expected, expressive rationality guided the decision-making in two debates that both strongly relate to our subjectivity. Stakeholder resistance and aversion was a good reason to postpone the exhibition of Santa Clause in a public space. Growing sympathy for the sculpture provided a good reason to give Santa Claus his public presence later on. Widely shared aversion, fear, feeling uneasy and taking offence due to the niqab were valid reasons to consider a veil ban. The importance of wearing a face veil as an expression of one's religious identity and religious commitment were seen as good reasons for not executing such a ban. Thus, expressive rationality guides both public and private actions, and reference to expressive-rational motives is a way to strengthen the legitimization of actions that affect our subjectivity.

However, the force of expressive-rational motivations is strongly dependent on variation in stakeholder sympathies. When they are different, they require tolerance. Our likings can be different and only that does not make them less rational. The degree of expressive rationality is more dependent on authenticity of feelings, on their proportionality versus oversensitivity, and on the absence of self-deception. When self-deception occurs, or disproportionality of feeling, right and balanced feelings need to get more priority. Public or more private intra-personal debate can support this process. These processes of challenging and prioritization, or being tolerant, are well illustrated in the two debates. Due to public debates, it has been considered more rational from an expressive point of view to give Santa Claus public presence; the fears for making a bad impression on children were assessed as irrational. The desire to wear the niqab was given priority over aversions of stakeholders with a different cultural preference; it was seen as a form of personal expression, which deserved tolerance.

Cross-rationality controversies related to expressive (ir)rationality

In the two debates focused on questions with strong subjective relevance, expressive rationality appears internally divided. People like and dislike the niqab. Similarly, there is liking and disliking of the abstract butt plug in the hand of Santa Claus. These oppositions stem from differences in subjectivity: what one person likes, another sees as bad taste. There are different opinions, but that is not sufficient to undermine expressive rationality. We can tolerate and appreciate differences.

As discussed, expressive arguments can be undermined internally by lack of authenticity, disproportional feelings or self-deception. Second, the two other types of rationality can challenge expressive rationality, as subjectivity is not all that counts when making a decision. In both discussed debates, expressive-rational arguments are mainly in conflict with social-rational arguments, which suggest inacceptable or illegitimate wishes as a form of irrationality. Next to that there are instrumental-rational challenges towards expressive-rational motives for wearing the niqab or appreciating Santa Claus, suggesting unrealistic or impractical wishes as a form of irrationality. To keep their strength, expressive-rational considerations should not become too disconnected from the other dimensions of rationality.

Social-rational opposition

Social-rational arguments appear to be most forceful in challenging the expressive-rational claims of proponents in the debate on Santa Claus. Shared values and principles claim a more universal validity than liking or disliking, which make them strong opposition. Social-rational arguments that claim that children have to be protected against obscenity have a broader scope than sheer liking or disliking. This argument was initiated by Christian parties, but shared by other religious groups as well. The political shift to the right after the elections in the city council in 2002 supported the social-rational opposition, as the voice of the critics became stronger. Other social-rational standards referred to were that art should not be too elitist and hermetic. These social-rational counterarguments for preventing obscenity in a public environment and the protection of children and their families, together with the intention of the artist not to provoke as an end in itself, favoured the temporary decision to not make the statue public as intended, at least for a while. Violating such accepted standards appears as irrational from a social-rational perspective. Also, artists have to respect certain norms and values when they want to make their work public. Their expressive freedom is bounded by social rationality, and the right balance had to be discovered along the way. It took some time to test the counter-claims, and to discover that the obscenity was mainly in the eyes of the critical beholders, and had no real impact on children. In the end, the expressive wishes of the artist and his supporters were not illegitimate at all. The critics were behaving irrationally, judged against expressive-rational standards by setting frustrating and upsetting norms and standards with their focus on obscenities.

In the niqab debate, the proposal of a veil ban in public environments is initially based on social-rational grounds. The UK government intended to stop this extreme expression of religious culture due to its problematic social consequences. Proponents of a veil ban challenged the expressive-rational arguments of opponents with arguments based on social values that Muslims should integrate, that the niqab is an undesirable barrier to identification and communication. Our common sense, not respect for import cultures, should guide our judgment on clothing. In addition, the unequal treatment of women is against Western standards and Muslims should not ask for special treatment. These wishes are illegitimate. As the face veil is not obligatory, even from an Islamic perspective, specifically the niqab as a means of expression was considered irrational from the social-rational perspective proponents identify with. However, in the end, the subject was still considered too much a subjective question, in spite of the negative social consequences. A ban did not get the required support. It did not seem the right approach to manage the identified problems. The ban was upsetting and frustrating, and, in itself, irrational judged against expressive-rational standards.

Instrumental-rational opposition

Instrumental-rational arguments against Santa Claus stress not to waste public money. The sculpture is said to be too expensive with its price of 280,000 Euros. The means are, therefore, seen as not suitable to reach the end, as the end is not worth so much effort. That makes the action irrational from an instrumental-rational perspective. However, the argument had little impact on those who wanted to spend the money.

Expressive-rational arguments for wearing the niqab were also challenged on instrumental-rational grounds. As the niqab covers the face it limits facial expression, and so influences communication negatively. Proponents of a veil ban argued that the niqab is a barrier to effective, open and pleasant communication, making wearing a niqab irrational on instrumental grounds, especially in the context of education, where it is really impractical. However, the countermove here was the denial of the suggested effect. Opponents argue that communication is still possible, like with telephone calls. The second instrumental countermove was making the debate a cause of the problem, as its controversial nature triggers major rifts in society.

Discussion: social construction of expressive rationality

Degrees of expressive rationality

Central emotions underpinning expressive rationality are liking and disliking, or appreciation and aversion, as these emotions give orientation to our actions. Dislike is a valid reason for avoiding or not doing something, whereas liking motivates engagement. Emotion-based reasons to motivate decisions are addressed in studies like Engelen (2006), Fisher and Freshwater (2014), Gaut (2012), Greenspan (2004), Hargreaves Heap (2001), Li *et al.* (2014) and Scherer (2011), arguing that they support rational decision-making. Other authors suggest, more generally, that we should pay attention to emotions in the context of rationality (Gigerenzer and Selten 2001; Greenspan 2004). However, until now, these emotional motives have hardly been explored empirically to flesh out the concept of expressive rationality. And even more common, emotions are not seen as being part of rationality at all and are a source of irrationality instead. Emotions that undermine rational decision-making due to loss of aversion or by the halo effect have also been studied (Kahneman 2011). Most rational would be, as Klamer (1987: 179) paraphrases, being like a robot, thus meeting the image of rational economic agents that are optimizing to best reach the goals they have set. This view on rationality is too limited.

The public debates about Santa Claus and the veil ban illustrate the positive contributions of expressive rationality to decision-making, thus adding a rich description to the studies by Engelen (2006), Gaut (2012), Gigerenzer and Selten (2001), Li *et al.* (2014) and Scherer (2011), who argue that emotions can have a positive role in decision-making. The findings from the Santa Claus and veil-ban debate illustrate how emotions are referred to in motivational arguments, thus expressing good reasons for action themselves. That makes emotions part of rationality (Engelen 2006; Gaut 2012; Scherer 2011), and not only a moderator in the deliberative search process (cf. Kim 2016: 17; Mellers *et al.* 2001: 263). The two debates illustrate how expressive-rational arguments guide decisions in a way that expresses the fit with the sympathies, desires and interests of the decision maker and relevant stakeholders. The emotions guide action in two directions: approval of proposed decisions is motivated by sympathy-driven emotions (liking Santa Claus) and disapproval of decisions is motivated by variations of negative emotions (disliking the veil ban). After all, it is common knowledge that we should ask ourselves if a decision we make also 'feels' right. The two debates illustrate that this common knowledge holds true when studying rationality in practice.

The better the fit between expressive rationality and the subjective context of the decision, the higher the impact of expressive-rational arguments. In this double case study, the questions about taste and expression carry great subjective relevance. Also, the more authentic and proportional the expressed emotions, the more impact they have when referred to in motivational arguments. Arguments about Santa Claus as being obscene and raising aversion proved to be less authentic and somewhat self-deceptive. They died out over time, after being challenged. Expressive arguments to ban the veil also lost force during the debate. Dislike was considered fine, but not grounds for banning the veil. Expressions of religious identity deserved tolerance in the UK, even if they were widely considered as too extreme and not good for the women involved; regardless, it should be their choice to free themselves. A ban would not be the right policy decision. Thus, debate was able to sort out which feelings should guide the decision, and which feelings should dominate less.

This double case study thus illustrates the process of improving expressive rationality by public debate. The classical economic and sociological rationality conceptions that dominate our current understandings of rationality cannot explain this process (Diesing 1976; March and Simon 1958; Mele and Rawling 2004; Tinbergen 1956; Weirich 2004) by their systematic disregard of expressive rationality. Also, Weber (1972) and Habermas (1988) are sceptical and exempt expressive considerations from the domain of rationality in their seminal works as mostly being too subjective. What this double case study adds to earlier studies on expressive rationality (Engelen 2006; Gaut 2012; Greenspan 2004; Hargreaves Heap 2001; Li *et al.* 2014; Scherer 2011) is the systematic exploration of expressive rationality in practice by studying motivational arguments, and by adding more detail to the single case study in Bouwmeester (2013).

Expressive (ir)rationality against standards of instrumental and social rationality

The findings in this chapter based on the argumentation analysis of two public debates on the niqab and on McCarthy's Santa Claus have illustrated situations in which motivational arguments referring to emotions can guide decision-making. In all situations, where the relevance of a decision mainly relates to our subjectivity, expressive rationality gives our decisions the best orientation we can get. In such contexts, we are well advised to act on our likings, enthusiasm, inspiration, intuition or other subjective motives that can guide us (Bouwmeester 2013; Calabretta *et al.* 2016; Engelen 2006; Gaut 2012; Greenspan 2004; Hargreaves Heap 2001; Li *et al.* 2014; Scherer 2011). Adding such nuance to the debate on rationality and bringing expressive rationality more to the forefront is the main contribution of this chapter. It helps to answer the research question Volz and Hertwig (2016: 111) conclude with – to better study the ecological rationality of emotions. That is, under what circumstances and in what situations can emotions be rational? However, the opposite can happen as well. That is, when decisions with subjective relevance based on expressive-rational arguments ignore instrumental- or social-rational considerations that are relevant to the question, resulting in impractical or illegitimate desires.

Violating instrumental rationality while acting in line with our subjectivity creates a rationality conflict that undermines expressive rationality based on standards of instrumental rationality. It is widely discussed how emotions can interfere with instrumental rationality and, thus, be at odds with optimization calculus (Elster 2009; Fessler 2001; Kahneman 2011). Emotions might, for instance, tempt us to focus on the short term while forgetting the long term (Boyd and Richerson 2001; Elster 2009). However, the studied public debates do not illustrate such forms of irrationality interfering with optimization, because optimizing is rare in real-life decision-making.

In the Santa Claus debate, some critics argue that Santa Claus is too expensive, a waste of resources and, thus, an impractical wish with low feasibility. Still, those who are happy to spend the money on the sculpture invalidate these arguments. Thus, expressive rationality reframes and renders the cost arguments irrational against the strong willingness to pay. Instrumental counterarguments in the veil-ban debate are stronger. They point out how common sense, communication and integration goals get undermined by the niqab, which is irrational against standards of instrumental rationality; again, this suggests an impractical wish. The instrumental criticism is relevant, but rebutted on instrumental grounds. What both debates confirm is that instrumental-rational opposition is of a bounded-rational nature by criticizing that some goals, like integration or open communication, are not satisfied (Gigerenzer and Selten 2001; March and Simon 1958).

Interactions between expressive rationality and social rationality are stronger in the two cases, both in pointing at irrationalities and in their mutual support. Looking at Santa Claus may be a nice and fun experience for adults, but it is framed as harming children. This social-rational argument has postponed public exposition by referring to the principle of banning obscene art from public space. Thus, Santa Claus was evaluated as irrational against such social standards, framing this form of artist expression as illegitimate – a form of irrationality earlier addressed in Scherer (2011: 334). The veil-ban debate started from a similar motivation. The attempt was made to frame the niqab as irrational, based on social-rational arguments in support of a veil ban – wearing a niqab was seen as socially unacceptable.

However, a ban would restrict subjective expression. Based on expressive rationality, the ban was challenged, suggesting irrationality of the ban itself. Social evaluations of expressive rationality are, thus, evaluated back. Similarly, the ban on Santa Claus, leading to a temporary exposition in a museum court, was seen as an irrational rule after some time, due to the growing sympathy towards the sculpture, also from the side of the families who did not see how Santa Claus would harm their children for something they could not even understand.

Recognition of the strong counter-influence of expressive rationality on critical instrumental- and social-rational arguments in the two debates is a clear invitation to pay more theoretical attention to the subjective aspects of our rationality, which remains a human construct in the end. Relating expressive reasons to instrumental rationality shows under what conditions instrumental rationality can frame expressive rationality as irrational. With debates selected for their subjective relevance, these are the exceptions, while the opposite was visible more often. Consequently, assuming that emotion-based rationality only tends to irrational decision-making in general (Habermas 1988; Kahneman 2011; Weber 1972) is a flawed assumption based on overgeneralization. Social standards also appear as somewhat flexible and subject to expressive-rational critique, as illustrated in the Santa Claus debate, or local, as visible in the veil-ban debate, showing different outcomes across nations and cultures (MacIntyre 1988). Countries have decided differently on banning the niqab or not. Some countries allow it and see it as a question of personal expression, other countries prohibit it in public spaces.

The changes in social standards due to challenges based on public debate inspired by expressive-rational opposition illustrate how the standards of rationality are socially constructed. Social construction determines when expressive-rational arguments cross the line of becoming irrational against social-rational standards and to what extent expressive rationality can push back. The evaluation perspective of reasonableness from a social perspective (Scherer 2011) is only one direction to evaluate, by making social rationality the norm. Debate determines which position gets priority and may dominate over the other. The interactions also show the mutual dependence of expressive and social rationalities, and how social rationality is grounded in and influenced by multiplied subjectivity. As we know, intersubjectivity requires subjectivity as input, and given the concept, this direction in the dependence is probably even stronger than the other way around. Still, reason is not only a slave of passions, as suggested by Hume, Smith and classical utilitarians (Diesing 1976: 246; Haidt 2001: 816; Sedlacek 2011). Social and expressive rationality do influence each other mutually, and instrumental rationality takes part in these rationality interactions as well, in spite of its modest role in the two discussed debates.

References

Abrahamson, E. (1996) Management fashion. *Academy of Management Review*, 21(1), 254–85.

Blaug, M. (1980) *The Methodology of Economics*. Cambridge: Cambridge University Press.

Bouwmeester, O. (2013) Field dependency of argumentation rationality in decision-making debates. *Journal of Management Inquiry*, 22(4), 415–33.

Boyd, R. and Richerson, P. J. (2001) Norms and bounded rationality, in Gigerenzer, G. and Selten, R. (eds), *Bounded Rationality: The Adaptive Toolbox*. Cambridge, MA: MIT Press, pp. 281–96.

Cabanac, M. and Bonniot-Cabanac, M.-C. (2007) Decision making: Rational or hedonic? *Behavioral and Brain Functions*, 3(1), 1–8.

Calabretta, G., Gemser, G. and Wijnberg, N. M. (2016) The interplay between intuition and rationality in strategic decision making: A paradox perspective. *Organization Studies*. DOI: 10.1177/0170840616655483.

Churchman, C. W. (1962) On rational decision making. *Management Technology*, 2(2), 71–6.

Dahms, H. F. (1997) Theory in Weberian Marxism: Patterns of critical social theory in Lukács and Habermas. *Sociological Theory*, 15(3), 181–214.

Davidson, D. (2004) *Problems of Rationality*. Vol. 4. Oxford: Oxford University Press.

Diesing, P. (1976) *Reason in Society: Five Types of Decisions and Their Social Conditions*. Westport, CT: Greenwood Press.

Eisenhardt, K. M. and Zbaracki, M. J. (1992) Strategic decision making. *Strategic Management Journal*, 13(S2), 17–37.

Elbanna, S. (2006) Strategic decision-making: Process perspectives. *International Journal of Management Reviews*, 8(1), 1–20.

Elbanna, S. and Child, J. (2007) Influences on strategic decision effectiveness: Development and test of an integrative model. *Strategic Management Journal*, 28(4), 431–53.

Elster, J. (2009) *Reason and Rationality*. Princeton, NJ: Princeton University Press.

Engelen, B. (2006) Solving the paradox: The expressive rationality of the decision to vote. *Rationality and Society*, 18(4), 419–41.

Esposito, E. (2011) Originality through imitation: The rationality of fashion. *Organization Studies*, 32(5), 603–13.

Fessler, D. M. T. (2001) Emotions and cost-benefit assessment, in Gigerenzer, G. and Selten, R. (eds), *Bounded Rationality: The Adaptive Toolbox*. Cambridge, MA: MIT Press, pp. 191–214.

Fisher, P. and Freshwater, D. (2014) Towards compassionate care through aesthetic rationality. *Scandinavian Journal of Caring Sciences*, 28(4), 767–74.

Gaut, B. (2012) Creativity and rationality. *The Journal of Aesthetics and Art Criticism*, 70(3), 259–70.

Gigerenzer, G. and Selten, R. (2001) Rethinking rationality, in Gigerenzer, G. and Selten, R. (eds), *Bounded Rationality: The Adaptive Toolbox* Cambridge, MA: MIT Press, pp. 1–12.

Gigerenzer, G. and Sturm, T. (2012) How (far) can rationality be naturalized? *Synthese*, 187(1), 243–68.

Green Jr, S. E. (2004) A rhetorical theory of diffusion. *The Academy of Management Review*, 29(4), 653–69.

Greenspan, P. (2004) Practical reasoning and emotion, in Mele, A. R. and Rawling, P. (eds), *The Oxford Handbook of Rationality*. New York: Oxford University Press, pp. 206–21.

Habermas, J. (1988) *Theorie des Kommunikativen Handelns, Band 1, 2*. Frankfurt: Suhrkamp.

Haidt, J. (2001) The emotional dog and its rational tail: A social intuitionist approach to moral judgment. *Psychological Review*, 108(4), 814–34.

Hargreaves Heap, S. (2001) Expressive rationality: Is self-worth just another kind of preference?, in Mäki, U. (ed), *The Economic World View: Studies in the Ontology of Economics*. Cambridge: Cambridge University Press, pp. 98–113.

Henderson, D. (2010) Explanation and rationality naturalized. *Philosophy of the Social Sciences*, 40(1), 30–58.

Kahneman, D. (2011) *Thinking, Fast and Slow*. New York: FSG.

Kilduff, M. and Mehra, A. (1997) Postmodernism and organizational research. *Academy of Management Review*, 22(2), 453–81.

Kim, N. (2016) Beyond rationality: The role of anger and information in deliberation. *Communication Research*, 43(1), 3–24.

Klamer, A. (1987) As if economists and their subjects were rational, in Nelson, J. S., Megill, A. and McCloskey, D. N. (eds), *The Rhetoric of the Human Sciences*. Madison, WI: The University of Wisconsin Press, pp. 163–83.

Li, Y., Ashkanasy, N. M. and Ahlstrom, D. (2014) The rationality of emotions: A hybrid process model of decision-making under uncertainty. *Asia Pacific Journal of Management*, 31(1), 293–308.

McCloskey, D. N. (2016) Max U versus Humanomics: A critique of neo-institutionalism. *Journal of Institutional Economics*, 12(01), 1–27.

MacIntyre, A. C. (1988) *Whose Justice? Which Rationality?* London: Duckworth.

Majone, G. (1992) *Evidence, Argument and Persuasion in the Policy Process*. New Haven, CT: Yale University Press.

March, J. G. and Simon, H. A. (1958) *Organizations*. New York: John Wiley.

Mele, A. R. and Rawling, P. (2004) Introduction: Aspects of rationality, in Mele, A. R. and Rawling, P. (eds), *The Oxford Handbook of Rationality*. Oxford: Oxford University Press, pp. 3–13.

Mellers, B. A., Erev, I., Fessler, D. M., Hemelrijk, C. K., Hertwig, R., Laland, K. N., Scherer, K. R., Seeley, T. D., Selten, R. and Tetlock, P. E. (2001) Effects of emotions and social processes on bounded rationality, in Gigerenzer, G. and Selten, R. (eds), *Bounded Rationality: The Adaptive Toolbox*. Cambridge, MA: MIT Press, pp. 263–79.

Scherer, K. R. (2011) On the rationality of emotions: Or, when are emotions rational? *Social Science Information*, 50(3–4), 330–50.

Sedlacek, T. (2011) *Economics of Good and Evil: The Quest for Economic Meaning from Gilgamesh to Wall Street*. Oxford: Oxford University Press.

Sen, A. (1993) Internal consistency of choice. *Econometrica*, 61(3), 495–521.

Smith, A. (1982) *The Theory of Moral Sentiments*. Indianapolis, IN: Liberty Classics.

Tinbergen, J. (1956) *Economic Policy: Principles and Design*. Amsterdam: Noord Hollandsche Uitgeversmaatschappij.

Volz, K. G. and Hertwig, R. (2016) Emotions and decisions beyond conceptual vagueness and the rationality muddle. *Perspectives on Psychological Science*, 11(1), 101–16.

Weber, M. (1972) *Wirtschaft und Gesellschaft: Grundriß der Verstehenden Soziologie*. 5th ed. Tubingen, Germany: JCB Mohr (Paul Siebeck).

Weirich, P. (2004) Economic rationality, in Mele, A. R. and Rawling, P. (eds), *The Oxford Handbook of Rationality*. Oxford: Oxford University Press, pp. 380–98.

Werder, A. von (1999) Argumentation rationality of management decisions. *Organization Science*, 10(5), 672–90.

4 Social rationality

Struggles with reality

Introducing social rationality

Since Weber's (1972) book *Wirtschaft und Gesellschaft* was published in 1921, we distinguish between the concepts of instrumental rationality and value rationality. Instrumental or goal rationality seeks to find the best means or ways to reach our goals. Value rationality sets the social principles and standards to evaluate and define our goals and values. These values have social legitimacy. Value rationality can thus be conceived as an early version of social rationality. Social values can be to fight poverty, to protect the weak, to consider the interests of future generations or, as illustrated in the previous chapter, to protect children from obscene images or to defend freedom of expression. Social and moral values inspire the principles, norms, rules and laws we act on in our bureaucracies (Gross *et al.* 2013). We use these norms to legitimize acts as rational. We consider it rational to follow the law, but also to take care of others' interests and to give men and women equal career opportunities, whereas the opposite needs much more explanation and might only be rational in exceptional situations like war. Thus, social rationality has a 'we' orientation in its reasoning (Gintis 2016: 96).

Our values need to be intersubjectively shared in order to get social validity (Habermas 1988). Usually, intersubjective reasoning is based on shared moral values and norms (Elster 1989, 2006; Satow 1975). It has more temporary visibility in fashions (Abrahamson 1996; Esposito 2011) and more local visibility in the majority arguments suggesting political rationality (Diesing 1976; Eisenhardt and Zbaracki 1992). Such different forms of socially shared reasoning can all be subsumed under the label 'social rationality' (Churchman 1962; Dahms 1997; Gintis 2016; Sen 1993). The label 'social rationality' fits the contested nature of this form of rationality, with a validity for specific groups of people (Diesing 1976; Gintis 2016; MacIntyre 1988; Zhu 2015). Value rationality as defined by Weber (1972) and Habermas (1988) articulates the most universal extreme within social rationality, expressing the ambition of being valid, at least, for mankind as a whole, with a long-time horizon.

Expressive rationality, as explored in the previous chapter, is in its content quite similar to social rationality. The main difference is that it is not grounded in inter-subjective agreement, but in our subjectivity. It refers to what I consider important as a subject or as a single person. Acting on personal desires, interests, motives and feelings can make my actions rational from a subjective perspective (Bouwmeester 2013; Engelen 2006; Gaut 2012; Greenspan 2004; Hargreaves Heap 2001; Li *et al.* 2014; Scherer 2011). It can, for instance, explain the rationality of career choices, how we dress, what music we listen to, etc. Regarding the content, the similarities with social rationality are that we can feel anger when something is against moral principles, feel sympathy for threatened animals that need protection or fear for dangers that need to be fought, such as global warming. Feelings and values can both point in the same direction. The difference is in the source for evaluation: subjective (me) versus social (we).

The third form of rationality is instrumental, aiming at optimizing effectiveness, efficiency or feasibility, which also gives good reasons for action. Most of us, and especially economists, consider it rational to reach one's objectives without using superfluous means (Majone 1992; Tinbergen 1956). Instrumental rationality can thus help to better act on our personal values and social standards by doing it effectively, efficiently and in a way that is feasible. It concerns the question of how we do things, whereas social and expressive rationality guide what we do. Instrumental rationality will get more attention in the next chapter.

As rationality is the ability to give good reasons to act on (Davidson 2004: 169; Elbanna 2006: 3; Elbanna and Child 2007: 433; Elster 2009: 2; Engelen 2006: 427; Gigerenzer and Sturm 2012: 243–5; Green 2004: 655; Henderson 2010: 32), social rationality is doing so by relating to reasons we intersubjectively agree on. The guiding norms and principles are socially constructed and repeatedly reinforced. Obviously, it is possible to deviate from such norms governing social action; otherwise these norms would be laws of nature (Elster 1989). But the social consequences of deviation can be severe within a community. Reasoning within an intersubjective argumentation field partly resembles the generality of instrumental arguments, as social norms or laws are external to our own subjectivity; this is clearly visible in the case of justification based on law (Diesing 1976; Mathiowetz 2007). However, even laws are not as universal as laws of nature, as they mostly only have national validity.

In philosophical debates related to social rationality, concepts like morality, principles or value rationality often share a universalistic pretence (Habermas 1988; Hegel 1986; Kant 1990; Schiller 1983; Weber 1972). Still, critiques on these more universalistic and deontological ways of reasoning abound as well (ten Bos and Willmott 2001; Gigerenzer 2010; MacIntyre 1988; Taylor 2016). Weber (1972: 12) has acknowledged some of these limitations by considering traditional and affective motives to act on, and they might even be rational in some cases, but not as a rule. Some Weber interpreters have argued to differentiate the concept of value rationality further in substantive rationality (the ability to make exceptions) and formal rationality (expressed in bureaucratic rules) to better handle situations where formal rules do not fit an individual case (Kalberg 1980; Townley 2002: 165). Substantive rationality could then refer to values like 'empathy, compassion and equity' (Gross *et al.* 2013: 96), which can be more tailored to the situation. Gigerenzer (2010: 550) has similar ideas when he argues for 'ecological morality'. He suggests using a social heuristic that best fits the situation, and to study such heuristics more in their natural environment.

The concept of social rationality also has in itself this possibility to change scope from more general communities with more general values to act on, to more local communities with their local values. Unfortunately, this possibility of scaling up and scaling down is not well explored yet in the context of social rationality. In addition, the nexus between expressive rationality and social rationality is under-explored, and the previous chapter has indicated strong mutual links. There might be a possibility of scaling up (inductively) from subjective feelings to shared values. Next to that, social values are commonly assumed to be leading in defining goals for instrumental-rational action (Habermas 1988; Weber 1972), which is a highly problematic assumption. Following fashion can be social rational, but quite irrational from an instrumental perspective. Esposito (2011: 604) gives the example of driving big cars in city centres due to fashion, while knowing that it is highly impractical. By studying the social aspects of rational decision-making in practice, as suggested by Gigerenzer (2010), this chapter seeks to add rich descriptions to the currently overly theoretical debate on social rationality.

As context to explore these questions, two public debates are selected based on theoretical sampling, in which social rationality is expected to have a central position. The first case is a critical debate about the development of multicultural integration policies in the Netherlands, where proponents argue for stricter policies. They state that multicultural policies have failed, whereas opponents in the debate defend the old integration policies and point at their successes. The sources to study the debate are 65 articles published in Dutch national newspapers and magazines written by journalists and opinion leaders during the years 2005–2014. This is a ten-year episode in a debate that started in the 1960s and still continues after 2015. The second debate is on settlement and pension rights of Gurkha veterans that have served in the British army. The government offers them only a limited rights extension compared to other Commonwealth veterans. Public opinion wants to give them a full rights extension. The sources to study this debate are 88 articles from national newspapers in the UK written by journalists and opinion leaders and all published in 2009, which makes the debate quite focused in time. After a cross-case analysis the chapter concludes with a discussion.

The first contribution of the current chapter is mapping the concept of social rationality as ranging from more local to more general social values, including value interactions. They show interactions like mutual value tolerance or opposition, and value prioritization. The Dutch integration debate, for instance, refers to giving priority to Western key values and principles such as gender equality, tolerance for homosexuals or atheists, the need for immigrants to speak Dutch and zero tolerance for criminal behaviour, as opposed to expressions of more fundamentalist Muslim values. In the Gurkha debate, Gurkha values like bravery and loyalty are admired, whereas the government is pushed by public opinion to not being treacherous and pay their debt of honour. These values are partly bound to national settings, partly to higher and lower classes and some are more Western in opposition to Muslim values. Thus, social rationality appears to be bound to social communities, implying that such general values are mostly not universal, as assumed by Weber (1972), Habermas (1988) or deontological ethics. High degrees of universal agreement are the exception and they appear, for instance, as human rights or laws against criminal behaviours that share great resemblances across nations. However, MacIntyre's (1988) relativism is also nuanced by this chapter. The cases illustrate different processes of creating value hierarchies by challenging prioritization, subordination or reconciliation values, which goes beyond value relativism.

Second, the chapter contributes to our understanding of rationality conceptualized more generally, by mapping in more detail mutual critical and supportive interactions between social and instrumental rationality (cf. Bergset 2015; Racko 2011; Townley 2002) or social and expressive rationality (cf. Engelen 2006; Fisher and Freshwater 2014; Scherer 2011). Opponents in both cases draw, for instance, on instrumental rationality to criticize the feasibility of acting on preferred social-rational values. They criticize each other's values as being utopian. Expressive rationality appears as mainly supporting social-rational values, especially in the Gurkha case, but there are also critical expressive evaluations that articulate anger and frustration with some rules, norms and values in the integration debate. These findings support earlier criticisms in Anderson (1983), Majone (1992) and Peacock (1992) against unidirectional relations between the rationalities, with value rationality always dominating. All kinds of interactions between social rationality and the other two rationalities appear to be possible, both in critical and supportive relations.

Multicultural policies have failed to realize cultural integration

History

In the Netherlands, and surrounding countries like Belgium, Germany, France and the UK, immigration policies have mainly focused on socio-economic integration since the 1970s. Since the 1960s, large numbers of Moroccan and Turkish labourers were invited to join the Dutch workforce. These were Muslims from the countryside, and mostly not the more liberal ones. Initially, the request was to come temporarily, but most of them never left. As soon as the Dutch economy developed more into a service economy, many of these low-skilled labourers became unemployed. Parents in this first generation were not able to support the education of their children as they could not understand their Dutch lives. This first generation hardly spoke the Dutch language. They also did not try very hard as it was more comfortable to stick to their own circles, and the idea was to go back. Still, hardly anyone believed it any more.

Dutch policies were mainly supportive, based on the facilities of the welfare state. There was, for instance, no obligation to learn Dutch. Tolerance was seen as a political virtue. However, Dutch society experienced more and more problems with the first- and second-generation immigrants; for example, high unemployment, starting in the 1980s and remaining high over the years. School performance of immigrant children was relatively low and youth criminality high. Increasing equality between men and women, a recent achievement in Western societies, was set back to the old days in circles of these Muslim immigrants. Emancipation of homosexuals, also a recent achievement in Western cultures, was not accepted in Dutch Muslim circles either. Their numbers increased: in the biggest Dutch cities, more than half of the schoolchildren have parents with a non-Dutch background. Today, many inhabitants with a Dutch background feel less and less at home in their own environments, where Turks and Moroccans are the two biggest groups of immigrants, each comprising more than 2% of the total population. It is the Turks and Moroccans that dominate the Dutch integration debate.

Surinamese (another immigrant group almost as big) or asylum seekers integrated well in the same political environment. Generally, they were not lower-class immigrants, and asylum seekers were not necessarily asked to come to the Netherlands; instead, it was their need to come to the Netherlands and start a new life that brought them there. The identified problems with Turks and Moroccans as economic immigrants made Scheffer criticize the Dutch integration policies in a landmark article in *NRC*, (January 29, 2000) about 'the multicultural drama'. It was followed up by a book in 2010, arguing a whole generation gets lost due to Dutch tolerance. Earlier in the 1990s, Bolkestein had argued the same in another landmark article in the *Volkskrant* (September 12, 1991) that Dutch policies should demand more from immigrants. Integration policies should be more courageous, was the title message.

The atmosphere got worse after 9/11. Then, on November 2, 2004, a Muslim extremist murdered Theo van Gogh in Amsterdam. The motive was his sharp critiques on Muslims and Islam, but van Gogh was critical towards all religions, actively exploring the limits of freedom of expression. The 7/7 metro attacks in London followed in 2005, partly performed by British-born Muslim terrorists. The Danish cartoonist Kurt Westergaard was attacked at home on January 1, 2010 for having drawn a critical Mohammed cartoon in 2006, picturing Mohammed as a terrorist. On July 4, 2014, there was even a pro-Islamic State (IS) demonstration in The Hague. Later attacks are not discussed in the newspapers here, as the selection only extends to the end of 2014. Still, Muslim terrorism was already growing worldwide, with Muslims born and educated in the West within their ranks. This had its impact on the Dutch integration debate. Muslim immigrants report that they are treated differently by the Dutch since these attacks, as Funda Müjde states: 'When I grew up in the Netherlands, it was like a warm bed. But my children who once felt inhabitants of Amsterdam, feel more Turkish than ever' (*Elsevier*, February 13, 2010).

Stakeholders and decision makers

The Dutch integration debate is polarized between old-school policymakers defending a multicultural society, and new-school politicians and opinion leaders aiming at more cultural integration. The divide between pro and con is visible across political parties and immigrants themselves. Immigrants participate less in the debate. The debate is more *about* them than *with* them. It is mainly Dutch ministers, policymakers, journalists, experts and opinion leaders that are debating. Still, immigrants and citizens with a Dutch background are the most important stakeholders, and immigrants are quite heterogeneous as a group. Ministers and the Dutch parliament are decision makers in this debate, but always subject to democratic control.

When immigrants are interviewed, many support the new, more demanding integration policies, and zero-tolerance approaches. The interviewed immigrants suffer because of the bad performance, criminal behaviour and bad reputation of their peer group. Atilay Uslu, Chief Executive Officer of the well-known travel agency Corendon, blames Dutch politicians for having paid insufficient attention to immigrants: 'They have ignored subsidy fraud while tolerating abuses. Only now immigrants have to integrate. That should have been said 20 years ago' (*Elsevier*, February 13, 2010). As a consequence, immigrants are held responsible for criminal behaviours they would never wish to support. Sabri Kocoglu, a successful cook, comments: 'my environment is not as typically described by journalist or politicians, but how often do they see us? They form their opinion based on a group of Moroccans that screw it up for the other Moroccans and Turks' (*Elsevier*, February 13, 2010).

Arguments used

In the Dutch integration debate we see a confrontation between instrumental-rational arguments stressing effects and social-rational arguments referring to values. Within each rationality perspective there are disagreements as well. While the rationality behind the 'pro case' (for making integration policies more demanding and restrictive) is more social rational (SR), the 'con case' consists more of instrumental-rational (IR) argumentation, defending the effectiveness of earlier policies. Expressive-rational (ER) arguments figure less prominently. They support, for both sides, the related social-rational arguments by referring to Muslim emotions like feeling excluded, supporting multiculturalism, or the Dutch experiencing problems and feeling angry or detached supporting stricter policies. As can be seen in Table 4.1, the last column presents the groundedness of grounds and rebuttals (their frequency of appearance in the newspapers). Pro arguments were expressed somewhat more often (419) than were contra arguments (345). Arguments of the con case are presented in italics, and those of the proponents in normal case. The pro case wins the debate, as policies change over time into more demanding ones, but this is an episode in an ongoing debate.

Arguments pro are mainly social rational

Table 4.1 starts with the arguments of proponents for stricter integration policies. They mention a number of problems that are insufficiently addressed by multicultural integration policies during the 1980s, 1990s and the start of the twenty-first century. Policy scientist Verhoogt finds, for instance, that social integration as practised in multicultural policies is no guarantee against Muslim fundamentalism (*Trouw*, April 22, 2006). Thus, exclusive focus on socio-economic integration is insufficient as a means for political and cultural integration. Scheffer criticizes the tolerance principle in the Dutch multicultural policies: 'A parliamentary inquiry is needed to

Table 4.1 Integration of Dutch Muslim immigrants

	Claim, grounds and rebuttals; con case in italics	IR	SR	ER	(N)
Claim	New integration policies have to improve on the failures and flaws of the old, open-ended, too easy multicultural policies				
Since	Multicultural (Mc) policies have failed to support integration				
Since	They focus on socio-economic integration, not on political Islam, fundamentalism, culture and feelings of own people	X			14
			X		18
Since	Mc policies have unintended effects: acceptance of minority segregation, homosexual/woman repression, radicalism	X			10
Since	Mc policies demand too little from immigrants, are too open-ended, tolerant and supportive		X		7
Since	Mc policies are too soft in fighting fraud, crime and intolerance	X			5
Since	Mc policies are not well executed, and are ill-managed and inconsistent	X	X		5
Since	Underlying assumptions are flawed and often need revision over time	X			6
Since	Islam immigrants are not seen as they really are (but as similar to Christians, as victims, as incapable)	X			6
Since	Support of Islamic identity is no good means for cultural integration, due to Muslims' own intolerance	X			6
But	*Multicultural policies have been effective regarding socio-economic integration and can be further developed*	X			14
Since	New, better integration policies, laws and regulations are needed		X		5
Since	New policies need to be more demanding regarding required assimilation and speaking of the Dutch language		X		20
Since	Immigrants need to internalize key norms and values in Dutch society		X		10
But	*The Dutch cannot define their key values*	X			7
But	*Political parties behave inconsistently: become harder but then softer again to keep immigrant votes*	X			10

(Continued)

Table 4.1 (continued)

Claim, grounds and rebuttals; con case in italics	IR	SR	ER	(N)
New policies need to be more restrictive				13
Since New immigrants need a completed education and a passed integration test		X		13
Since Zero tolerance is needed regarding over-proportional criminal behaviours of immigrants		X		10
Since Sharia, niqab, import imams, honour killings, sex inequality must be prohibited. They undercut our culture		X		18
But *Banning the niqab is counterproductive and intolerant itself*		X		*10*
But *The integration test has problematic questions and cannot only target at Muslim immigrants (discrimination)*		X		*4*
But *Hard restrictive policies undermine open debate and freedom of religion, which is counterproductive*	X			9
New policies need to foster and enforce democratic key values against conflicting Islam values				14
Since Tolerance, freedom of opinion and religious freedom deserve to be protected		X		21
Since Equal rights for men, women and homosexuals are to be defended		X		10
But *Integration still needs to be reciprocal and inclusive*		X		*15*
But *Tolerance of homosexuals is problematic in Western countries as well*		X		*2*
New policies need to be better operationalized and made less contradictory and less vague	X			27
Since Communication needs to be more open with room for acknowledging polarization and shared interests		X		17
Since Focus needs to be more general on lower-class problems, their low education and emancipation		X		8
Since Politicians should take responsibility for political integration and fostering the democratic power of reason		X		5
But *Political emancipation hard to achieve as it is incompatible with the more fundamental Islamic ideas*	X			*5*
Since Integration policies can be made more effective when aligned with EU policies	X			3
But *Integration policies can be made more effective when following co-creation and receptor approaches*	X			*4*

(Continued)

Table 4.1 (continued)

Claim, grounds and rebuttals; con case in italics	IR	SR	ER	(N)
But The new policies still need to remain supportive and facilitative to help realize benefits from immigration	X			8
Since *Facilitate integration by sharing experiences, connecting immigrants, supporting their communities*	X			7
Since *Facilitate integration by means of helping/defending suppressed liberal, critical or homosexual Muslims*	X			7
But State support of religious communities is not neutral and only helps integration within, not between, religions		X		4
But *Effect of most policies is limited and success is more due to immigrants themselves*	X			6
Since There are too many problems with immigrants		X		8
Since Immigrants are not politically integrated, intolerant towards Western democratic values, stick to their own circles		X		32
Since Muslims are superficially committed to Western values, use them only to their own advantage, have double loyalty		X		17
But *Double loyalty is inevitable, acceptable and easy to handle*		X		4
Since Radical Islam causes honour killings, terrorism, decapitation, intolerance for other beliefs/liberal Islamic traditions, obligate internal marriage, female circumcision, discrimination of women, restricted freedom of movement and fear		X		28
But *Radical Muslims have a minor influence: most Muslims do not even go to a mosque and attacks are incidental*	X			10
Since Islamic schools underperform and the Moroccan youth is aggressive and over-represented on criminality lists		X		16
Since Muslim states have a low standard of living. Muslim immigrants are lower class: high unemployment, low education	X			16
Since Integration takes three generations, which implies high costs	X			2
But *Part of the problem is due to the Dutch system with its complex rules and large impersonal schools*	X			3

(Continued)

Table 4.1 (continued)

Claim, grounds and rebuttals; con case in italics	IR	SR	ER	(N)
But *Immigrants have achieved a lot in the Netherlands*	X			7
Since Many immigrants are socially integrated as increasingly successful entrepreneurs, employees, students	X			22
Since Many immigrants are politically/culturally integrated and defend Western values like freedom, equality men/women		X		17
But There are differences between first/second generation, (non)Muslim immigrants, asylum seekers and youth	X			11
But *Immigrants experience severe problems with the Dutch attitude towards them*		X	X	9
Since There is little tolerance for Islamic habits and culture. Muslims feel excluded. Lack of nuance after 9/11			X	28
Since Many immigrants face a crude Dutch state, complex procedures, stereotyping, discrimination and racism		X		19
But Muslim-related problems (terrorism, disrespect homosexuals and women) cause fair emotions of fear, anger, detachment			X	24
But Within the EU, the Netherlands still has relatively positive attitude towards Muslim immigrants, entrepreneurs and labour force			X	17
But *Debate itself is also a way to defend liberal values, challenge religions, name problems, share information and convince*	X			45
But It is still turned to the negative, lacks nuance, is offensive, polarized (not left–right), fragmented, foggy; not open		X		38
But Debate needs to be more open (also to emotions), fact-based, with journalists and scientists being more conclusive		X		8
Groundedness (totals)	270	**416**	78	764
Pro (totals)	106	**272**	41	419
Con (totals)	**164**	144	37	345

Note: IR: instrumental rationality; SR: social rationality; ER: expressive rationality.

evaluate our immigration and integration policy. Now whole generations are wasted due to tolerance' (*NRC*, September 29, 2007). Both quotes refer to the effects of multicultural policies, starting with some instrumental-rational claims related to the old policies, but moving quickly into a social-rational discussion on principles.

An intensively debated concern is the clash between Western and Muslim values, as large groups of Muslim immigrants do not integrate well from a cultural perspective. The critique of the proponents is that they only show superficial commitment to Western values and mainly stick to their own circles. They are not well integrated politically and culturally. Frits Bolkestein criticizes the multicultural integration policy supporting this:

> The religious infrastructure supported by Cohen in 2002, was based on an illusion of 'integration via Islam'. To support dialogue in society, Cohen supported a couple of projects, and Westermoskee was the most important. This prestigious mosque had to be a 'symbol of integration' according to the mayor. He argued for a subsidy of two million euros. There were no question marks put as to how a mosque can be a symbol of integration.
>
> (*Volkskrant*, May 15, 2010)

Figure 4.1 shows the newly built Turkish mosque inspired by Aya Sophia in Istanbul. It has a small entrance on the left for women and the big main entrance in the middle is meant to be for men.

Such criticisms are based on social-rational arguments that refer to Western values as the norm. The value clash is illustrated by greater gender inequality, support for mutilative female circumcision, forced marriage, hate towards gays and lesbians, intolerance for other beliefs or atheism and honour killings, to name a few results of fundamentalist Muslim culture. While it is not the majority of the Dutch Muslims who are extreme in all such aspects, there is a substantial minority, growing in dominance.

Ruud Koopmans, head of the research group *Migration* of Wissenschaftszentrum Berlin für Sozialforschung, reports in an interview the findings of an inquiry among European Muslims in 2013. He reports that 45% can be labelled as fundamentalist, as they are not tolerant towards other religions or atheism (*Parool*, March 26, 2015). It is not the majority, but still quite mainstream among Muslims and much stronger than expected. Koopmans also finds that headscarves are absolutely no means of emancipation, because they are strongly associated with fundamentalist Islamic ideas, suggesting that women have the exclusive responsibility for seduction between men and women.

Wouter Bos, a left-wing politician, acknowledges the culture clash around 2008, and states that there is a need to 'name the problems and accept more polarization' (*Volkskrant*, November 22, 2008). Earlier, Parekh, a British professor in political philosophy, was invited to reflect on the Dutch situation. He states: 'Western society needs to prevent that we get a new underclass of immigrants with dangerous proportions' (*De Groene Amsterdammer*, June 8, 2007). Such lower-class problems are youth criminality, low school performance and relative high unemployment. Earlier

Figure 4.1 Entrances for men and women in the recently built Westermoskee in
Amsterdam.

wake-up calls by Bolkestein, Scheffer and Fortuyn are repeatedly remembered
during the debate (*De Groene Amsterdammer*, August 4, 2010; *Trouw*, September
28, 2011).

Expressive-rational pro arguments in the integration debate are based on feelings
of anger. Such feelings are legitimate in the current situation argues Van der Laan,
at that time the proposed new Dutch minister for integration. He counters the
assumption that Dutch intolerance stems from fear: 'The homosexual teacher who
has been bullied for years by many of his pupils and their parents is not scared, he is
angry. Like the girls who find out they do not count' (*Volkskrant*, November 22,
2008). It is these Muslim girls that suffer a lot. Hirsi Ali had already pointed this out
in 2005: 'this year six girls are murdered in Berlin. And according to a recently
published report of the Dutch government eleven girls are murdered by family
members in one province the previous year' (*Volkskrant*, June 10, 2005). Hirsi Ali
refers to a stable trend, as there are between ten and 20 such murders yearly in the
Netherlands. It is not only girls who are the victims, but it starts with them. The
Dutch police report such crimes separately (see Politie 2016).

Arguments con are mainly instrumental and social rational

Opponents of more demanding policies defend the old multicultural policies by pointing at what is achieved over the last 40 years. Table 4.1 shows they mention the positive effects of earlier policies when rebutting the first main pro argument and they put the negative effects into perspective by using instrumental-rational counterargumentation. They argue socio-economic integration has improved over the years, which still is a positive effect. Participation of immigrant youth in higher education is increasing as well. They argue that Muslim extremism is incidental in Western countries and not the biggest threat we face, although it scares us most as it targets Western people. However, Muslim girls suffer more and they need our support, like the repressed liberal and critical Muslims. They also argue the debate should be used more to challenge Muslims in a positive way (see the last main rebuttal in Table 4.1). Problems with the debate itself are also stressed by the opponents. The tone is far too negative. This supportive orientation is social rational, and refers to values like helping, caring and protection.

Conditions for integration and competing policy ideas

We do see a shift in the debate over time towards increasing acknowledgement that socio-economic integration is not enough and that multicultural policies are not sufficient conditions for real integration. However, Table 4.1 also shows how opponents argue that immigrants suffer under the Dutch attitude that is not open anymore and that Muslims feel excluded. They feel no tolerance for their culture and habits, and they experience a lack of nuance on the side of the Dutch after 9/11, which is no good condition for integration either. Still, the Dutch do remain relatively tolerant and positive towards Muslim immigrants compared to other European Union countries. As the sociologist Pollock reports in *NRC* (December 3, 2010), from his research: 62% of the Dutch still has a positive impression of Muslims, compared to 56% in France and 34% in West Germany. The more personal contact people have with Muslims, the more positive is their judgment.

The debate is about policies. It is about the most effective way to handle the integration problems. And also it is about what incidents or exceptions will ease out over time, and what are the more fundamental integration problems. It is not about the seriousness of the acknowledged value clash. Bas Heine, therefore, ridicules Donner's criticisms on multiculturalism as creating a strawman: 'Who argues in the Netherlands for a multicultural society, and what should that mean? Who argues immigrants should not adapt to the Dutch society? Who argues female circumcision is a beautiful cultural tradition?' (*NRC*, June 18, 2011).

Whereas proponents focus on stricter policies, and on naming problems, opponents still believe in more supportive policies. They suggest co-creative policies as they are best tailored to immigrant needs. They try to prevent insider–outsider dynamics. They want to support liberal, critical and homosexual Muslims against the threats they face in their Muslim communities as a means to influence Muslim culture from the inside. Another policy suggestion made is that debating integration is itself an effective force in influencing Muslim values. However, proponents argue that Muslims are quite convinced about their Muslim values as outlined by Parekh in *NRC* (May 5, 2007): 'many Muslims feel superior compared to our secular and in their eyes immoral society'. Parekh underlines that the integration trajectory of Muslims is different from that of Sikhs, Jews and Hindus in the nineteenth and twentieth centuries in Europe. Still, addressing these differences is not possible by general rule-based policies, irrespective of how strict they might be, as they will apply to all immigrants equally.

Gurkha fighters deserve equal settlement and pension rights, whatever it costs!

History

Gurkhas, Nepalese army men, served for over 200 years in the British army but were never allowed to settle in the UK and were not given equal pensions to British soldiers. That remained so after the re-stationing of the Gurkha bases from Hong Kong to the UK due to the transfer of sovereignty over Hong Kong to the Chinese in 1997. It was only in 2004 that the government announced allowing the Gurkhas' settlement in the UK after retirement, but only if they had served after 1997. In 2007, a high-court judge declared this policy to be illegal, as the process to determine pre-1997 applications was deemed arbitrary. The Labour government agreed to change the rules, and later that year agreed that the Gurkha veterans would receive an equal pension to other soldiers in the army. However, there were some important caveats: only Gurkhas that had served 20 years would be eligible; a common Gurkha rifleman, however, only served 15 years. Nor were settlement rights granted. Only after a heated public debate and lots of stakeholder pressure, and a quite critical public opinion, things changed for the better for the Gurkhas in 2009.

Stakeholders and decision makers

The limited rights were a trigger for the rise of a Gurkha-rights movement led by actress Joanne Lumley and supported by large newspapers, and an accompanying large public debate on the issue of Gurkha-rights extension in the first half of 2009, that eventually led the government to grant almost all Gurkha veterans equal pension and settlement rights as compared to other British soldiers. Though decision-making authority belonged to the government, public opinion influenced by interest groups had great impact.

Arguments used

In the Gurkha case we see a clear confrontation of instrumental-rational arguments criticizing social rationality. While the rationality behind the 'pro case' (for expanding the rights of the Gurkhas) is strongly social rational, based on values like being honourable and supporting equal rights, the 'con case' consists of both defensive social- and critical instrumental-rational argumentation, stressing the cost effects of a rights extension. Expressive-rational arguments are used less, but they play a strong role in support of the social-rational arguments in the pro case based on feelings like a deeply felt care for the Gurkhas by the British public. As can be seen in Table 4.2, the last column presents the groundedness of grounds and rebuttals (their frequency of appearance in the newspapers). Pro arguments were expressed a lot more often (622) than were contra arguments (206). Contra arguments are presented in italics and those of the proponents in normal case. The pro case wins the debate.

Social pro arguments versus instrumental counterarguments

The most important argument for extending the rights of the Gurkhas is social rational. It is based on their alleged bravery and willingness to fight for Britain: 'Many of these brave soldiers have given . . . their lives in the service of this country' (readers' reactions in *the Herald*, May 2, 2009). The British share a moral impulse to reward them: '[The Gurkhas] put their lives on the line for our country and have therefore earned the right to live among us' (*The Express*, May 22, 2009). Such quotes are summarized in the first and most reported pro argument that is listed in Table 4.2.

Opponents never disputed the alleged bravery of the Gurkhas. In the words of Field Marshal Edwin Bramall, 'they [the Gurkhas] are marvelous, the very best and most loyal of fighting men' (*The Independent on Sunday*, April 26, 2009). But they did point out that:

> should there be a large influx of [. . .] ex-Gurkhas and their families, their pensions [. . .] would be quite inadequate to live on in this country. This would mean either that these pensions would have to be increased or that the government would be having to deal with large numbers of welfare claims.
>
> (Tony Gould in *The Guardian*, May 2, 2009)

However, this instrumental cost argument questioning the feasibility of such a policy failed to impress the proponents of a rights extension, who called it 'beneath contempt' (*The Express*, January 15, 2009) and 'disgraceful' (*The Express*, January 16, 2009). 'Whatever it costs, however much we owe them in pensions, however many NHS beds they take up we want them all here as a debt of honor' (Lumley quoted in *The Sun*, May 6, 2009). Proponents of an expansion of rights for Gurkhas thus forcefully rejected the relevance of cost-related considerations in favour of a classic value-rational justification, so redefining the debate into a social-rational one. Thus, proponents of an extension were both able to discharge the most important cost arguments of their opponents by rebutting their instrumental rationality on instrumental grounds, and by referring to social-rational arguments to which the opponents of a rights extension did not dare challenge them, because they were government officials and army officers who were the first to expand the rights of the Gurkhas in 2004, even before Lumley started the debate. This might explain why the opponents were never able to give a convincing

Table 4.2 Gurkha debate in the UK

Claim, grounds and rebuttals; con case in italics	IR	SR	ER	(N)
Claim The Gurkha veterans who served before 1997 should be given pension and settlement rights equal to other army men				
Since The Gurkhas always have been brave and honourable fighters, prepared to make sacrifices for Britain		X		62
Since The Gurkhas have always played a vital role in the British army		X		11
Since The bravery of the Gurkhas is illustrated by the fact that they won no fewer than 13 Victoria Crosses (the army's top honour for bravery), more than any other regiment		X		26
Since If someone is prepared to die for this country, then surely they deserve to live in this country		X		7
Since Heroically, some Gurkhas will go on hunger strikes to persuade the government			X	4
Since Officers will refuse to come to the UK if it means that they should leave their men behind			X	3
Since The government acted treacherously and dishonestly towards the Gurkhas in not giving them equal rights		X		58
Since Government policy of providing unequal rights is ruled unlawful by the high court		X		40
Since There are multiple examples of Gurkhas or their widows cruelly being denied medical attention, despite their needs		X		24
Since Many retired Gurkhas live in poverty		X		8
Since Government regulations for settlement and pension rights are impossibly stringent		X		23
Since A typical Gurkha rifleman is only allowed to serve 15 years, while for a full pension 20 years of service is required. This is unfair		X		6
Since The exclusion of Gurkhas is nothing but discrimination		X		7
Since The Gurkhas have – as it stands – far fewer rights than non-British Commonwealth soldiers.		X		11
Since They want equality		X		
Since Westminster has always treated the Gurkhas as if they were cheap brown labourers		X		4
***But** No government has done more for the Gurkhas than this one*		X		19
***Since** This government already gave the Gurkhas a major increase in their pensions*		X		12
***Since** The government acted in good faith and realistically in this case*		X		9
***Since** This government was the first to provide settlement rights*		X		6

(Continued)

Table 4.2 (continued)

Claim, grounds and rebuttals; con case in italics	IR	SR	ER	(N)
Since Equal rights for the Gurkhas are fair and just; it is a matter of honour for Britain		X		40
Since Exclusion of the Gurkhas is the betrayal of true friends		X		8
Since A 200-year friendship exists between the Gurkhas and the British army		X		12
Since Active Gurkhas already have these privileges; it is unfair towards the veterans			X	4
Since The British public cares deeply for the fate of the Gurkhas			X	34
Since The British public has overwhelmingly supported this case in many ways		X		16
Since The campaign on behalf of the Gurkhas is supported by big tabloid newspapers, The Sun and the *Daily Express*, which have millions of readers between them		X		17
Since The House of Commons has voted to extend the rights of the Gurkhas		X		14
Since The campaign on behalf of the Gurkhas is supported by a member of the Royal family		X		14
Since The campaign on behalf of the Gurkhas is led by the prominent and popular actress Joanna Lumley		X		5
Since The campaign on behalf of the Gurkhas is backed by many decorated (ex)soldiers		X		2
Since Many immigrants that contribute nothing to society are allowed in, but brave and loyal soldiers are let down		X		28
Since Gurkhas are very loyal people			X	23
Since The Gurkhas will make outstanding British citizens, being loyal to British values		X		8
Since The government is scaremongering by hammering on about costs and immigration		X		17
Since The numbers of veterans coming to the UK and the related costs are small when compared to total immigration	X			13
But *Between 36,000 and 100,000 Gurkhas and their family members may settle, leading to immense pressure on the immigration system*	X			15

(Continued)

Table 4.2 (continued)

Claim, grounds and rebuttals; con case in italics	IR	SR	ER	(N)
But Extending Gurkha rights will cost the taxpayer through the social services they will be entitled to, and the Ministry of Defence, which is already on a tight budget	X			35
Since The cost of these proposed measures is so high that it jeopardizes the future existence of Gurkha regiments	X			22
Since The army is seriously overstretched already; losing more soldiers will lead to underperformance	X			6
Since Any change in settlement rights will open the way for change in pension rights for the veterans	X			9
Since Extending the rights of the Gurkhas will lead to a review of the rights of all non-British forces	X			3
But Britain has a debt of honour towards the Gurkhas, whatever the costs		X		26
Since Without the Gurkhas, the UK would not be what it is now	X			8
But Costs will not be that high, as only a limited number of Gurkhas will settle in Britain	X			15
Since The extra costs associated with extending Gurkha rights are marginal; the government is grossly exaggerating	X			11
Since The cost associated with extending Gurkha rights pales in comparison to those used to bail out banks	X			3
But As retired soldiers, the Regiment veterans are entitled to make use of social services like the National Health Service		X		6
But The use of the cost argument by the government is shameful		X		4
But If all Gurkhas are allowed into Britain the Nepalese government may ban any further recruitment		X		11
Since The payment of army pensions is a great stimulant for the Nepalese economy	X			6
But Gurkhas are mercenaries who should not be allowed into Britain		X		7
But The Gurkhas knew that they would have to live in Nepal on a good pension for Nepalese standards when they signed up		X		15
Since Letting the Gurkhas settle is unfair immigration policy		X		5

(Continued)

Table 4.2 (continued)

Claim, grounds and rebuttals; con case in italics		IR	SR	ER	(N)
Since	Britain is overcrowded already; no more immigrants should be let in, including the Gurkhas		X		4
Since	Nepal is not a member of the Commonwealth, so the Gurkhas never have been subjects of the British Crown		X		6
Since	Before 1997 the Gurkhas were stationed in Hong Kong and, thus, did not experience British life	X			7
Since	Only people with strong links to Britain should be allowed to settle		X		5
Since	Extending the rights of the Gurkhas is public policy based on populism and demagogy		X		4
	Groundedness (totals)	153	**607**	68	828
	Pro (totals)	50	**504**	68	622
	Con (totals)	**103**	103	0	206

Source: adapted from Bouwmeester 2013: 422.

Note: IR: instrumental rationality; SR: social rationality; ER: expressive rationality.

legitimation for the decision not to expand rights further – despite the fact that the authority to decide was fully in their hands.

Overrated conditions and adjusted policies

Policies aimed initially to give Gurkha veterans a limited rights extension, due to the involved costs of a full rights extension referred to in the first rebuttal in Table 4.2. Financial means were considered an unfulfilled condition for full rights. Also, the expected response by the Nepalese government was pictured as negative. Fulfilled conditions for partial rights extension were the contracts signed, which clearly stated the limited rights beforehand, and they even got somewhat extended. However, under pressure from the proponents of a full rights extension these objections became fluid. Proponents argued that:

> stories that say letting retired Gurkhas live in the UK will cost billions and be a drain on services like the NHS are simply MoD [Ministry of Defence] scaremongering. The numbers of retired Gurkhas that are likely to come to the UK are small when compared to immigration into this country.
>
> (Lumley quoted in *The Express*, January 22, 2009)

The result was a policy change towards granting a full rights extension due to public opinion and stakeholder pressures in 2009, which settled the debate.

Cross-case analysis

Social rationality and the force of opposite values or principles

Due to the topics of integration and Gurkha rights, we find in the double case study that social rationality dominates both in importance and number of arguments presented in the two cases as based on their groundedness. The fit between social rationality and an intersubjective context for legitimating or challenging decisions is as assumed by Bouwmeester (2013). Social rationality is grounded in what communities of people consider valuable, important or attractive. Social-rational arguments in the cases refer to justice and fairness, to law, to majority values and interests, and to standards belonging to Western civil society, to name a few. They also illustrate many value conflicts (MacIntyre 1988).

In the Dutch integration debate, the social norms, values, laws, etc. referred to in social-rational arguments are, in the pro case, about the importance of tolerance, freedom of expression and liberty to follow your own sexual inclinations. More recently, participants in the debate also refer to values like standing up, protecting and defending our safety and the importance to fight criminal and intolerant Muslim behaviours. Gay and young liberal Muslims, for instance, who want to enjoy the freedom in a Western society need such protection. Another group of values is about the importance of demanding more from immigrants, that they should learn the language, not behave like victims or blame Western society for their problems.

Contrary to this Western orientation, Muslims and their Western allies stress in their social-rational arguments the importance of preventing discrimination, stereotyping and general hostility towards Muslims in general, due to terrorist attacks like 9/11, London 7/7, etc. Muslims have the right to be different as long as they obey the law. The con case also stresses the importance of care and support during the integration process.

In the Gurkha debate, pro-case arguments refer to the social-rational values of taking responsibility for Gurkha veterans. For having been prepared to give your life for the UK, you deserve the right to live there. Another value is being honest and not treacherous about what rights Gurkha veterans deserve. It should be equal rights regarding settlement, medical care and pensions, as compared to non-British Commonwealth veterans and Gurkha soldiers today. Not allowing the Gurkha veterans such rights feels like a betrayal of good friendship. Moreover, Gurkhas have proven to be loyal to British values. To the majority, such values are extremely appealing and they serve as an argument towards a government that is unwilling to extent rights further than it had done already. On the contrary, the principles the UK government refers to in their con case are the need to balance interests between stakeholder groups and spending money wisely – you can spend it only once. Table 4.3 summarizes the main stakeholders and summarizes what kind of values and principles are at the core of social rationality as advocated by opponents and proponents in the two debates.

The first observation from the two debates dominated by social-rational arguments is that the social-rational arguments affect different stakeholder groups

Table 4.3 Different group values backing social rationality in immigration and Gurkha debate

Stricter Dutch integration policies	Gurkha rights extension
Main stakeholders: politicians/parties defending multicultural policies (con) or new integration policies (pro), Dutch society, 'own' people (pro), homosexuals (pro), Muslim women and girls, liberal/critical Muslims (pro), first/second generation, Muslim communities, radical Muslims (con), asylum seekers, journalists, experts.	**Main stakeholders:** British government (con), Ministry of Defence (con), House of Commons, British public (pro), Joanna Lumley (pro), Gurkha veterans (pro), decorated (ex)soldiers (pro), Nepal.
Proponents' values: no intolerance to other sexual inclinations. No inequality of rights men/women. Intolerance towards other beliefs and atheism is unacceptable. Zero tolerance for criminal behaviours immigrants.	**Proponents' values:** Gurkha veterans deserve equal rights compared to non-British Commonwealth soldiers. Loyalty and bravery need to be rewarded. Britain has a debt of honour, whatever the costs.
Opponents' values: give those who need it socio-economic support, legal/police support or care. Not tolerating religious practices Muslims is intolerant itself.	**Opponents' values:** interests need to be balanced. Extending Gurkha rights can only be at the cost of other expenses.

differently. The controversies between opponents and proponents in the integration and Gurkha debate are grounded in principles (equal rights for men and women, or Gurkhas and other soldiers, or interests that need to be balanced), values (liberty, tolerance, care) and commitments (debt of honour). In the debates, we see tolerance for such differences, but also examples of challenging each other's values, setting priorities or establishing a value hierarchy.

The Gurkha debate progresses towards a value hierarchy, with more local economic values advocated by the Ministry of Defence subordinated to the more general moral values referred to by the British civil society. The principles of being frugal and prudent referred to by the Ministry of Defence are contested by public opinion, which gives voice to the majority of British citizens. Saving money is considered not very relevant in relation to what Gurkhas have done for the UK, and what responsibility the UK has for them. Proponents argue that such costs do not matter as much as our debt of honour. Pressed by public opinion, the Ministry of Defence has to accept that their money interests need to be given less weight, as they are perceived as less rational from a social perspective.

The integration debate is split between those who defend multicultural policies and new policymakers who challenge them and defend stricter integration policies. A solution to the value conflict is less obvious here. The opposition is Western tolerance towards non-Western cultures versus defending own key values like gender equality, gay rights and freedom of speech and religion. Tolerance of Muslim intolerance is more and more seen as a dead end. The social rationality of multiculturalism is criticized as contradictory, by welcoming intolerant cultures that undermine its own conditions. The counterargument is that the new, more restrictive policies are intolerant themselves. They set a bad example. During the debate, a value hierarchy gradually develops, where multicultural policies end up being as less rational and where Western values like gender equality and gay tolerance need to get more priority. Other splits in the integration debate are between Western values and Muslim values, where a basic tolerance remains, and within Muslim communities between values of radical and liberal Muslims. Liberal or gay Muslims especially experience hard times and are repressed. The more conservative Muslim judgments about them have great impact. There is little Muslim tolerance for their choices and within Muslim communities their choices are considered less rational; they are in conflict with well-accepted Muslim standards, resembling the situation of Western societies about more than 50 years ago.

Social rationality can solve these value tensions in different ways: by tolerance, by challenging them, by giving priority to values and subordinating others or by reconciliation. After decades of experiences with a multicultural approach, the conclusion is that tolerance by multiculturalism can undermine itself when importing intolerant cultures and religions. As a consequence, priority is given to Western key values, like equal rights for men and women, over multicultural tolerance. In the Gurkha debate we see a process of subordinating economic values for being prudent under the moral value of paying the debt of honour, which gets priority in the debate. Value tolerance is still attractive when one culture can add to the other. We can observe this in the integration debate for economic examples like different kitchens that coexist and where consumers enjoy the variety. We see the same in the British respect for Gurkha fighters, who, with their skills and bravery, add to the force of the British army. The debate on integration also illustrates attempts of value reconciliation; for instance, full acceptance of key Western values by liberal, emancipated and tolerant Muslims.

Cross-rationality controversies related to social (ir)rationality

Social rationality can be divided in itself like expressive rationality, but more on the level of different groups or community values. There are clashes within social rationality, many of them visible in the integration debate, and little in the Gurkha debate. Opposition from other rationality perspectives is mainly instrumental, by criticizing the costs of plans, or their effectiveness. Expressive rationality is mainly supportive towards the social-rational arguments in the Gurkha debate. Only in the integration debate is the expressive-rational opposition quite substantial. The emotional motives work on the internally divided value clusters and vice versa, thus making one side more legitimate by mutual reinforcement, while challenging the other side as irrational.

Expressive-rational opposition

In the integration debate, the controversy is about setting boundaries for youth criminality and intolerant behaviours performed by fundamentalist Muslims versus values aimed at helping and supporting the more tolerant and liberal Muslims and not stigmatizing the whole group because of the problematic behaviours of some of them. This social-rational controversy is mirrored in expressive-rational arguments: on the one hand, the authentic feelings of repulsion towards inacceptable Muslim practices like forced marriage, women's one-sided responsibility for seduction, the headscarf obligation and inequality of sexes, hating homosexuals, youth criminality, etc. The feelings of anger support the values behind more restrictive policies as rational from an expressive perspective, and multicultural policies as more irrational. On the opposite side, we see authentic feelings of dislike towards stereotyping, discrimination and Muslim exclusion, making the stricter policies irrational from the expressive-rational perspective of the more care-oriented opponents. Within social rationality the conflicting clusters of shared values are thus fuelled and supported by motivational arguments grounded in feelings that express a similar conflict.

The Gurkha debate does not show a strong internal controversy of a social-rational nature: both proponents and opponents want extension of pension and settlement rights, and both feel grateful and positive about what Gurkhas have done for the UK. There is only controversy about the degree to which rights should be extended. Expressive rationality merely supports a rights extension, because all participants feel sympathy towards extending pension and settlement rights. When proponents of a full rights extension use expressive rationality in their motivational argumentation, it is not rebutted by government officials based on contradictory feelings and so there are no suggestions of social irrationality projected on Gurkha supporters based on expressive-rational arguments. Thus, the feelings of opponents and proponents are quite aligned.

Instrumental-rational opposition

Between instrumental rationality and the social-rational value clusters there are supporting and also strong undermining relationships. The values of proponents of stricter integration policies receive support from their instrumental-rational arguments claiming the effectiveness of a zero-tolerance approach towards immoral immigrant behaviours that are visible, for example, in the repression of women or homosexuals and in youth criminality. Multicultural policies are criticized on instrumental-rational grounds as ineffective and utopian. However, opponents, in turn, point at the irrationalities of making integration policies stricter based on their instrumental-rational evaluations; the impact of integration policies has always been low, whatever was tried. The biggest immigrant successes were mainly due to their own efforts. Moreover, stricter policies are counterproductive regarding freedom of religion and open debate, whereas, for realizing integration, open debate might be the most effective in the end. Opponents of stricter integration policies thus argue by means of instrumental rationality for the effectiveness of their own multicultural policies, which is, for instance, supporting liberal streams in the Muslim community, co-creative approaches and celebrating the socio-economic achievements of the second generation. Thus, the debate about what are the best policies to realize the higher aims of integration, on which both parties fundamentally agree, is quite intense.

The controversy between social and instrumental rationality in the Gurkha debate is about the amount of money that is needed to be paid for their pensions and settlement rights. The Ministry of Defence and its political supporters do not want to invest too much for extending Gurkha rights, as their budgets are tight. That would be irrational from an instrumental perspective and as ideal rather utopian. Moreover, different interests need to be balanced, and money can only be spent once. However, according to the proponents, the debate should not be about money, or the necessary means; it should be about the goal, first and foremost. And this goal of granting equal pension and settlement rights is fully justified based on a couple of moral arguments: equality towards non-British Commonwealth veterans and towards current Gurkha fighters. That Gurkhas have signed a different contract in the past is not a convincing counterargument – with the current knowledge, that contract is unfair. In addition, the expected settlement of up to 100,000 Gurkhas and, consequentially, the increased immigration costs are rebutted on instrumental grounds. The numbers are grossly exaggerated. The debate thus illustrates a strong controversy between social and instrumental rationality, and proponents consider instrumental rationality off limits here, given what values are at stake. Even the government is attacked for that way of thinking in this situation. It is arguing from the wrong rationality perspective and, in doing so, this view is reframed as irrational on social-rational grounds.

Discussion: social construction of social rationality

Social rationality in kinds and degrees: mitigating
controversies by debate

Social rationality includes what Weber (1972) calls value rationality. For Weber, value rationality has a universal pretence. Habermas (1988: 41–5) follows up on this, and excludes therapeutic and aesthetic critique from moral discourse, because it is too subjective and too local, imitating Weber who excluded traditional and affective motives to act on. However, legitimate values referred to as social rational always include in their conception the boundaries of a community, which is mostly not mankind in general (MacIntyre 1988). As in Freeman's (2010) stakeholder approach, a social universe can be smaller or bigger, and the active values within such communities can be contested by values that guide behaviour in other social universes, like values in Western culture versus Eastern or Muslim cultures (Zhu 2015). The concept of social rationality (Churchman 1962; Dahms 1997; Sen 1993) helps locating value conflicts at the borders or intersections of these social spaces, a phenomenon also acknowledged by Weber (1972: 16).

Differentiations in the concept of social rationality that follow from differences between social spaces are illustrated in the two debates. There is political rationality visible in the massive public critiques supporting the Gurkhas, pushing the UK government to change policies. Group rationalities are also based on higher- or lower-class views, Western or Muslim and liberal or fundamentalist views, and these rationalities compete in the debates. Legal and moral rationality is also used to argue claims in both debates, and they try to establish the more general value claims, but are still bound to national or cultural context.

Different social rationalities are illustrated in the Dutch integration debate, where some Muslim values clash with Western values. More radical Muslim interpretations legitimate honour killings based on the sharia. So are certain punishments for women, who have a one-sided responsibility for seduction or for having sex. In this social universe, inequality between men and women is accepted, while homosexuality is off limits. The Sociaal en Cultureel Planbureau (Netherlands Institute for Social Research) reports in a study on integration that especially Turkish and Moroccan immigrants stick to their cultural roots. Half of them are partially segregated, and about 25% are either fully segregated or isolated, which means not willing to accept Western standards such as equality between men, women and LGBTs (lesbian, gay, bisexual and transgender) (Sociaal en Cultureel Planbureau 2015: 9). Within the social universe of Western culture, such unwillingness to accept our key values due to Muslim ideology feels anachronistic. Still, gay tolerance is only a recent value for us, and some forms of gender inequality also exist in the West, but we aim more strongly at equality.

Social rationality is internally divided as the rule, which makes it a local and also historical category, with values developing over time. Social rationality is thus subject to social construction within time, disciplinary field and social community or stakeholder boundaries (Bouwmeester 2013; MacIntyre 1988; Toulmin 1994; Toulmin *et al.* 1984). The kind of values and principles referred to can be many, extending political, legal or organizational values, as suggested by Diesing (1976). The two studied debates cannot give a full overview of all social-rational universes, but do they illustrate the differences between Western (the Dutch) and Muslim values (Turkish and Moroccan immigrants), the military value of bravery and loyalty that is so special for the Gurkhas and the economic value of being frugal (Ministry of Defence) versus paying a debt of honour in the UK (citizens). The debates suggest that social rationality has to be defined more broadly than in Diesing (1976), thus following Churchman (1962), Dahms (1997), Gintis (2016) and Sen (1993), but also more differentiated per community than assumed in Weber (1972) or Habermas (1988). Still, there remain clear conceptual boundaries with expressive rationality that is based on subjective instead of social motivations, and with instrumental rationality grounded in means–end argumentations as based on caus- alities. The different ways social rationality appears in the two debates and over time hints at the ecological differentiations addressed by Gigerenzer (2010), but it is beyond the scope of this study to interpret specific underlying social heuristics and their ecological fit.

Given these differences in social rationality, the analysis still provides insights into the reasons why some social-rational arguments are considered more rational in a public debate than other ones, thus nuancing MacIntyre's (1988) value relativism. In the Dutch integration debate, becoming more restrictive and demanding in complying with Western key values is considered more rational in the end, due to a learning process of trial and error, and many reflections on such experiences in various settings. These reflections result in tolerance, challenges, value prioritization, subordination and value reconciliation. These are ways to respond to value conflicts which detail a process called norm setting in Majone (1992: 23). The responses to value conflict add nuance to the coping strategies available to opponents that accept that social rationality relates to the right field for debating their questions, as found in Bouwmeester (2013). The response processes to value conflicts socially construct degrees of rationality, with the higher-ranked values given a higher degree of social rationality than the lower-ranked ones.

Social (ir)rationality against standards of instrumental and expressive rationality

In spite of the differentiated nature of social rationality, when applying values in their relevant context they can guide you well. Military values guide your behaviour in the army, higher-class values in higher-class contexts and academic values when working in academia, as suggested before (Boltanski and Thevenot 2006; Diesing 1976; MacIntyre 1988; Satow 1975). However, value conflicts do not only appear at the intersections of social spaces, or when applying them in the wrong context. It is also possible that norms, values or principles underlying social rationality get evaluated as problematic from the perspective of expressive or instrumental rationality (Bouwmeester 2013; Gaut 2012). Some values can be upsetting or frustrating from an expressive-rational perspective, or they can seem unrealistic or utopian from and instrumental perspective, which makes them irrational evaluated against the standards of these two other rationality perspectives. If the evaluation turns out positive, mutual support between different rationalities is possible as well.

People can discover they share subjective impulses, emotions or interests. The Gurkha debate illustrates how personal feelings referred to in expressive rationality support and prioritize values used in social-rational arguments: many British feel for the Gurkha veterans and wish them equal rights. That way social rationality receives bottom-up support, and values are also established by using inductive logics (Smith 1982: 319–20). This bottom-up support creates an expressive reconfirmation of social-rational values and principles, which is little discussed in ethics or social philosophy, where deontological views frame the way we think about norms, principles and values (cf. Habermas 1988; Kant 1990; Weber 1972).

Social-rational principles can also be framed as irrational from an expressive-rational perspective, as when citizens of liberal Western societies do not like some radical Muslim principles, or feel angry about them. Irrationality is usually seen as acting on emotions, on first impressions, on preferring the short run over the long run or own interests over shared interests (Boyd and Richerson 2001; Elster 2009; Fessler 2001; Kahneman 2011). This chapter has illustrated, like the previous chapter, that the opposite form of irrationality is possible too, meaning that social norms or values do not feel right, that they frustrate us or make us angry, as with unequal rights for Gurkhas, Muslim women and homosexuals, or with banning the veil or banning Santa Claus from public spaces due to the abstract butt plug reference. Such interactions between expressive and social rationality challenge value relativism (MacIntyre 1988) by pointing at the inductive mechanisms that are able to ground, recalibrate or correct social norms, principles and values. Detailing these interactions also helps to disentangle the somewhat mixed conceptions of social and expressive rationality in Diesing (1976) or Engelen (2006).

Social-rational motivations can also be evaluated as irrational from an instrumental-rational perspective; that is, when they are seen as utopian, too difficult to realize or impractical. This perspective is as unusual in academic debates on rationality as evaluating social rationality from an expressive-rational perspective. In theory, we consider norms, values and principles as the guiding instances for an instrumental-rational argument, which resembles the classical deontological view that rules should guide our decisions and policies, as articulated by Habermas (1988), Tinbergen (1956) or Weber (1972), and which is critically discussed in Anderson (1983), Majone (1992) or Peacock (1992). Instrumental rationality is usually seen as sub-ordinated to goals, norms and values, as based in a social-rational argument. The cases demonstrate how the opposite can happen as well.

The integration debate offers the best examples of critical instrumental-rational evaluation. Multicultural policies were based on the value of tolerance, but this value proved to be counterproductive. Tolerant policies were ineffective in supporting integration, as they did not fight Muslim intolerance towards Western values. Tolerance was sympathetic as a value, but irrational from an instrumental perspective by not reaching the intended consequence of integration. However, opponents returned the criticism. They argued that no integration policy has ever really been effective: all the bigger achievements of immigrants – and there are many – are due to their own efforts. Deeper fundamentalist Muslim beliefs cannot be changed by restrictive policies. They will be ineffective and such policies have to be rebutted as irrational as well. New policies will not be better, and maybe even worse, as a means to realize immigrant acceptance of Western values. The many ambitions in the integration debate are, thus, criticized as lacking realism, as being over-idealistic and naïve. A similar attempt of critique based on standards of instrumental rationality is made in the Gurkha debate, but it ends up as being flawed itself. The evaluation is reframed as irrational against social rationality, and instrumental arguments like insufficient means and too high costs are forcefully rebutted.

Support of social rationality by instrumental-rational arguments would mean evaluating socially shared values and objectives as feasible and realistic, effective in their execution and not too costly, nor based on wishful or utopian thinking. Thus, instrumental evaluation as studied here appears quite intertwined with the values and principles that underpin social rationality. In addition, the study adds a multiple rationality perspective that shows how both expressive and instrumental rationality can influence and limit what is constructed as socially rational, or what becomes irrational evaluated against standards of social rationality. These findings challenge the traditional views of Weber (1972), Habermas (1988) or Tinbergen (1956) that goals and values are only the starting point for instrumental-rational arguments. Moreover, the findings add new rich descriptions to the discussions found in Anderson (1983), Majone (1992) or Peacock (1992) by showing how these logics work far more interactively, especially when adding the perspective of expressive rationality.

References

Abrahamson, E. (1996) Management fashion. *Academy of Management Review*, 21(1), 254–85.

Anderson, P. A. (1983) Decision making by objection and the Cuban missile crisis. *Administrative Science Quarterly*, 28(2), 201–22.

Bergset, L. (2015) The rationality and irrationality of financing green start-ups. *Administrative Sciences*, 5(4), 260–85.

Boltanski, L. and Thevenot, L. (2006) *On Justification: Economies of worth*. Princeton, NJ: Princeton University Press.

Bos, R. ten and Willmott, H. (2001) Towards a post-dualistic business ethics: Interweaving reason and emotion in working life. *Journal of Management Studies*, 38(6), 769–93.

Bouwmeester, O. (2013) Field dependency of argumentation rationality in decision-making debates. *Journal of Management Inquiry*, 22(4), 415–33.

Boyd, R. and Richerson, P. J. (2001) Norms and bounded rationality, in Gigerenzer, G. and Selten, R. (eds), *Bounded Rationality: The Adaptive Toolbox*. Cambridge, MA: MIT Press, pp. 281–96.

Churchman, C. W. (1962) On rational decision making. *Management Technology*, 2(2), 71–6.

Dahms, H. F. (1997) Theory in Weberian Marxism: Patterns of critical social theory in Lukács and Habermas. *Sociological Theory*, 15(3), 181–214.

Davidson, D. (2004) *Problems of Rationality*. Vol. 4. Oxford: Oxford University Press.

Diesing, P. (1976) *Reason in Society: Five Types of Decisions and Their Social Conditions*. Westport, CT: Greenwood Press.

Eisenhardt, K. M. and Zbaracki, M. J. (1992) Strategic decision making. *Strategic Management Journal*, 13(S2), 17–37.

Elbanna, S. (2006) Strategic decision-making: Process perspectives. *International Journal of Management Reviews*, 8(1), 1–20.

Elbanna, S. and Child, J. (2007) Influences on strategic decision effectiveness: Development and test of an integrative model. *Strategic Management Journal*, 28(4), 431–53.

Elster, J. (1989) Social norms and economic theory. *The Journal of Economic Perspectives*, 3(4), 99–117.

Elster, J. (2006) Fairness and norms. *Social Research: An International Quarterly*, 73(2), 365–76.

Elster, J. (2009) *Reason and Rationality*. Princeton, NJ: Princeton University Press.

Engelen, B. (2006) Solving the paradox: The expressive rationality of the decision to vote. *Rationality and Society*, 18(4), 419–41.

Esposito, E. (2011) Originality through imitation: The rationality of fashion. *Organization Studies*, 32(5), 603–13.

Fessler, D. M. T. (2001) Emotions and cost-benefit assessment, in Gigerenzer, G. and Selten, R. (eds), *Bounded Rationality: The Adaptive Toolbox*. Cambridge, MA: MIT Press, pp. 191–214.

Fisher, P. and Freshwater, D. (2014) Towards compassionate care through aesthetic rationality. *Scandinavian Journal of Caring Sciences*, 28(4), 767–74.

Freeman, R. E. (2010) *Strategic Management: A Stakeholder Approach*. Cambridge: Cambridge University Press.

Gaut, B. (2012) Creativity and rationality. *The Journal of Aesthetics and Art Criticism*, 70(3), 259–70.

Gigerenzer, G. (2010) Moral satisficing: Rethinking moral behavior as bounded rationality. *Topics in Cognitive Science*, 2(3), 528–54.

Gigerenzer, G. and Sturm, T. (2012) How (far) can rationality be naturalized? *Synthese*, 187(1), 243–68.

Gintis, H. (2016) Homo Ludens: Social rationality and political behavior. *Journal of Economic Behavior & Organization*, 126(PB), 95–109.

Green Jr, S. E. (2004) A rhetorical theory of diffusion. *The Academy of Management Review*, 29(4), 653–69.

Greenspan, P. (2004) Practical reasoning and emotion, in Mele, A. R. and Rawling, P. (eds), *The Oxford Handbook of Rationality*. New York: Oxford University Press, pp. 206–21.

Gross, M. A., Hogler, R. and Henle, C. A. (2013) Process, people, and conflict management in organizations: A viewpoint based on Weber's formal and substantive rationality. *International Journal of Conflict Management*, 24(1), 90–103.

Habermas, J. (1988) *Theorie des Kommunikativen Handelns, Band 1, 2*. Frankfurt: Suhrkamp.

Hargreaves Heap, S. (2001) Expressive rationality: Is self-worth just another kind of preference?, in Mäki, U. (ed), *The Economic World View: Studies in the Ontology of Economics*. Cambridge: Cambridge University Press, pp. 98–113.

Hegel, G. F. W. (1986) *Grundlinien der Philosophie des Rechts*. Frankfurt am Main: Suhrkamp.

Henderson, D. (2010) Explanation and rationality naturalized. *Philosophy of the Social Sciences*, 40(1), 30–58.

Kahneman, D. (2011) *Thinking, Fast and Slow.* New York: FSG.

Kalberg, S. (1980) Max Weber's types of rationality: Cornerstones for the analysis of rationalization processes in history. *American Journal of Sociology*, 85(5), 1145–79.

Kant, I. (1990) *Kritik der Praktischen Vernunft.* Hamburg: Felix Meiner.

Li, Y., Ashkanasy, N. M. and Ahlstrom, D. (2014) The rationality of emotions: A hybrid process model of decision-making under uncertainty. *Asia Pacific Journal of Management*, 31(1), 293–308.

MacIntyre, A. C. (1988) *Whose Justice? Which Rationality?* London: Duckworth.

Majone, G. (1992) *Evidence, Argument and Persuasion in the Policy Process.* New Haven, CT: Yale University Press.

Mathiowetz, D. (2007) The juridical subject of interest. *Political Theory*, 35(4), 468–93.

Peacock, A. (1992) The credibility of economic advice to government. *The Economic Journal*, 102(414), 1213–22.

Politie (2016) *Terugblik op 2015: Jaarverslag van het landelijk expertisecentrum eer gerelateerd geweld.* Den Haag: Politie.

Racko, G. (2011) On the normative consequences of economic rationality: A case study of a Swedish economics school in Latvia. *European Sociological Review*, 27(6), 772–89.

Satow, R. L. (1975) Value-rational authority and professional organizations: Weber's missing type. *Administrative Science Quarterly*, 20(4), 526–31.

Scherer, K. R. (2011) On the rationality of emotions: Or, when are emotions rational? *Social Science Information*, 50(3–4), 330–50.

Schiller, F. (1983) *Über die Ästhetische Erziehung des Menschen: In einer Reihe von Briefen.* Stuttgart: Reclam.

Sociaal en Cultureel Planbureau (2015) *Werelden van verschil: Over de sociaal-culturele afstand en positie van migrantengroepen in Nederland.* Den Haag: Sociaal en Cultureel Planbureau.

Sen, A. (1993) Internal consistency of choice. *Econometrica*, 61(3), 495–521.

Smith, A. (1982) *The Theory of Moral Sentiments.* Indianapolis, IN: Liberty Classics.

Taylor, B. J. (2016) Heuristics in professional judgement: A psycho-social rationality model. *British Journal of Social Work.* DOI: 10.1093/bjsw/bcw084.

Tinbergen, J. (1956) *Economic Policy: Principles and Design.* Amsterdam: Noord Hollandsche Uitgeversmaatschappij.

Toulmin, S. E. (1994) *The Uses of Argument.* Cambridge: Cambridge University Press.

Toulmin, S. E., Rieke, R. J. and Janik, A. (1984) *An Introduction to Reasoning.* New York: Macmillan.

Townley, B. (2002) The role of competing rationalities in institutional change. *Academy of Management Journal*, 45(1), 163–79.

Weber, M. (1972) *Wirtschaft und Gesellschaft: Grundriß der Verstehenden Soziologie.* 5th ed. Tubingen, Germany: JCB Mohr (Paul Siebeck).

Zhu, Y. (2015) The role of Qing (positive emotions) and Li 1 (rationality) in Chinese entrepreneurial decision making: A Confucian Ren-Yi wisdom perspective. *Journal of Business Ethics*, 126(4), 613–30.

5 When instrumental rationality appears as irrational

Introducing instrumental rationality

Being rational is commonly understood as having good reasons to act on (Davidson 2004: 169; Elbanna 2006: 3; Elbanna and Child 2007: 433; Elster 2009: 2; Engelen 2006: 427; Gigerenzer and Sturm 2012: 243–5; Green 2004: 655; Henderson 2010: 32). However, these good reasons always depend on context. Some good reasons can relate to our subjectivity by fulfilling our desires, passions, personal interests, intuitions or likings. Such reasons are expressive rational (Bouwmeester 2013; Engelen 2006; Greenspan 2004; Hargreaves Heap 2001) and help us to decide on decisions with great subjective relevance; that is, when we want to decide what to do for ourselves. That can be reading a book, watching a movie or having a cup of coffee. It can also be decisions with more long-term impact, such as asking someone out for dinner to begin a deeper relationship, or quitting your job and starting your own business. Personal motives are quite relevant here. Also, the cases from Chapter three illustrate how in debates on public decisions these subjective motives can dominate decision-making; for instance, when many stakeholders are personally affected by a decision.

Good reasons can also stem from socially shared values, goals, principles, norms or national and international laws. When our actions get support from socially shared values or principles, we can consider these acts rational from a social-rational perspective (Churchman 1962; Dahms 1997; Diesing 1976; Gintis 2016; Sen 1993). Social rationality suggests what is good for us to do, based on intersubjective agreement. We reach such agreement when deciding on laws, but we also share a lot of values based on our culture, or on our professional socialization. They support certain kinds of behaviour. For referencing and quotation, there are rules within the academic community. For journalistic writing, there are different rules, and for novelists as well. These community-based rules inform writing decisions of the different kinds of authors, and they help to legitimize their decisions in front of others. The cases in Chapter four illustrate many norms, principles and values that are referred to as good reasons to act on; for instance, when fighting the decision to give older Gurkha veterans only a limited extension of their pension rights – it is said to be unfair, it is treacherous and Britain has a debt of honour towards them that needs to be paid.

Still, there also is a well-known type of rationality that helps us to realize our personal or social goals by choosing a rational approach. Such an approach is rational by its focus on *how* to realize our goals, and is referred to as instrumental rationality (Elster 1989; Racko 2011; Stewart 1995; Tomer 2008; Weber 1972). Instrumental rationality is dominant in the understanding of economists and scholars in public or business administration when they refer to rationality. Rational choice analysts consider it a synonym for rationality in general (Cabantous *et al.* 2010; Elbanna 2006; Sandberg and Tsoukas 2011). They aim for intentional action, most efficient or effective goal realization, and the full representation of alternatives, their consequences, likelihoods and utilities. Economists also assume goals to be directed at utility, profit or welfare, and the effort goes in to selecting the right means to reach the predefined goals as efficiently or effectively as possible. Thus, instrumental rationality is effect- or goal-oriented and based on means–end argumentation (Habermas 1988: 127). What matters for instrumental rationality is a correct understanding of relevant causalities and their contingencies, as the selected means must serve as the cause to realize an intended effect most effectively or efficiently. Irrational would be not choosing the right means for realizing the effects you are aiming at (Gigerenzer and Sturm 2012: 262), thus creating unintended consequences (Argyris 1996; Majone 1992; Mason 1969; Tinbergen 1956). Inconsistencies thus appear between intended ends and used means, which can imply the irrationality of acting against your own best judgment (Davidson 2004).

Instrumental rationality is commonly understood among economists and rational choice theorists as aiming at optimization (Cabantous *et al.* 2010; Weirich 2004). Henderson (2010: 35) calls rational choice theory a principle-based 'apriorist approach', with a focus on consistency, implications and calculability. However, this view is widely criticized as too theoretical (Gigerenzer and Selten 2001a; Klamer 1987; Klein 2001; Stewart 1995; Tomer 2008). First attacks came from March and Simon (1958) who argued that human beings are bounded rational, and, thus, not able to optimize efficiency and effectiveness to the maximum. Elster (2009: 64) follows up on this with a critique on 'hyperrationality', saying the costs for optimization are often much higher than the possible benefits of being fully rational. It takes too much time to investigate all alternatives and calculate their utility or expected profits, compare them and choose the best one – overall, it is hardly better than a second-best approach and not worth the extra search efforts. Gigerenzer and Selten (2001b) argue likewise, based on the benefits of using heuristics when making decisions. Gigerenzer and Sturm discuss many situations where heuristics lead to better results than optimization ever could, given the uncertainties of the large and complex real world. The application of optimization procedures is irrational in such cases (Gigerenzer 2010: 534; Gigerenzer and Sturm 2012: 262). Sandberg and Tsoukas (2011) also criticize the dominant concept of rationality as being too theoretical. However, Cabantous *et al.* (2010) and Racko (2011) show that instrumental rationality including optimization does still have a strong presence in our organizations, and that its principles are enacted by decision analysts and teachers at universities, in spite of the well-known criticisms. Based on such studies, we know a lot about instrumental rationality and about the more realistic versions of bounded rationality, but much less about instrumental rationality in interaction with expressive- and social-rational argumentation, as practised when decision makers prepare complex strategic decisions.

When studying interactions between instrumental, social and expressive rationality, social rationality is understood more broadly than in Diesing (1976) or Weber (1972), as argued in the previous chapter. It can include legal, moral, value and political rationality, as long as values are socially shared (Churchman 1962; Dahms 1997; Gintis 2016; Sen 1993). Political rationality (Eisenhardt and Zbaracki 1992; Harrison 1993) aims, for instance, at getting sufficient stakeholder support, but shared values, principles, norms, rules or interests do not need to have universal validity as assumed by Weber (1972) and Habermas (1988). Their nature can be more local and time-bound, as illustrated in Chapter four. When relating instrumental rationality to expressive rationality the findings from Chapter three are taken as the point of departure, defining expressive rationality as based in our subjectivity, with motives that stem from our feelings, emotions, intuitions and other subjective impulses (Bouwmeester 2013; Engelen 2006; Greenspan 2004; Hargreaves Heap 2001; Li *et al.* 2014; Scherer 2011).

As context to explore instrumental rationality in interaction with social and expressive rationality, two public debates are selected based on theoretical sampling. Instrumental rationality is expected to have a dominant position in both debates. The first debate is on Heathrow's extension with a third runway. Extension is seen as means to better facilitate the travellers. The debate is reported in 309 articles published in national newspapers in the UK between 2003 and 2009 and it concludes with extension, as Heathrow operates on 99% of its capacity and cannot meet more traveller demands. The second debate is on 'flex work', or 'tele work' in the Netherlands, which is presented as a means to accommodate the wishes of employees to work when and where they want by using the possibilities of new cloud-based information technologies. In addition, it is a means for companies to save office space, and for society to reduce traffic and greenhouse gases. The debate is reported in 79 articles published in Dutch national newspapers and magazines between 2007 and 2014. The chapter continues with a cross-case analysis and discussion.

The concept of instrumental rationality is more discussed than expressive and social rationality, especially by scholars who have studied bounded forms of instrumental rationality (Elster 2009; Gigerenzer and Gaissmaier 2011; Gigerenzer and Selten 2001a; March and Simon 1958; Mason 1969). Given this mature knowledge, the main contribution of this chapter lies in deconstructing instrumental rationality as the central and archetypical form of rationality, which it is mostly not. Moreover, it is quite vulnerable to internal inconsistencies resulting in unintended effects, sometimes due to forms of tunnel vision (Kahneman 2011) or overlooking conditions necessary to make assumed causalities work (Argyris 1996). It requires debate instead of optimization and calculation procedures to reduce our boundedness, and to increase our instrumental rationality. This makes realizing higher degrees of instrumental rationality a result of social construction in the studied real-life settings.

Second, when ignoring the perspectives of social or expressive rationality, decisions motivated by instrumental reasons alone can be quite disappointing. These other rationality perspectives need to be included by seeking interaction with relevant stakeholders (Fischer and Forester 1993; Majone 1992; Rieke and Sillars 2001). In such debates, instrumental rationality can even be framed as irrational, in spite of high degrees of efficiency, effectiveness or feasibility, as illustrated in both the Heathrow and flex-work debate. Without considering the social- and expressive-rational perspectives, instrumental rationality makes us narrow-minded and partially blind. Approaching rationality as socially constructed helps to overcome these limitations.

Heathrow's extension: balancing social and economic objectives

History

The debate about Heathrow's third runway began with the 2003 government white paper '*The Future of Air Transport*', in which the building of a small third runway was proposed, given that targets on the reduction of noise and pollution and better public transport could be met. In January 2009, however, the then secretary of transport, Geoff Hoon, announced that government would support the plans for a big third and fully operational runway for Heathrow, saying: 'Doing nothing will damage our economy and will have no impact whatsoever on climate change' (*Guardian Unlimited*, January 16, 2009). He suggested growth would move to other airports. Over the course of six years, the Labour government that was then in power had almost made a complete volte-face by finally fully supporting the extension, stressing that the environment would not benefit from staying passive, thus repeating the argumentation of his predecessor:

> If Heathrow is allowed to become uncompetitive, the flights and routes it operates will simply move elsewhere [...]. All it will do is shift capacity over the Channel. It will make us feel pure, but with no benefit to the rest of the planet.
> (Transport Secretary Ruth Kelly quoted in
> *The Observer*, January 27, 2008)

This episode in the debate on Heathrow's growth ended with positive intentions to build the third runway, but many steps in the decision-making process were still pending in 2009, which made the future still uncertain. The debate illustrates how environmentalists and local opposition had impact as well, by criticizing many 'unintended consequences'.

Stakeholders and decision makers

Decision-making authority in the case is divided between the Department for Transport (DfT) and BAA Airports Ltd, which owns Heathrow. The abbreviation

BAA is a relic from the past and means British Airport Authority. The company was renamed Heathrow Airport Holdings in 2012, which is after the time period studied here that runs until 2009. BAA needed to get official permission from the Department for Transport (DfT) to expand Heathrow, but the investment decision was completely its own. The loudest advocates of expansion were the Labour government and the British aviation sector (BAA, British Airways, Virgin Airlines, etc.), who lobbied extensively for the permission to extend. Local opposition started with citizens living in a village near Heathrow that would not survive the third runway, and with critical environmentalists, later followed by opposition parties combined with civil interest groups against aviation in general, or against Heathrow in particular, and local government including the mayor of London.

Arguments used

The discussion in the Heathrow case concentrates mostly upon the positive economic and negative environmental effects of expansion. The arguments are summarized in Table 5.1. The last column presents the groundedness of grounds and rebuttals (their frequency of appearance in the newspapers). Arguments belonging to the 'con case' are in italics and those of the proponents in normal case. The rationality behind the 'pro case' is strongly instrumental rational (IR), indicated, for instance, by arguments referring to growth effects or measures to realize them. The 'con case' has more social-rational (SR) arguments that refer, for instance, to the law, emission regulations or procedures that need to be followed. There are no expressive-rational (ER) arguments in this case. If they could have been given, they are turned into social-rational ones, like arguing that noise levels are too high and illegal, instead of irritating, probably to give the argument greater force in this case. Overall, there are more arguments counted against extension (1543) than in favour of it (1075).

Arguments pro are mainly instrumental rational

The main arguments pro suggest Heathrow's expansion is vital for the economy, as indicated by the first main argument in Table 5.1. If not, as stated in the second main argument, minor incidents can have giant knock-on effects. Third, London's infrastructure needs to be upgraded, as illustrated by a quote from BA Chief Executive Officer (CEO) Walsh: 'we remain absolutely convinced that Heathrow is a critical piece of national infrastructure. At a time of difficult economic conditions we need to be building it' (*Guardian Unlimited*, November 7, 2008). However, the economic significance of airport expansion, which is the proponents' most given argument, is rather played down by opponents rebutting the economic growth argument: 'most airline users are outbound leisure travellers. Curbing such travel, through taxation or slot rationing, would benefit domestic tourism' (*The Guardian*, January 14, 2009). It is thus questioned if Heathrow's extension is really vital for the economy, as claimed by the proponents. Economic growth pops up somewhere else if Heathrow cannot extend.

Table 5.1 UK debate on Heathrow's third runway

Claim, grounds and rebuttals; con case in italics	IR	SR	(N)
Claim Heathrow airport should have a third runway			
Since Expansion of Heathrow is vital for the British economy	X		127
Since If no capacity is added Heathrow will lose much of its business to continental hubs or even airports farther away	X		87
Since The current state of Heathrow undermines London as a world-class city and hurts the UK plc	X		48
Since BAA's monopolistic way of doing business has caused under-capacity and a low level of service	X		24
But Heathrow should be made better, not bigger		X	16
Since The UK is hugely reliant on Heathrow as the country's only international hub airport	X		42
Since Heathrow expansion is good for the development of British regions, by improving air links	X		17
Since There is a strong economic case for Heathrow expansion	X		41
Since Construction of a new runway will create jobs; without expansion many jobs could be lost	X		38
Since The economic benefits of a new runway outweigh the environmental costs	X		19
Since If Heathrow is not expanded the government will face legal challenges from the aviation industry		X	9
Since Without adequate airport facilities, Britain will be less attractive to businesses	X		21
But Only a minority of travellers use Heathrow for business purposes	X		10
Since There is a strong consensus among business-minded people that a new runway should be built		X	61
But The BAA has massive debts and is losing money; it is unlikely it will be able to finance a project of this kind	X		11
But The economic significance of Heathrow expansion is marginal	X		59
Since Expansion would only serve transfer passengers, who are worth as much as a cup of coffee to the economy	X		13
But The high number of transfer passengers ensures many destinations from Heathrow	X		14
But As long as many claims are contested a definitive decision is undesirable		X	12

(Continued)

Table 5.1 (continued)

Claim, grounds and rebuttals; con case in italics		IR	SR	(N)
Since	Heathrow operates at 99% capacity, so even minor incidents have giant knock-on effects	X		91
Since	Passenger numbers are set to double before 2030; the best way to accommodate that is to expand Heathrow	X		52
Since	Demand already outstrips supply, leading to congestion, fewer choices and higher prices	X		41
But	*Due to noise and emission regulations, the runway cannot be used on full capacity for the first years of service*		X	17
But	*Passenger numbers are falling instead of rising at the moment*	X		16
Since	The whole London transport infrastructure should be updated; airport expansion is an integral part thereof		X	49
But	*Expansion with a new runway would cause much environmental damage and contribute heavily to climate change*	X		159
Since	*Expansion will detrimentally effect air quality in the area, which is already in breach of European standards*	X		77
Since	*Expanding Heathrow will cause mass congestion on the roads leading to the airport as well as on the tube*	X		36
Since	*The British government is committed to cutting 80% of greenhouse-gas emissions by 2050; an extra runway will not benefit reaching that target*	X		64
Since	*The quality of life in West London will suffer unacceptably if the new runway is built*		X	64
But	The new runway can be built and function within agreed-upon environmental targets		X	95
Since	Heathrow with a new runway will have to meet some very strict environmental criteria		X	92
Since	*Only low energy-emitting and quiet planes will be allowed to use the third runway*		X	21
Since	Airplanes will become progressively cleaner and quieter	X		38
But	*Aircrafts will for the foreseeable future be neither fuel-efficient nor quiet*	X		19
But	*The increase in flights will overwhelm any benefit from more fuel-efficient planes*	X		8

(Continued)

Table 5.1 (continued)

Claim, grounds and rebuttals; con case in italics	*IR*	*SR*	*(N)*
Since By insufficient airport capacity, airplanes have to wait to land or depart, burning enormous amounts of fuel	X		14
But Aviation should be curbed as it is the fastest growing source of greenhouse-gas emissions in the country		X	26
But To enable the airport's expansion, some very harsh emission controls will have to be enforced in other sectors		X	17
But *The consultation process for the new runway was flawed with the government in the hands of BAA from the start*		X	110
Since The government and BAA alike have been dishonest with the residents		X	104
But The government has been honest and impartial at all times		X	8
But *The local community is against a new runway, and is prepared to fight against the construction*		X	89
Since The runway will displace a whole village of 700 homes, some schools, a church, a graveyard and – most importantly – a community		X	79
Since A legal challenge against expansion is raised by organizations representing millions of residents between them		X	22
But *Noise levels will continue to grow: even today they are unacceptable and possibly illegal*	X	X	65
Since The new runway will be likely to provide up to 500 extra flights above London, causing congestion, (noise) pollution	X		46
But *There are decent alternatives for Heathrow expansion, like better management, expansion of other airports or a new airport*	X	X	80
Since High-speed rail is a viable and environmentally friendly alternative to short-haul flights	X	X	41
Since Efficient taxation would reduce congestion, improve the environment and boost domestic tourism	X		16

(Continued)

Table 5.1 (continued)

Claim, grounds and rebuttals; con case in italics		IR	SR	(N)
But	Building a new airport as an alternative is neither environmentally nor economically viable	X		26
But	*Environmental groups are against an extra runway*		X	79
But	*The coalition against a new runway is now extremely broad*		X	52
Since	*If the Conservatives win the next election, as seems increasingly likely, there will probably be no new runway*		X	48
Since	*The Labour party, including the cabinet, is split about the issue of expanding Heathrow*		X	34
	Since Approval of Heathrow expansion will cost Labour important votes in marginal constituencies		X	25
Since	*Across all parties, MPs and other politicians are against Heathrow expansion*		X	19
Since	*In a democracy, the government should follow the wishes of the majority of its people*		X	10
	Groundedness (total)	**1395**	1223	2618
	Pro (totals)	**740**	335	1075
	Con (totals)	655	**888**	*1543*

Source: adapted from Bouwmeester 2013: 420.

Note: IR: instrumental rationality; SR: social rationality.

Arguments con are more often social rational

Stakeholders against extension are mainly local and environmental interest groups. Environmentalists argue against Heathrow's extension due to the negative effects it causes, such as environmental damage, climate change and noise levels that are much too high. This argument is the first main rebuttal in Table 5.1 and is found most often in all of the newspaper articles. The argument is illustrated by a quote from the *Financial Times*: 'Our planet and the people who live on it are in danger. Climate change can be beaten but not by almost doubling the size of the airport' (*Financial Times*, February 26, 2008). This critical instrumental reasoning is also visible in a quote showing an argument from cause by pointing at the effects of extension: 'By giving this runway the go-ahead Gordon Brown is effectively holding a giant blow torch to the polar ice-caps and saying "Melt, Melt!"' (*The Guardian*, January 13, 2009). This clearly is an effect of a growth policy, but unintended. It makes this policy irrational on instrumental grounds, next to socially unacceptable. We do not want to live in danger. Next to that we want to keep our international agreements, and follow the right procedures as indicated by the second main rebuttal. Local opposition is visible in the third main rebuttal and its supporting grounds. An illustrative quote hints at the village that will be displaced by the third runway: 'Historic buildings aren't replaceable. Once they're gone, they're gone forever. This would destroy a huge amount of heritage. It's not justifiable' (*The Guardian*, May 26, 2003). However, the first main rebuttal stated by the con case is, in turn, also challenged. Proponents counter rebut that 'there is a sound environmental case for a third runway. If aircraft can land more promptly, hundreds of planes a day won't have to circle overhead for hours' (*The Times*, June 30, 2008). The consequence would be saving a lot of fuel, and a reduction of greenhouse gases compared to doing nothing. By diving into each other's arguments, opponents and proponents seem to prepare for a compromise.

Unfulfilled conditions and policies balancing interests

Opponents mention some unfulfilled conditions that undermine the rationality of the decision, like not staying within the limits of environmental agreements or a consultation process that was flawed. On the side of the proponents, the claim is put forward that promises were made about the extension which should also be kept. As these conditions need to be fulfilled, parties search a middle way of green growth. Over time, the debate arrives at the compromise to expand, while also sufficiently acknowledging environmental concerns.

Alternative policies are only discussed in the margins of the debate, suggesting better taxation, or high-speed rail, but they remain more theoretical exercises, not real alternatives for Heathrow's extension. Still, they work, as pressure towards the pro camp in considering a more green approach. By remaining competitive they make such green alternatives less appealing.

The (in)conveniences of flex work

History

In 1995, Erik Veldhoen *et al.* published a book with the provocative title: *The Demise of the Office* (in Dutch: *Kantoren Bestaan Niet Meer*). He envisioned a future where people work online on their own laptops when and wherever they want. The need to be physically in the office would decrease due to new technologies like wireless Internet and the possibility of working in the cloud. Workers could share documents while working at different places. As the office would not necessarily be a place to stay anymore, office space could be reduced and desks could be shared, resulting in substantial cost savings. The office would be the place to meet colleagues or clients, but not necessarily the place to do work. For work that requires concentration you could choose the most convenient time and place. Veldhoen was inspired by Ericsson in Sweden:

> Ericsson had found out that 70% of all desks where not in use. People were at home, sick, in a meeting, at a client. Use of desks could be organized more efficiently. Savings were invested in mobile technology that enabled people to work at distance.
>
> (*Elsevier*, August 16, 2014)

Pioneers in the Netherlands who experimented with a new office design were guided by Veldhoen and his consulting company. He started in the 1990s with redesigning a police office in Maastricht and he helped to develop the interior of the new headquarters of Interpolis, an insurance company in Tilburg. During the start of the twenty-first century, more big companies followed: consultancies and IT firms like IBM, Oracle, Microsoft, Deloitte, Accenture, banks like Rabo and SNS, insurance companies and telecom companies. More and more Dutch companies started to accept the possibilities of new technologies.

The trend also developed internationally, and some companies started to report critically as they experienced the downsides of the new ways of working. In 2013 Marissa Mayer from Yahoo forced her employees to work from their Yahoo offices again, and not from home anymore: 'quality and speed of work decrease if we work from home' (*Volkskrant*, March 16, 2013). This decision was reported in the Netherlands where it had an impact on the Dutch debate. Companies started to seek a better balance between office work and flex work. Disadvantages became more and more visible, and companies found out that the possible advantages required tailored policies to be realized. So, 'before its peak – 20% of the Dutch companies have flex-work arrangements now – growth is slowing down according to trendwatcher Richard Lamb' (*Volkskrant*, March 16, 2013).

Stakeholders and decision makers

Consultants are the stakeholder that started the debate on flex work, as they introduced the concept in the Netherlands. They have sold their ideas to companies, who are the main decision makers. They decided to implement these consultant ideas due to the advantages they could realize: cost savings due to the reduced need for office space, less waste of traffic time, higher productivity and more employee satisfaction. Employees are an important stakeholder. Many of them like the concept, as it allows them to combine work and care more easily, which helps to improve their work–life balance. Environmental organizations and the Dutch government are stakeholders that supported flex work from the start, due the reduction of carbon dioxide: fewer offices have to be heated and fewer workers have to travel to their work. Still, not all companies decided to embrace flex work. And despite initial enthusiasm, many workers in newly designed offices did not feel too happy with the new work arrangements. Labour associations criticized growing burnout and increase in long-term sick leave. Middle managers resisted, as they could not manage their employees well as there is too little face-to-face contact. Some companies, like Yahoo, started to reconsider and adjust their policies. But all in all, flex work was growing in the Netherlands over a period of 20 years, most visible in the professional service industries, as indicated in the debate.

Arguments used

The flex-work debate in the Netherlands concentrates on the benefits for different stakeholders and the negative side effects of flex work. The arguments are summarized in Table 5.2, with the last column presenting the groundedness of all grounds and rebuttals (their frequency of appearance in the newspapers). Arguments belonging to the 'con case' are in italics and those of the proponents of flex work in normal case. While the rationality behind the 'pro case' is strongly instrumental by referring to conditions that need to be fulfilled for realizing the positive effects, the 'con case' has mainly expressive-rational arguments to explain the misfit between employee character and flex work, or dislike of the anonymous work spots as downsides of flex work for the flex workers. Social-rational arguments refer to the idealistic principles behind the concept, like giving workers autonomy. It is rebutted by suggesting employers have far more pragmatic principles, which mostly support cost saving. Overall, there are more arguments counted in favour of flex work (465) than against it (269). However, we see this optimism mainly during the introduction of flex work, and in the early years. While experiences grow, the counterarguments start to gain more influence in the debate.

Arguments pro are mainly instrumental and expressive rational

Proponents of flex work present their ideas as a social philosophy, including social-rational assumptions that workers benefit from autonomy, can plan their work independently and are able to meet objectives and agreements as made with their management. Based on this philosophy, stated in the first main argument in Table 5.2, proponents present the different benefits that can be realized as their next main argument. These are detailed in sub-grounds. For instance, many employees (50%) feel happier in flex work, and they consider it an important condition for a job

Table 5.2 Dutch debate on flex-work arrangements

Claim, grounds and rebuttals; con case in italics	IR	SR	ER	(N)
Claim Flex-work arrangements are wrongly implemented and do not reach their potential				
Since Flex-work ideology wants to favour autonomous workers who choose their own time, place and way to meet work objectives		X		27
Since Flex offices better support different activities with IT to work when and where you want and without your own desk	X			22
But *Flex-work ideology reduces in practice to home office only, for saving office space*		*X*		5
Since In 2010, 30% of employees chose home office for 6 hours a week and 67% for at least 1 hour a week			X	14
Since Flex work got popular by commitments from Accenture, Deloitte, Microsoft, HP, Rabo, ING, KPN, Interpolis			X	13
Since It is popular in sectors like insurance, banks, consultancy, lawyer firms, IT, oil companies, journalism			X	10
But *It is not popular in shops, factories, call centres requiring control or creative industries requiring interaction*			*X*	5
Since Flex work is caused by the digital revolution, a need to consolidate offices and a need to combine care with work	X			14
But *As a consequence, the rights of overtime payment, part-time work and traditional offices are eroding*		*X*		4
But *Economic crisis and lack of egalitarian culture (as outside the Netherlands, Australia, Sweden) limit appeal of flex work*			*X*	5
Since Flex work has advantages for employees, companies, society and suppliers of flex-work infrastructure			X	26
Since 80% of employees want flex work, 50% feel more happy as a flex worker and for 50% it is an important job-search condition			X	33
Since It offers better work–life balance, more autonomy, freedom, possibilities to care for family, less traffic stress			X	37

(Continued)

Table 5.2 (continued)

Claim, grounds and rebuttals; con case in italics	IR	SR	ER	(N)
But The self-employed, as trendsetters of flex work, combine autonomy with an unacceptable social security level		X		7
Since More than 50% of companies have flex work to become a more attractive employer and increase performance	X			36
But Employer values mainly support cost saving (less office space, travelling, sick leave) and higher productivity		X		51
But Still unknown is if and how much savings or benefits can be realized per saldo	X			3
Since Society welcomes flex work due to CO2 reduction, fewer traffic (jams) and fewer traffic accidents		X		33
Since Suppliers of flex-work solutions benefit by having more business			X	5
But Flex work has also disadvantages for employees, companies and society				
Since 60–70% employees dislike hot-desking and prefer office work over home office			X	6
Since Flex work invites overworking, more burnout and disturbed work–life balance, and it does not fit everyone well			X	12
Since Labour conditions get worse both at home and at work due to distraction, lacking quiet work spots, privacy			X	42
Since Employees dislike anonymous offices, lack of personal contact/feedback from manager or colleagues			X	11
Since Employees suffer under digital overload and changes of proven routines			X	22
Since Families of flex workers do not like it, have to keep quiet, get less attention at home			X	6
Since Many companies like Yahoo, Microsoft, PWC, ING, Rabo, KPN, Philips became less optimistic since 2013			X	5
Since Some consequences are unintended like more burnout, higher rates of longer sick leave, lower productivity, quality	X			14
Since Unacceptable consequences are less knowledge sharing, innovation, company identity and office use	X			10

(Continued)

Table 5.2 (continued)

Claim, grounds and rebuttals; con case in italics	IR	SR	ER	(N)
Since *Managers resist due to falling control: their people work too hard or not enough and get too little attention*			X	8
Since *Society faces more permanent stress as labour regulations do not prevent the downsides of flex work yet*		X		3
Since *Real estate loses value, which creates an unacceptable risk, like the one that caused the bank crisis*		X		3
But Compared to traditional work, new conditions need to be fulfilled to implement flex work effectively	X			2
Since Flex work cannot be implemented as one-size-fits-all solution. It requires a tailored approach and voluntariness	X			20
Since Implementation takes time and needs coaching as people cannot change so many habits overnight	X			16
Since New culture needs to be institutionalized with min/max availability rules, management by objectives and trust	X			28
Since Flex concept requires sufficient employee commitment based on agreement and an eye for employee interest	X			9
Since Flex concept requires good home-office facilities, IT infrastructure and hardware implying substantial investments	X			22
Since Workers need to be autonomous, good time managers and have a clear understanding of the benefits for them	X			11
Since Managers need to be inspirational, setting feasible objectives; caring, without control reflex and not resisting	X			22
Since The type of work should allow for time and place independence	X			6
But *Not all conditions are or can be fulfilled: some cannot change into ideal flex workers/ managers, and implementation is often a one-size-fits-all obligation, while necessary facilities are lacking, as focus is only on saving*	X			15

(Continued)

Table 5.2 (continued)

Claim, grounds and rebuttals; con case in italics	IR	SR	ER	(N)
But New business policies and personal strategies are vital to fulfil necessary conditions and to manage negative side effects	X			5
Since New personal strategies are needed to improve own time management and management of home-office conditions	X			13
Since New business policies are needed to realize several conditions	X			4
Since Workload employees can be managed by server shutdown during evenings, limiting home-office days, close monitoring, joint definition targets and encouraging employees to relax when possible	X			9
Since Bonding can be fostered by organizing meetings and better seducing people to come to the office	X			11
Since Flex work can be supported by investing in better facilities (office design, IT, phones, digitalized archive)	X			9
Since New rules needed like flex work for all (including management), clean desk, own day planning employees	X			8
But *Flex work is hyped, does not develop and Yahoo's policy is even to stop with the flex-work possibility*			X	7
But *First, institutions need to improve and modernize with help of new government policies and the influence of labour unions*		X		4
Since *Government has to improve social security and labour laws for flex workers and the self-employed*		X		12
Since *Unions should modernize new collective labour agreements to improve flex-work conditions*		X		4
Groundedness (totals)	**309**	153	272	734
Pro (totals)	**267**	60	138	465
Con (totals)	*42*	*93*	*134*	*269*

Note: IR: instrumental rationality; SR: social rationality; ER: expressive rationality.

search. Some 80% like the possibility of working from home – it helps them to improve their work–life balance, it means less traffic stress and they can better manage care tasks. These are the important expressive-rational arguments. For employers, this opportunity is not only a means to become a more attractive employer, but also to improve company performance by increasing productivity while lowering costs, which is instrumental-rational thinking. Society benefits from less greenhouse gases, less traffic and, thus, fewer traffic accidents. Consultants and IT firms benefit as the supplier of flex-work solutions. When discussing the benefits, the pro argumentation is quite expressive rational. Pro arguments also focus on conditions that need to be fulfilled for realizing the positive effects. There the argumentation also turns instrumental rational.

Arguments con are mainly expressive rational

However, opponents among employees and employers see important downsides (see the first main rebuttal presented in Table 5.2). Many employees dislike the anonymity of hot-desking and the home office, as a consequence of most flex-work designs. Some long to return to their own personalized work spot, like Sandrine Willemars, a consultant at Accenture: 'Sometimes I would like to have my own desk back, with pictures of my own children [. . .] and no obligation to clean it up every evening' (*Financieel Dagblad*, June 28, 2010). Or, as the Dutch poet Nico Dijkshoorn writes: 'An office only works well if it has your own smell' (*De Pers*, October 18, 2010). Flex work also increases potentials for overworking and burnout, and offers worse labour conditions both at the office that is less quiet and at home where facilities are worse. It implies less contact with colleagues and managers, digital overload and families that suffer when employees work from home: 'Compared to normal office workers flex workers more often admit that friends and family get less attention due to their work, finds Karolus Kraan from TNO' (*NRC Handelsblad*, December 28, 2010). These are all expressive-rational counter-arguments on behalf of the employees. Employers see increasing costs due to more long-term sick leave, more burnout, lower productivity and lower quality of the work provided. Another issue is that knowledge sharing becomes more difficult with anyone working from home. It hinders innovation and building a company identity. Managers say they cannot manage the workload of their people anymore so they resist, but still cannot prevent the burnouts. CEO of Microsoft NL, Theo Rinsema, admits: 'In the past we could see our employees during the whole day, but today we have difficulties to see if someone does not feel well' (*NRC Handelsblad*, December 29, 2010). For society at large, there are drawbacks as well. Labour regulations do not protect flex workers well enough, so increased burnout and high stress levels are the result, which is unacceptable referring to social rationality. These arguments are also used to rebut more specific advantages of flex work, due to the focus on cost saving. Germany even prepares new legislation, as it sees downsides for the economy: 'some estimates suggest the German economy loses 6 billion euro per year due to permanent stress' (*De Groene Amsterdammer*, March 6, 2013).

Crucial conditions

As the ultimate proponents, flex-work consultants respond to the critics by pointing at important conditions that need to be fulfilled in order to make flex-work arrangements effective. They argue it cannot be a one-size-fits-all solution. It should be voluntary, and tailored to companies and workers. Implementation also takes time and needs coaching. Company routines and leadership culture need to change, implying more trust and management by objectives. In addition, to make the flex concept work, people should still be committed to coming in to the office, and the anonymous hot-desk must be compensated by a good coffee bar and sufficiently well-designed work spots that accommodate different kinds of activities, such as meetings, concentration work, relaxation, video conferencing, etc. At the same time, IT facilities for working from home or elsewhere should be made perfect by substantial investments. Further conditions are that managers need to be inspirational; when they manage by objectives, these need to be feasible.

Opponents like middle managers and employees are mostly not convinced that these conditions are sufficiently fulfilled in their firms, which creates negativity. So, fewer people come to the office, as it is not attractive to be there due to lack of privacy or workspaces, as in the case of Ingeborg:

> I am big. In the past I could hide my legs behind my desk [. . .] today everyone sees me as I always work in an open space. At least, if there is a work spot available [. . .] Sometimes I have to return and go home.
>
> (*Volkskrant*, March 13, 2013)

IT investments also lack backing, causing trouble during the work. And, aside from that, a quote from TNO research illustrates why productivity also decreases, as not all employees have the right attitude for flex work:

> I was lately at my neighbors place for a coffee told Tahlia (42, career coach), where my neighbor was moving her mouse every five minutes to show her colleagues she was online. When I reacted somewhat surprised she said: 'but everyone is doing that'.
>
> (*Volkskrant*, March 16, 2013)

Policies lagging behind

Flex-work supporters remain optimistic, as companies can develop better policies to fulfil the relevant conditions and manage the unwelcome side effects. Flex work should not aim at saving money, but at new and better ways of working. And if workers have sufficient autonomy and managers manage inspirationally, even then the work is not done. The need for better time management becomes paramount as well. Employees play a crucial role in preventing their own burnout and they are also important in managing their own home-office conditions. Still, employers can also develop policies to prevent burnout by defining realistic targets in agreement with their employees and by defining a maximum for the home-office days. Bonding can be fostered by organizing social events and by investing in an attractive office with sufficient workspace and concentration rooms. Microsoft discovered, for instance, that 'it was a mistake to plan concentration rooms next to meeting rooms [. . .] or to remove message boards in the different units' (*NRC Handelsblad*, January 4, 2011). Paperless work can be facilitated by digitalizing archives and by making the IT facilities as convenient as working with paper. Flex work also requires new rules that apply to both management and employees. At the insurance company UVIT, they have as a rule: 'empty desk and if you are not working at your desk for more than one hour you take your laptop with you' (*NRC Handelsblad*, September 1, 2010).

However, for some workers these trial and error policies are not enough to manage the downsides of flex work. In addition, labour laws and social security lag behind the new flex-work developments and cannot protect employees sufficiently. Labour unions should focus more on the improvement of collective labour agreements regarding flex-work conditions, by negotiating better home-office facilities, as suggested by De Unie:

> I claim a home office allowance, to design the home office in a way that meets our regulations on labor conditions. It needs a good chair and desk, but also a compensation for coffee that the employee drinks at home instead of at the office. The savings due to reduction of office space should be reinvested in employees.
>
> (*De Telegraaf*, October 2, 2010)

That this does not happen also makes the Dutch flex-work pioneers pessimistic: 'Veldhoen claims that flex work "fails in 75% of all cases". Van Laarhoven even adds that Veldhoen is rather soft in this judgment' (*Elsevier*, August 14, 2014). Great challenges still await flex-work consultants.

Cross-case analysis

Instrumental rationality and its debated inconsistencies

In the two debated topics – airport extension and introducing flex-work arrangements in organizations – instrumental rationality dominates both in number of arguments presented in the articles (groundedness) and in the importance of instrumental-rational arguments that support the decision. More than half of the arguments stated in the debates are based on arguments that connect causes to effects and means to ends. The assumed fit between the economic context with a focus on cause-based questions about how to realize intended effects efficiently or effectively is apparent in both cases. Instrumental rationality as defined by Weber (1972) or Diesing (1976) is neutral in terms of preferences for values or objectives as they are given. It only looks for the best means to realize them. Instrumental or economic rationality can also point at inconsistencies between means and ends, between different means to reach one end or between higher- and lower-order ends (Bouwmeester 2010; Majone 1992; Tinbergen 1956).

Instrumental rationality in the Heathrow debate is visible in arguments by proponents that stress the positive economic effects caused by expansion. The main effects discussed are, for instance, how business increases due to a bigger airport, including more jobs on and around the airport and due to a better service level, more destinations and higher frequencies that can be offered. These positive arguments are all based on airport extension as their cause. Opponents respond based on the same rationality by questioning the size of the suggested positive effects, and by pointing at other, unintended effects caused by extension like lower air quality, climate change and increased noise levels. Opponents also suggest that negative effect sizes are bigger than the positive ones to strengthen their argument. Thus, the debate is not about existence, but about the kind of effects and their right estimation.

In the debate on flex work, instrumental arguments used by proponents focus on how flex work has the effect of making employers more attractive for young employees and for employees with young children, due to its effects on work–life balance. Flex work also causes better performance in terms of productivity. Other instrumental arguments are visible in outlining the conditions that need to be fulfilled to make flex work more successful, and policies to realize its full potential. Opponents mention that some companies have changed policies drastically and have stopped flex work due the unintended effects. They also criticize that some firms reduce flex work to the home office only, interested in saving office space and, thus, undermining most of the possible positive effects. The effects in the two debates are summarized in Table 5.3, together with the main stakeholder groups.

Instrumental rationality has in its logic an aspect of universality (Habermas 1988), as it assumes that the underlying causalities to make a means–end claim are universal. The means to reach ends should always be independent of time and place. However, we know such causalities can be overruled by unfulfilled conditions (Argyris 1996). When different causes are in conflict with each other, they can level each other out, making the instrumental reasoning weaker or even inconsistent. Both debates illustrate such inconsistencies.

Heathrow's extension will cause more emissions, but at the same time less congestion and waiting time for airplanes circling around in the air, thus implying less emissions. These are contradictory effects. Proponents in the Heathrow debate focus on positive economic effects, while opponents question their size as overoptimistic, and add negative effects in reply. Such perspectives contradict each other. Opponents rebut the suggestion of positive effects by claiming there are mainly negative effects. The contradiction gets partly resolved over time by the view that the negative effects can be managed and limited, in order to realize a more positive overall effect.

A contradiction in the flex-work debate is the positive short-term effect of lower sick leave next to the long-term effect of higher sick leave, but there are more contradictions. In the flex-work debate, consultants stress the positive effects of flex work to convince employers of the attractiveness of the concept. Over time, opponents more and more rebut the suggested positive effects. They see less innovation and knowledge sharing, people coming in less to the office, a disturbed work–life balance, higher stress levels and more burnout. They thus doubt the positive overall

Table 5.3 Stakeholders and discussed causalities backing instrumental rationality

Extension of Heathrow	Introduction of flex work
Main stakeholders: aviation industry (pro), leisure travellers, business travellers, environmental groups (con), inhabitants of sentenced village (con), residents, national government, local government and mayor of London (con)	**Main stakeholders:** flex-work consultants (pro), (top) management flex-work companies, employees in flex-work companies, their families, environmental organizations (pro), government (most stakeholders internally divided)
Means–end focus proponents: growth of Heathrow is a means to create economic effects (more employment, economic growth) and fewer negative environmental effects due to greater air traffic efficiency	**Means–end focus proponents:** flex work is a means to attract employees, to increase productivity, to improve work–life balance, to save costs (office space), to reduce traffic and greenhouse gases
Means–end focus opponents: growth of Heathrow causes environmental effects (air pollution, noise), negative social effects (cultural heritage), which are not consequences to aim at and that seem bigger than the positive effects	**Means–end focus opponents:** many conditions to realize intended effects are not fulfilled. There is more burnout, long-term sick leave and lower productivity. There is less innovation and knowledge sharing. Unknown if the benefits outweigh the costs per saldo

effect. Their arguments contradict those of the proponents by showing many ends are not realized. Flex-work consultants do not give up though. They argue that problems stem from implementation, not from the concept. They argue that the necessary conditions are not fulfilled. For instance, flex work as an instrument to realize benefits for employees, employers and society cannot be a means for savings only. This new way of working needs investments. Flex work needs a supporting culture, another management style, new rules and some coaching for employees and managers. Even more importantly, the type of work and the degree of autonomy of employees should allow for place and time independence. Flex work is not a one-size-fits-all solution. It cannot be applied in every sector or firm, and it needs to be tailored in order to avoid means–end inconsistencies. Still, for many employers who implement the model, cost saving seems to be the primary focus, which is at odds with managing the necessary conditions. Thus, employers are responsible for creating the means–end inconsistencies and the painful unintended consequences.

Instrumental rationality is cause-based, but still complex enough to end up in many conflicting beliefs about causes for effects, effect sizes or kinds of effects that are realized. When they are unintended, they might have been overlooked due to wishful thinking or bounded rationality. However, this boundedness seems to be strategic when proponents overlooked Heathrow's negative effects. In the case of a new concept like flex work, learning is necessary and bounded rationality is more than likely. That savings on short-term sick leave have turned into an increase in long-term sick leave must have surprised many. However, employers who only seek to save on costs misuse the concept. Over time, the degree of instrumental rationality improves due to the debates. Means–ends consistency gets stronger, and there are fewer unintended consequences that surprise, due to a better management of the necessary conditions to realize the intended effects. Heathrow's growth perspectives get greener and flex-work designs get more tailored. If they still fail we get a better understanding of why.

Instrumental rationality framed as irrational on social and expressive grounds

Instrumental rationality has a neutral focus as long as it argues based on effects realized in terms of size or kind, or when means are discussed in terms of their effectiveness or efficiency. The discussion is objective in the sense that we can measure the effect sizes attributed to causes and that we can reach agreement on them. If effects were overlooked, we can later include them in our considerations and act on them, inspired by critical opposition and debate. Such debate improves instrumental rationality of the decision. Next to that there is also critical interaction between instrumental- and social-rational arguments or between instrumental- and expressive-rational arguments. In the Heathrow debate, effects and means are considered irrational against standards of social rationality. The flex-work debate shows this irrationality as well, but also irrationality of means and effects against standards of expressive rationality. How means and effects are valued from a social or personal perspective is different between social communities in the studied debates, and here opponents and proponents get into the most heated debates, about more than the effect sizes or means effectiveness.

In the case of Heathrow's extension, the environmental effects are socially contested by opponents due to a quality of life decrease in London, a substantial increase in the biggest source of greenhouse-gas emissions in London and because the interests of the local community are harmed (one entire village will disappear). Overall, a large national coalition of environmental, local and political interest groups, seemingly a majority, evaluate this extension as irrational. Arguments based on an instrumental logic aimed at economic growth are good for no one if it means the planet will be damaged. Still, there are also some positive social-rational evaluations of these means for economic growth put forward by the aviation industry. If expansion will be denied, they predict legal claims, as many promises for extension have been made already. They argue it is possible to stay within emission levels agreed upon earlier, so extension will be legitimate and, thus, social rational. As in the earlier debates, we see controversy within social rationality itself, due to different values; here, the economic 'good' of more growth and welfare versus the environmental and social 'good'. It makes extension partly rational and partly irrational on social-rational grounds, and further policy development is thus required. Too many expected effects are now immoral (displacement of village), illegitimate (environmental damage) or unacceptable (increasing noise levels).

There are also consequences of flex work that interfere with established rights from a social-rational perspective, like the disappearing payment of overtime or unacceptable labour conditions as evidenced by the increasing level of burnout and permanent stress. Realizing them is now only grounded in instrumental-rational arguments, which feels irrational and not sufficient as good reasons to act on. And there are even more expressive-rational counterarguments in the flex-work debate, adding to the irrationality of flex work evaluated against standards of expressive rationality.

Expressive-rational grounds for embracing flex work are that the concept fits your personality, that you like working when and where it suits you, while managing your own work autonomously. There are such employees who like flex work, feel happier as flex workers and even make it a criterion for a job search. It helps them to improve their work–life balance and it reduces their traffic stress. Such proponents value the consequences of flex work as positive from their personal perspective. For them it is an expressive-rational decision to participate in flex work. However, for workers who like their own desk in their own office better than hot-desking, or working in a café, there is a mismatch. Such employees dislike flex work and can experience a work–life balance disturbance due to more overwork and lack of self-management skills. Some even lose their homes as a place for relaxation, as work more and more enters their private space, which makes flex work even more irrational for them. Engaging in flex work is for them the opposite of acting on good reasons. For them, flex work makes no sense at all. These employees experience burnout more often, they have more difficulties in concentrating in a flex office, dislike its anonymity and miss contact with their manager and direct colleagues. In addition, families of home-office workers suffer, as they have to adapt their behaviours. Middle managers complain, as they cannot do their jobs well. These examples indicate the irrationality of flex work for these groups when evaluated against their standards of expressive rationality. The flex-work effects receive labels like upsetting and frustrating. As a consequence, expressive rationality mainly stresses that flex work is no one-size-fits-all solution, and, also, that the initial one-size-fits-all sales approach is very irrational seen from an expressive perspective.

The debates illustrate how social and expressive rationality can evaluate instrumental rationality. The means–effect relations are cause-based and have their own logic which can be valid in itself, but the means and effects also have value for society, groups or individuals, as they are more or less acceptable or attractive to them. In the Heathrow case, instrumental-rational arguments thus provide a basis for social evaluation, causing a negative judgment and inviting adjustment to improve the overall rationality of the decision. In the case of flex work, some effects are attractive for some people, while others are not. Flex work fits some people better than others, some organizations better than others. Expressive evaluations are more local here, and less general compared to social evaluations.

Discussion: instrumental rationality and the social construction of its irrationality

Instrumental rationality in degrees: mitigating internal irrationalities by debate

Instrumental rationality is usually seen as a synonym for rationality as such. Especially procedures of maximizing and optimizing utility, welfare or profit are popular goals among economists, and seen as ultimately rational. However, the studied debates do not illustrate any form of such hyperrationality as taught by economists (Racko 2011) or as implemented by decision analysts (Cabantous *et al.* 2010). It is often a too theoretical ambition, earlier criticized by Elster (2009), Gigerenzer and Selten (2001a), Gigerenzer and Sturm (2012), Klamer (1987), Klein (2001) and Tomer (2008), among many others, and probably only visible in rather exceptional contexts. What the debates show are forms of bounded rationality, as suggested by March and Simon (1958). Bounded rationality is explored in experimental settings (Kahneman 2011), but rarely in complex real-life settings (Gigerenzer and Selten 2001b). The Heathrow and flex-work debates show for complex questions how bounded forms of instrumental rationality support decision makers with decision preparation and legitimization. Discursive processes are critical here for detailing how intended effects can be better realized (Habermas 1988; Majone 1992; Mason 1969), far more than optimization calculus.

Instrumental rationality provides the reasons to explain to others why decision makers chose this way or this alternative to realize their decisions. It gives opponents the arguments to critically assess means–end inconsistencies or unintended consequences, due to bad decision execution. All stakeholders can point critically at unfulfilled conditions, or at alternative policies to better realize the purpose of a decision, as illustrated in the flex-work debate. The debates both demonstrate a fit between instrumental rationality and questions that aim at realizing effects in the outside world as earlier suggested in Bouwmeester (2013), resembling what Gigerenzer and Selten (2001b: 9) and Gigerenzer and Sturm (2012) call ecological rationality: choosing a rationality that best fits to its context. However, this ecology also implicates a far more limited field of application for instrumental rationality than assumed by economists. It provides only one type of good reason to act on (Diesing 1976), best suitable for well-defined small-world problems where information is available, not too overwhelming and relatively certain (Gigerenzer and Gaissmaier 2011; March and Simon 1958; Mason 1969). If not, its application easily results in irrationality (Gigerenzer and Sturm 2012: 262).

When there is a rationality fit, our boundedness offers a second explanation for why decisions can be less rational, seen from an instrumental perspective. The discussed examples of instrumental inconsistencies in the two cases were, for instance, realizing lower labour productivity by flex work instead of the intended higher labour productivity. Unintended side effects in the Heathrow debate were the pollution effects, and in the flex-work debate, higher burnout and stress. Unfulfilled conditions were most prominent in the flex-work debate. Critical stakeholders or consultants can challenge such inconsistencies. The cases illustrate how a higher degree of instrumental rationality develops over time, as a consequence of combining different opinions. Deliberation due to debate can, thus, somewhat reduce our boundedness (Bouwmeester and van Werven 2011; Mason 1969; Saxton 1995). The debates present bounded rationality as a relative concept, which shows instrumental rationality in degrees.

Stakeholders can, for instance, be bounded by what they want to see. The aviation industry in the Heathrow case has a focus on its own interests. That makes it difficult to see the interests of other powerful stakeholders, which resonates with the WYSIATI (What You See Is All There Is) principle in Kahneman (2011: 85). Opponents can push the debate towards the ignored side, by stressing all kinds of instrumental inconsistencies like unintended effects (opposite and overlooked effects) and unfulfilled conditions. The debate brings ignored points of view to the forefront, and pushes the aviation industry to emulate environmental interests in their own reasoning, to create a better outcome for all parties. If they did not, resistance might explode, which then, in turn, would hurt aviation interests. Similarly, employers that embrace flex work start to pay more attention to long-term effects over time, due to their own learning and critiques by key stakeholders. That reduces inconsistencies and thus increases instrumental rationality. A too-narrow focus on their interests also hurts employers in the end. Thus, debate helps to better perform on the three rationality criteria mentioned by Elster (2009: 13): impartiality regarding time, persons and better-founded beliefs.

Overlooking conditions to enable causalities is something that also happens a lot in practice, and undermines instrumental-rational arguments in particular. Means–end relations assume what Argyris (1996) calls 'design causality'. When you observe causality, and interpret it after the fact, you would assume it also works as a design principle. But conditions between the context of discovery and the context of application are never exactly the same, so causalities often do not hold due to unfulfilled and often unknown conditions (Argyris 1996). The flex-work debate gives a perfect illustration of Argyris' critique that management knowledge is not often actionable. For increasing the degree of instrumental rationality, managing these conditions deserves the highest priority, especially in a context of change as illustrated by flex-work implementation. Again, debate is the primary force here that leads to higher degrees of instrumental rationality.

If we can assume that there is an ecological fit, and instrumental rationality fits the debated question to decide on, we can postulate that realizing higher degrees of instrumental rationality is a process of social construction. Debate, first, helps address instrumental-rational inconsistencies, unintended effects and ignored conditions. Second, it helps with finding a way out by exchanging arguments and ideas. The debates on Heathrow's extension and on implementing flex work both show the developments towards a consensus about the effects of the decisions. The initial disagreements are on what effects need to be considered (like short-term or long-term sick leave) and how big they are, which get settled more and more due to learning. Both debates also help to discover important ignored but unfulfilled conditions, by reflecting on experiences. Discussing different degrees of instrumental irrationality, including ways to socially construct and reduce them internally, is the first contribution of this chapter. It is a process independent of a public- or private-sector setting. We see the process in both settings independently where flex work is implemented, while Heathrow offers a mixed setting to demonstrate this process.

Instrumental (ir)rationality against standards of social and expressive rationality

Next to the internal instrumental inconsistencies visible in the cases, the two instrumental-rational debates show rationality alignment and controversy finding their origin in evaluating instrumental rationality based on standards of other rationalities (Bouwmeester 2013; Gaut 2012). These evaluations can support instrumental logics based on expressive arguments when used means or realized ends are attractive based on subjective grounds, or based on social-rational arguments by contributing to the greater good. The opposite can happen as well, when the used means and realized ends are evaluated as upsetting and frustrating, or immoral and illegitimate. In such cases, the used means and ends can appear rational from an instrumental perspective but irrational seen from the two other perspectives.

The Heathrow debate refers to promises made to reduce greenhouse gases in an international context. It is considered socially irrational to break these promises, despite the economic attractiveness of a growth strategy. A similar social-rational critique originates from the consequence for the inhabitants of the village that will lose their homes and houses. It is considered as immoral to let this happen. These evaluations can be seen as value rational within the spectrum of social rationality, given the general moral principles applied (Bergset 2015; Weber 1972), implying that the instrumental way of thinking is itself too limited. An end to better serve the travel interest of passengers is fine, as long as there is no conflict with other basic values and objectives relevant to stakeholders. A similar evaluation is visible in the flex-work debate. Flexible work arrangements undermine the enforcement of labour laws regarding time regulations, thus increasing the risks for employee health. This is socially irrational. Saving office space, reducing greenhouse gases and reducing traffic is fine, but not at the costs of labour, law enforcement, more illness and burnout.

In recent discussions on instrumental rationality, there is some awareness that instrumental rationality needs to be complemented by social rationality, or, as some argue, altruistic motives (Bergset 2015; Diesing 1976; Weber 1972; Weirich 2004). How these two rationalities should interact remains unclear. Weber assumes instrumental rationality is neutral in supporting accepted ends, but more recent work criticizes this assumption (Anderson 1983; Majone 1992; Peacock 1992) because means have an implied value themselves. If means really were neutral, they could not work as irrational on social-rational grounds. However, it is by their negative impact – damaging the planet or undermining employee health – that the means in an instrumental argument are considered irrational. Against standards of social rationality, they are evaluated as unacceptable, illegitimate or immoral.

Next to social evaluation, instrumental rationality can be evaluated against standards of expressive rationality. In the flex-work debate, the main opposition is expressive rational, whereas this rationality is not expressed in the Heathrow debate. The claim stating general applicability of flex work is deemed irrational against the standards of expressive rationality, because the pre-requirements for flex work do not apply to most workers; workers lack the necessary autonomy and planning skills and they need a manager that takes care. The concept does not fit these workers well. Only a small part of the labour force, specific sectors and some functions within organizations can really benefit from flex-work arrangements. Flex work is, thus, severely criticized for being implemented as a one-size-fits-all solution. Too many people do not like it or cannot handle it. That makes the flex-work concept irrational for them from a subjective, expressive-rational perspective. They cannot work this way or do not like it, thus missing out on good reasons to act on, when forced into this choice. However, others really like flex work, and for them there are expressive-rational reasons to choose an employer that facilitates it. For them, this choice is in harmony with the instrumental-rational choice of their employer.

Until now, the role of expressive rationality in decision-making is under-explored in most work on rationality. Still, there are calls to pay more attention to emotions and subjectivity in relation to rationality (Engelen 2006; Gaut 2012; Gigerenzer and Selten 2001b; Li *et al.* 2014; Scherer 2011). As illustrated, emotions not only disturb rational decision-making as sources of irrationality (Elster 2009; Kahneman 2011). Expressive rationality is also able to evaluate instrumental rationality based on its own standards of rationality; that is, when evaluating applied means critically for generating upsetting, frustrating or unpleasant effects (Calabretta *et al.* 2016; Fisher and Freshwater 2014). Likewise, social rationality can evaluate used means and generated effects as illegitimate, unacceptable or immoral (Bergset 2015; Colic-Peisker 2016). Discussing this influence of social and expressive rationality on instrumental rationality in two debates focused on instrumental questions is the second contribution of this chapter. It is an insight that, so far, is only sparsely acknowledged, as instrumental rationality is assumed to be neutral, quite robust and uncontroversial in most scholarly debates.

We can conclude that two types of irrationality attributed to instrumental arguments stem from conflicts with social and expressive rationality. As these irrationalities are uncovered and emphasized by means of public debate, they get socially constructed – a process also stressed by Majone (1992), Fischer and Forester (1993) or Rieke and Sillars (2001). Expressive rationality can, thus, construct instrumental rationality as irrational if there is a mismatch with the subjectivity of certain individuals or many of them. Social rationality does the same on a more general level, by referring to the violation of social norms, principles, values or laws accepted within a community. However, these community values can differ, just like personal taste can differ. What is expressive rational for one, can be irrational for somebody else. And what is acceptable in one community can be challenged in another. Still, these local rationalities do help to differentiate between good and bad reasons for acting in these contexts.

References

Anderson, P. A. (1983) Decision making by objection and the Cuban missile crisis. *Administrative Science Quarterly*, 28(2), 201–22.

Argyris, C. (1996) Actionable knowledge: Design causality in the service of consequential theory. *The Journal of Applied Behavioral Science*, 32(4), 390–406.

Bergset, L. (2015) The rationality and irrationality of financing green start-ups. *Administrative Sciences*, 5(4), 260–85.

Bouwmeester, O. (2010) *Economic Advice and Rhetoric: Why Do Consultants Perform Better Than Academic Advisers?* Cheltenham: Edward Elgar.

Bouwmeester, O. (2013) Field dependency of argumentation rationality in decision-making debates. *Journal of Management Inquiry*, 22(4), 415–33.

Bouwmeester, O. and Werven, R. van (2011) Consultants as legitimizers: Exploring their rhetoric. *Journal of Organizational Change Management*, 24(4), 427–41.

Cabantous, L., Gond, J. P. and Johnson-Cramer, M. (2010) Decision theory as practice: Crafting rationality in organizations. *Organization Studies*, 31(11), 1531–66.

Calabretta, G., Gemser, G. and Wijnberg, N. M. (2016) The interplay between intuition and rationality in strategic decision making: A paradox perspective. *Organization Studies*. DOI: 10.1177/0170840616655483.

Churchman, C. W. (1962) On rational decision making. *Management Technology*, 2(2), 71–6.

Colic-Peisker, V. (2016) Ideology and utopia: Historic crisis of economic rationality and the role of public sociology. *Journal of Sociology*. DOI: 10.1177/1440783316630114.

Dahms, H. F. (1997) Theory in Weberian Marxism: Patterns of critical social theory in Lukács and Habermas. *Sociological Theory*, 15(3), 181–214.

Davidson, D. (2004) *Problems of Rationality*. Vol. 4. Oxford: Oxford University Press.

Diesing, P. (1976) *Reason in Society: Five Types of Decisions and Their Social Conditions*. Westport, CT: Greenwood Press.

Eisenhardt, K. M. and Zbaracki, M. J. (1992) Strategic decision making. *Strategic Management Journal*, 13(S2), 17–37.

Elbanna, S. (2006) Strategic decision-making: Process perspectives. *International Journal of Management Reviews*, 8(1), 1–20.

Elbanna, S. and Child, J. (2007) Influences on strategic decision effectiveness: Development and test of an integrative model. *Strategic Management Journal*, 28(4), 431–53.

Elster, J. (1989) Social norms and economic theory. *The Journal of Economic Perspectives*, 3(4), 99–117.

Elster, J. (2009) *Reason and Rationality*. Princeton, NJ: Princeton University Press.

Engelen, B. (2006) Solving the paradox: The expressive rationality of the decision to vote. *Rationality and Society*, 18(4), 419–41.

Fischer, F. and Forester, J. (eds) (1993) *The Argumentative Turn in Policy Analysis and Planning*. Durham, NC: Duke University Press.

Fisher, P. and Freshwater, D. (2014) Towards compassionate care through aesthetic rationality. *Scandinavian Journal of Caring Sciences*, 28(4), 767–74.

Gaut, B. (2012) Creativity and rationality. *The Journal of Aesthetics and Art Criticism*, 70(3), 259–70.

Gigerenzer, G. (2010) Moral satisficing: Rethinking moral behavior as bounded rationality. *Topics in Cognitive Science*, 2(3), 528–54.

Gigerenzer, G. and Selten, R. (eds) (2001a) *Bounded Rationality: The Adaptive Toolbox*. Cambridge, MA: MIT Press.

Gigerenzer, G. and Selten, R. (2001b) Rethinking rationality, in Gigerenzer, G. and Selten, R. (eds), *Bounded Rationality: The Adaptive Toolbox*. Cambridge, MA: MIT Press, pp. 1–12.

Gigerenzer, G. and Gaissmaier, W. (2011) Heuristic decision making. *Annual Review of Psychology*, 62, 451–82.

Gigerenzer, G. and Sturm, T. (2012) How (far) can rationality be naturalized? *Synthese*, 187(1), 243–68.

Gintis, H. (2016) Homo Ludens: Social rationality and political behavior. *Journal of Economic Behavior & Organization*, 126(PB), 95–109.

Green Jr, S. E. (2004) A rhetorical theory of diffusion. *The Academy of Management Review*, 29(4), 653–69.

Greenspan, P. (2004) Practical reasoning and emotion, in Mele, A. R. and Rawling, P. (eds), *The Oxford Handbook of Rationality*. New York: Oxford University Press, pp. 206–21.

Habermas, J. (1988) *Theorie des Kommunikativen Handelns, Band 1, 2*. Frankfurt: Suhrkamp.

Hargreaves Heap, S. (2001) Expressive rationality: Is self-worth just another kind of preference?, in Mäki, U. (ed), *The Economic World View: Studies in the Ontology of Economics*. Cambridge: Cambridge University Press, pp. 98–113.

Harrison, E. F. (1993) Interdisciplinary models of decision making. *Management Decision*, 31(8), 27–33.

Henderson, D. (2010) Explanation and rationality naturalized. *Philosophy of the Social Sciences*, 40(1), 30–58.

Kahneman, D. (2011) *Thinking, Fast and Slow*. New York: FSG.

Klamer, A. (1987) As if economists and their subjects were rational, in Nelson, J. S., Megill, A. and McCloskey, D. (eds), *The Rhetoric of the Human Sciences*. Madison, WI: The University of Wisconsin Press, pp. 163–83.

Klein, G. (2001) The fiction of optimization, in Gigerenzer, G. and Selten, R. (eds), *Bounded Rationality: The Adaptive Toolbox*. Cambridge, MA: MIT Press, pp. 103–14.

Li, Y., Ashkanasy, N. M. and Ahlstrom, D. (2014) The rationality of emotions: A hybrid process model of decision-making under uncertainty. *Asia Pacific Journal of Management*, 31(1), 293–308.

Majone, G. (1992) *Evidence, Argument and Persuasion in the Policy Process*. New Haven, CT: Yale University Press.

March, J. G. and Simon, H. A. (1958) *Organizations*. New York: John Wiley.

Mason, R. O. (1969) A dialectical approach to strategic planning. *Management Science*, 15(8), B403–14.

Peacock, A. (1992) The credibility of economic advice to government. *The Economic Journal*, 102(414), 1213–22.

Racko, G. (2011) On the normative consequences of economic rationality: A case study of a Swedish economics school in Latvia. *European Sociological Review*, 27(6), 772–89.

Rieke, R. D. and Sillars, M. O. (2001) *Argumentation and Critical Decision Making*. New York: Longman.

Sandberg, J. and Tsoukas, H. (2011) Grasping the logic of practice: Theorizing through practical rationality. *Academy of Management Review*, 36(2), 338–60.

Saxton, T. (1995) The impact of third parties on strategic decision making: Roles, timing and organizational outcomes. *Journal of Organizational Change Management*, 8(3), 47–62.

Scherer, K. R. (2011) On the rationality of emotions: Or, when are emotions rational? *Social Science Information*, 50(3–4), 330–50.

Sen, A. (1993) Internal consistency of choice. *Econometrica*, 61(3), 495–521.

Stewart, H. (1995) A critique of instrumental reason in economics. *Economics and Philosophy*, 11(01), 57–83.

Tinbergen, J. (1956) *Economic Policy: Principles and Design*. Amsterdam: Noord Hollandsche Uitgeversmaatschappij.

Tomer, J. (2008) Beyond the rationality of economic man, toward the true rationality of human man. *Journal of Socio-Economics*, 37(5), 1703–12.

Veldhoen, E., Piepers, B., Musch, F., Groenendijk, P. and Wheeler, R. (1995) *Kantoren Bestaan Niet Meer: De Digitale Werkplek in een Vitale Organisatie [The Demise of the Office: The Digital Workplace in a Thriving Organisation]*. Rotterdam: 010 Publishers.

Weber, M. (1972) *Wirtschaft und Gesellschaft: Grundriss der Verstehenden Soziologie*. 5th ed. Tubingen, Germany: JCB Mohr (Paul Siebeck).

Weirich, P. (2004) Economic rationality, in Mele, A. R. and Rawling, P. (eds), *The Oxford Handbook of Rationality*. Oxford: Oxford University Press, pp. 380–98.

6 Rationality interplays

From mutual support to critical evaluation

Introducing a full cross-case analysis of rationality in public debates

Earlier studies on rationality have shown differentiations between instrumental and economic rationality, between social, political and legal rationality (Diesing 1976), and also how expressive and aesthetic rationality are different from value rationality and instrumental rationality (Engelen 2006; Fisher and Freshwater 2014; Habermas 1988). Others have stressed that rationality is perceived differently within social communities, social traditions and time periods (Esposito 2011; MacIntyre 1988). The differences between these rationalities are explained by disciplinary rules of reasoning and social or historical contexts (Corvellec 2007; Diesing 1976; MacIntyre 1988; Toulmin 1994). All these different rationalities appear somewhat fragmented, but also overlapping at times. Instrumental and economic rationality have much in common, and so have value, legal, political and social rationality, or expressive and aesthetic rationality. What these sets have in common is that the first relies on cause-based reasoning, the second on intersubjective logics and the last one on subjective grounds to motivate decisions. Such commonalities hardly get attention, as most studies implicitly or explicitly focus on specific rationalities and not on the inter-actions and relations between them.

When studies mention the relations between rationalities, this relationship is commonly assumed to be fixed: value rationality defines the goals, instrumental rationality the best means, which makes instrumental rationality always sub-ordinated (Bouwmeester 2010; Majone 1992; Weber 1972). When discussing the role of emotions in decision-making, they are assumed to have the lowest position in terms of hierarchy; as 'hot' sources of irrationality (Elster 2009: 40), emotions are said to disturb rational decision-making (Kahneman 2011), or moderate it at best (Kim 2016; Mellers et al. 2001). Still, in our daily lives we can laugh about how irrational mainstream economists are in assuming that we always want to optimize our choices, or that feelings can only disturb rational decision-making; for instance, when deciding what piece of art we want to buy, or when deciding on how to celebrate our marriage. Assumptions of economists seem to be misleadingly narrow when we attempt to make rational decisions in practice.

The study of six public debates performed in the previous chapters has illustrated how decisions that relate to different kinds of contexts demonstrate different forms of rationality that dominate in preparing and legitimating decisions. Decisions that affect our personal lives are mainly grounded in expressive rationality, decisions with great social relevance demonstrate a focus on social rationality, and for decisions that intend to realize effects we mainly use instrumental rationality to explain our decisions. The theoretical sampling of the six debates along these lines has illustrated how context, being subjective, intersubjective or more objective, matters for what we consider as rational. The cases also illustrate how the different rationalities can mutually interact, both in critical and supportive ways, and in all possible directions.

This chapter seeks to explore which critical and supportive interactions appear within and between rationalities, and how these interactions are grounded in different types of argumentation. To do so, the typology in Brockriede and Ehninger (1960) helps to differentiate between arguments. By building on the three double case studies, this chapter can show all patterns of interaction, based on the possible relations between the three rationalities, as well as the internal rationality interactions. To answer these questions, the chapter first shows which rationality evaluations are apparent in the six cases. Then it discusses in three mains sections per type of rationality, first, the critical interactions within a type of rationality and then cross-rationality evaluations from the perspective of this type of rationality. The last main section before the discussion gives an overview of the types of argumentation that support these rationality interplays. The chapter concludes with the theoretical contributions of the whole study, followed by limitations.

The first contribution of this chapter lies in better mapping all possible inter-relations and interactions between different rationalities, as called for by Townley (2002). Expressive, social and instrumental rationality are three autonomous but interrelated extremes in a more complex rationality concept. This threefold rationality concept can better guide decision makers and their stakeholders in practical decision-making than each single rationality. The threefold concept also explains why we consider decisions as irrational in many more ways (Gaut 2012) than only as deviations from instrumental rationality (Kahneman 2011) or from logical and consistent reasoning (Davidson 2004; Henderson 2010). Second, this understanding of rationality offers an explanation for the variety of rationality types between the two poles of expressive and social rationality, like aesthetic, political or legal rationality. They all have a different position between full sub-jectivity and full intersubjectivity. This insight adds more perspective to the discussions on multiple rationalities (Bouwmeester 2013; Diesing 1976; Eisen-hardt and Zbaracki 1992; Harrison 1993; van Houwelingen and Bouwmeester 2008; MacIntyre 1988; Schipper 1996; Weber 1972). Third, the study as a whole relates rationality back to having good reasons to act on. It details the construction of good reasons as rational or irrational against different standards of rationality. The means to do so can be analogical, inductive, deductive, causal or motivational arguments. These findings extend earlier work on argumentation and decision-making by Bouwmeester (2013), Fischer and Forester (1993), Majone (1992), Mason (1969), Rieke and Sillars (2001) and von Werder (1999).

Internal and cross-rationality tensions

Six controversial debates in which good reasons for strategic decisions are publicly discussed offer rich empirical material for analysing what arguments are considered more and which are considered less rational in support of a decision. Differentiating between expressive, social and instrumental rationality helps to illustrate the nature of internal contradictions within each type of rationality. However, it also helps to map the tension between the rationality perspectives, labelled as irrationalities that stem from cross-rationality evaluations. Table 6.1 summarizes the origin of the main tensions and irrationalities that are socially constructed in the six studied debates. The column with primary cross-rationality tensions depicts the most prominent critical rationality evaluation in each case.

Table 6.1 Socially constructed irrationalities in the six cases

Debated decision	*Internal tensions*	*Primary cross-rationality tensions*	*Secondary cross-rationality tensions*
Santa Claus publicly exposed	Expressive rational: Opposite likings and taste	Expressive image evaluated as *socially* irrational (is obscene)	Expressive image evaluated as *instrumentally* irrational (is too costly)
Banning/ wearing the veil	Expressive rational: Opposite likings and religious expression	Expressive image evaluated as *socially* irrational (under-mines integration and gender equality)	Expressive image evaluated as *instrumentally* irrational (hinders communication)
Strict integration policies	Social rational: Communities with opposite values	Social norms evaluated as *instrumentally* irrational (stricter norms are not the right means)	Social norms evaluated as *expressively* irrational (Muslims feel excluded, stereotyped)
Rights extension for Gurkhas	Social rational: Communities with opposite values	Social norms evaluated as *instrumentally* irrational (rights extension too costly)	Only confirmation by *expressive*-rational arguments
Heathrow's extension	Instrumental rational: Means–end inconsistencies	Realized effects evaluated as *socially* irrational (pressure on environmental agreements)	No third rationality perspective
Implementing flex work	Instrumental rational: Means–end inconsistencies	Effects evaluated as *expressively* irrational (many workers do not like flex work)	Effects evaluated as *socially* irrational (flex-work concept undermines labour laws)

In some cases, there is secondary critique from a third rationality perspective, as summarized in the last column. In one case, this third perspective only supports the dominant rationality perspective (Gurkha case). In one case, the third perspective is missing (Heathrow case). Table 6.1 shows left internal tensions and irrationalities within one type of rationality; for instance, means that do not help to reach the intended effect, which is internal criticism based on the criteria of instrumental rationality.

The next sections compare in more detail the social construction of internal irrationalities and crossover irrationalities, based on cross-case analysis. When arguments intending to be rational are considered irrational based on grounds that

Table 6.2 Different interplays between and within rationalities

Influences by: *Evaluations of:*	*Expressive rationality (Motivational arguments and generalization)*	*Social rationality (Applying arguments from classification)*	*Instrumental rationality (Applying means–end arguments)*
Expressive rationality	• Sharing of likings • Challenge opposite likings • Tolerance opposite likings • Dominance over opposite likings *Also: arguments from analogy*	• Supporting likings • Challenging likings • (Re)framing likings • Prioritization and subordination of likings • Temporization and mitigating expression	• Effectiveness check means for expressive desires • Efficiency/cost check means for expressive desires • Feasibility check of realization expressive ends
Social rationality	• Supporting values • Challenging values • Realizing value shift • Realizing shift in prioritization and subordination of values	• Sharing of values • Challenge opposite values • Tolerance opposite values • Prioritization and subordination of values • Value reconciliation *Also: arguments from analogy*	• Effectiveness check means for value realization • Efficiency/cost check means for value realization • Feasibility check of value realization
Instrumental rationality	• Expressive prioritization and selection of *ends* • Expressive evaluation of *means* and (unintended) *consequences* with support or challenge • Redirecting policies	• Social prioritization and selection of *ends* • Social evaluation of *means* and (unintended) *consequences* with support, challenge or framing • Redirecting policies	• Check unintended consequences • Check consistency between ends and means • Or between higher- and lower-level ends *Also: arguments from sign and analogies*

belong to another rationality, it assumes some hierarchy between the rationalities. An example is acting on emotions and not using your head. That is often seen as irrational against social norms, or against instrumental-rational considerations (Davidson 2004: 192; Elster 2009: 42; Kahneman 2011). Such relations are socially constructed in the debates, indicating subordination or tolerance, etc. All possible relations in response to the constructed tensions and irrationalities for the different combinations of rationality evaluation are summarized in Table 6.2. The diagonally ordered fields presented in grey (starting in the upper-left field, moving through the middle of the table and ending in the lower-right field) summarize the interactions within one rationality perspective. The other fields summarize the interactions of cross-rationality evaluation.

The next three sections focus first on expressive rationality, then on social rationality and finally on instrumental rationality as leading in the evaluations. Each section starts with the internal tensions within that rationality perspective, before moving to the two cross-rationality evaluations.

Rationality evaluations by expressive rationality

Degrees of internal expressive-rational controversy: from sharing to challenging emotions

In five out of the six debates, expressive-rational arguments have a prominent role: the veil-ban and Santa Claus debates are both mainly grounded in expressive rationality, but also the Gurkha debate, the integration debate and the flex-work debate show strong signs of expressive rationality. Cross-case analysis indicates what can be considered as rational from an expressive point of view. Expressive rational is what fits to someone emotionally, but not necessarily to someone else. Expressive inconsistencies are that taste can be different, sympathies can be different and interests can be conflicting. Still, they can be grounds that explain what someone does, or what another does not. Balanced authentic judgments can be considered more rational than letting only one emotion rule, as when being too angry (Davidson 2004: 170; Elster 2009: 40; Engelen 2006; Habermas 1988; Scherer 2011). Likewise, it can be irrational when moods such as feeling down determine motivations, as they are disconnected from the event that can be more properly assessed by immediate or anticipated emotions (Li *et al.* 2014; Scherer 2011).

In the Gurkha and the Santa Claus debates, expressive rationality is developing towards consensus. Consensus in the Gurkha debate becomes the most outspoken. Expressive-rational arguments express sympathy towards Gurkha veterans for what they have done for Britain. People feel bad if Gurkha veterans do not get a full extension of their rights. People share these feelings. In the Santa Claus debate, the development of consensus takes more time but in the end people want him close, which means not in a museum court anymore. Both debates reach an expressive-rational consensus based on a shared basis of sympathy – in the Gurkha debate, from the start, which created strong expressive-rational grounds for challenging the policies and values of the British Ministry of Defence, which, in fact, fundamentally shared these sympathies. The Santa Claus debate illustrates a process of learning and the development of taste. However, reaching consensus after disagreement on the sculpture took many years, and there were strong debates until shared sympathy eventually dominated.

The opposite to sharing emotions is challenging them. Resistance and antipathy towards the sculpture challenges the feelings of those who like Santa Claus. The British veil-ban debate, which is also mainly grounded in expressive rationality, refers to feeling uneasy and offended on the side of the people identifying with Western culture, whereas the Muslim population feels under siege. Both groups have completely different feelings towards the debated question and challenge each other. They do not reach consensus on the level of expressive rationality. However, the British tolerate the Muslim preferences in the end and accept the veil as a legitimate religious expression. In the Dutch integration debate, the Western anger about lack of integration and intolerant Muslim behaviours is also challenged by Muslims who complain about the lack of nuance due to stereotyping and by feeling excluded. In the flex-work debate, some workers appreciate flex work and for them it is a reason to choose an employer that offers such facilities. Other workers do not like it, complain or even get sick. This debate concludes with tolerance for such differences between employees, and against the one-size-fits-all approach. In the three debates that do not reach consensus, expressive rationality is not able to find one solution for all, as different stakeholders feel differently due to their backgrounds and interests. These patterns of interaction are summarized in the left-hand upper field of Table 6.2.

The first outcome of internal expressive-rationality assessment is mutual support. People discover by comparison and analogical reasoning that they share likings. All supporters of Santa Claus, of the niqab or of the Gurkhas do. Their likings are referred to in motivational arguments suggesting to act in support of what they like. The second form of internal interplay aims at challenging such likings, meaning that people are pushed to like or dislike something they did not before. Santa Claus illustrates this interplay between those who like and those who dislike him, based on a 'do like what I like' argument illustrating analogical reasoning. Tolerance of different expressive-rational positions grounded in subjectivity is a third form of interacting. People acknowledge by comparison and analogical reasoning that people feel differently about Santa Claus or a niqab. However, to wear a face veil is seen as a personal choice. Tolerance suggests it is sufficient that the person wearing the veil wants it. You do not need to like it and you may want different things. Dominance is the last observed form of interaction; for instance, regarding Santa Claus. Over time, dislike eases out and people learn to appreciate it. The dominant conclusion develops based on generalization and inductive reasoning. The Dutch integration debate illustrates how more liberal Muslims or homosexuals have hard times to free themselves from the dominance of more fundamental Muslim communities with preferences that dominate over those of the gay Muslims. However, history also shows that concluding for the whole group of homosexuals based on inductive reasoning establishes a dominant preference within their group, and over time it also creates more tolerance for their preferences outside their group because this inductive statement gathers strength by the increase in numbers.

When building an expressive-rational argument from analogy, outcomes like sharing of likings or a challenge are grounded in an argument suggesting that what feels good for me is good for you, whereas this same analogy is negated in an argument for tolerance; what is good for you is not the same as what is good for me. Creating dominant preferences requires a stronger and more broadly shared inductive argument. The most critical interactions challenge expressive irrationalities like self-deception and lack or authenticity (Davidson 2004; Habermas 1988), as visible in the veil-ban debate, where some Western critics cannot believe that wearing a niqab is something you can even like, as people seem imprisoned.

Social- and instrumental-rational opinions supported and challenged by expressive rationality

In three cases, there are crossover evaluations based on expressive rationality judging the other main perspectives. The two expressive cases are excluded, as they are discussed above based on the internal tensions. In the Heathrow case, the expressive-rational perspective is missing. Table 6.3 summarizes for the three remaining cases how the pro arguments with the dominant rationality in the debate (first row) are supported (second row) or challenged (third row) by expressive-rational arguments (see the left-hand side of the table for the social-rational cases and the right-hand side for the instrumental ones). Interactions based on the pro case give the best illustrations of the possible relations and influences between the rationalities.

Social-rational views evaluated by expressive rationality

In both cases presented in the left-hand columns of Table 6.3, expressive rationality is supporting social-rational principles, a relation discussed in Haidt (2001) and, earlier, by Adam Smith (1982); but there is also critical evaluation – a possibility that is addressed in Gaut (2012) and Fisher and Freshwater (2014). In the integration debate, we see expressive-rational criticisms towards the values behind stricter policies expressed by those more in favour of multiculturalist values (see the bottom row of Table 6.3). Expressive rationality is the secondary critical perspective in the integration debate.

Anger and fear related to fundamentalist Muslim practices and criminality support the development of new Dutch integration policies, which are more restrictive and demanding. These emotions of anger support the value shift towards being more demanding and help to set new priorities. Deeply felt sympathy for Gurkhas in the UK supports the principle to grant Gurkhas a full rights extension. Positive emotions support the claim that equal rights for all Commonwealth veterans are the most legitimate option. The observable value shift is towards treating Gurkhas as equals. Emotions of collective anger related to the earlier partial rights extension initiate this shift. These shared emotional judgements expressed by many people form a basis

Table 6.3 Rationality evaluations by expressive rationality

Integration of Dutch immigrants	Gurkha rights extension	Extension of Heathrow	Implementation of flex work
Social-rational opinions **Stricter integration policies (pro case):** Old multicultural policies demand too little. All immigrants need to internalize Western key values. Muslim intolerance to other sexual inclinations, rights women, other beliefs and atheism, is unacceptable. Zero tolerance for criminal behaviours. New immigrants need to be sufficiently educated.	**Social-rational opinions** **Full rights extension (pro case):** Equal rights for Gurkha veterans compared to non-British Commonwealth soldiers are fair and just. Loyalty and bravery needs to be rewarded. Government should not act treacherously and dishonestly towards Gurkhas. Gurkhas have many supporters in society. Britain has a debt of honour, whatever the costs.	**Instrumental opinions** **Extension (pro case):** Growth of Heathrow is a means to create economic effects (economic growth, more employment, better infrastructure) with less environmental effects (noise, emissions) due to more air-traffic efficiency.	**Instrumental opinions** **Flex work (pro case):** Flex work is a means to increase productivity, to save costs (office space), to reduce traffic and greenhouse gases, to attract employees and to improve their work–life balance.
Expressive-rational support: Fear, anger and feelings of detachment among the Dutch due to intolerable behaviours of Muslim immigrants.	**Expressive-rational support:** British public deeply cares for the Gurkhas. Gurkhas feel loyal to the British, but also committed to fight for their own rights.		**Expressive-rational support:** Flex work is popular in professional service firms. Employees like it for gaining more autonomy, freedom, reduction of traffic stress and better work–life balance.

(Continued)

Table 6.3 (continued)

Integration of Dutch immigrants	Gurkha rights extension	Extension of Heathrow	Implementation of flex work
Expressive-rational objections: Immigrants feel excluded, experience lack of nuance.			**Expressive-rational objections:** Many employees dislike hot-desking, anonymity, stress, noise, distraction. Families dislike the lack of attention by home-office workers, who experience a disturbed work–life balance. More companies dislike flex work as they discover it does not fit every sector, company or culture.

to ground and prioritize social-rational principles; in this case, of being more generous towards the older Gurkha veterans, and subordinating economic prudence principles.

However, there is not only expressive-rational support for the pro case in the integration debate. Quite disturbing is that Muslims feel excluded by the new Dutch policies – this does not help integration. Their unpleasant experiences with over-generalization and stereotyping are discussed as well. The social values behind integration cannot be valued entirely positive on expressive grounds, if it means Muslims feel excluded. Thus, the challenge is that the ones causing the real problems are not addressed by the stricter rules of the new more demanding policies, as radical Muslims are not affected. It is mainly the good ones who suffer, which is a large majority. Their new negative feelings obstruct the integration process, which is irrational from an expressive point of view. These four forms of interaction, based on expressive rationality evaluating social-rational reasoning, are summarized in the left-hand middle field in Table 6.2. The four forms are: support, challenges, value shifts and shifts in prioritizing or subordination of values.

What kind of expressive-rational argumentation supports social-rational values as the first type of interaction is most clearly illustrated in the Gurkha debate. Shared sympathy among the British for Gurkhas' military performance in the past supports their rights extension. Similar shared sympathy is visible in the Santa Claus debate. The supporting motivational arguments of these individuals work inductively when combined in arguments from generalization. They generalize from the moral feelings of individuals to more general social principles. Challenging social values is a second way in which expressive rationality works on social rationality inductively. The veil-ban debate gives several examples. When Western people express they feel sorry for Muslim women 'caged' in their niqab, they challenge this Muslim practice and its underlying rules. They cannot feel for themselves how Muslim women could really appreciate this. The intended consequence is a value shift, as a third form of interaction. The integration debate offers the best example, but so too does the Santa Claus debate, with its downplaying of the obscenity argument. Finally, in the integration debate, worries about lack of integration and the many unsolved problems give people the feeling that something needs to change. The principle of tolerance has to give in, whereas Western values of gender equality and freedom of expression need to be prioritized. These four interactions based on the force of expressive-rationality evaluations are all grounded in inductive reasoning. The basis of the argument is in individual motivational assessments. It is the number of individuals with shared feelings and desires that gets more and more substantial, that influences moral values and social rights over time, illustrated by the impact of substantial minorities like Muslims, Gurkhas and their supporters or the Santa Claus supporters. What happens is that moral sentiments create, support and influence moral principles bottom-up (Smith 1982).

Instrumental-rational claims evaluated by expressive rationality

The right hand columns in Table 6.3 indicate that the Heathrow debate lacks expressive-rational argumentation. It does not get a personal, expressive twist.

Maybe expressive arguments are considered less convincing than critical social-rational evaluations, which do abound. However, expressive rationality appears as the primary critical perspective in the flex-work debate for evaluating instrumental-rational views in the pro case. As the new ways of working affect the personal lives of many workers, they are more than willing to express their positive and negative experiences. Similar irrationalities of instrumental logics evaluated against standards of expressive rationality have been argued before related to a healthcare context (Fisher and Freshwater 2014). The relevance of affective evaluations regarding cause–effect logics are also reported in a qualitative study about intuition and rationality in strategic decisions about design innovations (Calabretta *et al.* 2016: 19).

The flex-work debate shows many accounts of people liking flex-work arrangements due to autonomy, less traffic stress and because it is a means to improve work–life balance. These positive experiences help to support flex work and frame it as an attractive way of working, to prioritize and select it as a new and good option. However, contradictory experiences illustrate why other people dislike flex work due to its effects: the anonymity of offices, the noise and the distraction at the workplace. Families of flex workers object as well because they have to keep quiet to accommodate the home-office worker. Home-office workers run into serious problems when they are not able to stop working due to emails and phone calls that continue to come in during weekends and evenings. These workers report that their work–life balance becomes negative. People become unwilling to work at flex-work companies and their numbers are substantial. They challenge the concept, based on their feelings. Companies like Yahoo report that they stop with the concept. It does not fit their type of organization, which requires more contact and interaction at work to foster innovation and creativity. For them it is no good means, based on expressive evaluation, as it does not fit. All these critical expressive-rational evaluations challenge the universal applicability of the flex-work concept, and show where and for whom it gets irrational. Expressive-rational evaluation provides a basis for assessing which workers might benefit from flex work and who might not, thus setting priorities for where to implement and how to tailor the concept. It is the main inspiration to conclude that flex work is no one-size-fits-all solution. Table 6.2 summarizes the expressive evaluation of ends, means, (unin-tended) consequences and policies in the left-hand bottom field. They result in supporting, challenging or prioritizing them.

The flex-work debate also illustrates the argumentation behind the interplay of expressive rationality evaluating instrumental-rational policies, which is based on motivational reasoning. Working where and when you want is an important objective for many knowledge workers. They say it is a reason for them to apply for jobs where these facilities are offered. Thus, they aim for flex work, give it priority over normal ways of working and select it as an attractive work context for making their living. Parents with young children evaluate flex work also as a good means to combine work with care tasks at home. These positive feelings act as grounds in motivational arguments to engage in flex work, and to evaluate it as a positive means to fit around their own plans. However, other people evaluate the flex-work effects as problematic, and they challenge the unexpected and unintended consequences based on motivational arguments. They feel the concept is not right for them due to their increased concentration problems, burnout, lack of contact with managers and workplace anonymity. These expressive-rational evaluations lead them to conclude that it cannot be a one-size-fits-all solution, as it does not suit everyone. More tailored flex-work policies that pay more attention to the differences between workers are needed. This implies a redirection of policies based on motivational reasoning. The force of these motivational arguments increases by the number of people who feel the same, which is input for an argument from generalization.

Rationality evaluations by social rationality

Degrees of internal social-rational controversy: from sharing to challenging values

Social-rational argumentation can be controversial as well (MacIntyre 1988; Majone 1992; Townley 2002: 170) based on conflicting values and social groups that identify with opposite values. Another discussed type of internal criticism is, for instance, the evaluation of decisions based on formal or bureaucratic rationality, when arbitrators argue for exceptions based on substantive rationality (Gross *et al.* 2013: 97). Rule application is in conflict with a principle like fairness then. Social-rationality conflicts reveal more possibilities for working towards a solution than the expressive-rational controversies. By arguing that some values are more universal and more fundamental than others, the lower values can be subordinated and sometimes values can be reconciled to reach more consistency. All studied debates refer to social rationality in legitimating the debated decisions, and in all cases there are opposite values that require internal debate based on social rationality.

Social-rational argumentation develops towards shared values based on growing consensus in the Gurkha and Heathrow debate. Most people agree that principles of taking care and paying the debt of honour to Gurkhas have to be given priority over cost-saving principles. In the Heathrow debate, there is consensus about taking care of the environment and taking care of passengers as well. During the debate, consensus develops about making improvements towards both objectives, thus reconciling the values. However, in these controversial debates, value conflicts abound as well and shared values get much less attention. The Santa Claus debate remains controversial from a social-rational perspective. Allowing culture criticism aimed at overconsumption gets highest priority, but producing decent art while banning pornographic elements still remains a challenging principle. The principle is not fully applicable though, and a growing majority can acknowledge that and tolerate the artist's freedom of expression. The UK veil-ban debate reaches even less consensus. By finally giving highest priority to freedom of religious expression as principle and by subordinating other principles like favouring open communication or integration, a conclusion is reached. Still, there remain social-rational challenges as the veil remains problematic in many respects: as a barrier to communication, integration and identification, as a sign of unacceptable special treatment and for discriminating certain groups. Similar challenges remain in the Dutch integration debate, where Western principles get more priority over time, like aiming at gender equality and freedom of religion, including atheism. On the other hand, there also remains tolerance for cultural diversity. Strong tensions also remain in the flex-work debate, where it is seen as a positive value to give workers autonomy and save the environment from greenhouse gases on the one hand, but on the other hand critics argue that managers cannot care for their employees sufficiently, and labour regulations lose their protective power. These critics argue that employee protection should get highest priority and values like autonomy for workers and reducing greenhouse gases need to be subordinated. However, protection is seen as good only for one type of employee, whereas autonomy is considered better for more independent employees. The flex-work debate thus offers a good example of tolerance of value opposition, given the accepted differences between stakeholder groups. Table 6.2 summarizes these five patterns of internal social-rationality interaction in its centre field: sharing, challenging, tolerating values, value subordination or prioritization and value reconciliation.

Just like there are different personal likings, there are also different values related to different social communities or different traditions, as illustrated by the debates. Good reasons to act on based on social values or principles work deductively, in arguments from classification. When there are overlaps in values, they can be discovered based on analogical reasoning. Groups of people can find out by comparison that they share them. Sharing as the first type of relationship is illustrated by the different stakeholder groups that share values regarding Gurkha treatment, or those that aim at environmental care in the Heathrow debate. Second, examples of challenging values are visible in the Santa Claus debate where the value to prevent obscene images in public challenges the artist's right of expression, including his criticism on overconsumption by means of an abstract butt plug. The defence of Santa Claus is based on analogical reasoning, claiming that more obscene billboards are accepted as well, so why not Santa Claus which is a much less obscene image? Third, tolerance of values that belong to different community cultures is best visible in the aims of the multicultural integration policies. Fourth, internal social-rationality interactions also move towards something like dominance as within expressive rationality; however, social rationality shows value subordination. While group values differ, some have a more general nature than others. If tensions are first challenged based on analogical reasoning, more local values can be subordinated under more general values based on deductive reasoning by using classification arguments. Examples are visible in the veil-ban debate in the UK, where freedom of expression is prioritized as the more general value and the principle of integration in a Western culture gets subordinated. The Dutch integration debate shows different priorities, as cultural integration becomes the higher value, and Muslim values may, for instance, not support inequality between men and women. The fifth observed form of internal social-rationality interplay of value reconciliation is best illustrated in the Heathrow debate, where improvements on two values need to be realized simultaneously – better travel possibilities and less environmental damage. Based on an argument from classification, they are syn-thesized under a higher value, and realizing both values at the cost of each other becomes a no-go. The most critical interactions challenge social irrationalities, like applying the wrong standards or 'acting against one's own best judgment' (Davidson 2004). Such criticisms appear in the Gurkha debate when the Ministry of Defence is applying standards of cost saving, where moral standards of paying the debt of honour are socially far more rational.

Expressive- and instrumental-rational opinions supported and challenged by social rationality

In four cases, there are crossover evaluations based on social rationality judging the other main perspectives. Excluded are the cases where social rationality dominates the case. They are discussed above based on the internal social-rational tensions. Table 6.4 summarizes for the other four cases how the main pro arguments in the debate (first row) are supported (second row) or challenged (third row) by social-rational arguments, first in the expressive-rational cases (left) and second in the instrumental cases (right). Interactions based on the pro case better illustrate the possible relations and influences between the rationalities than the con case.

Expressive-rational claims evaluated by social rationality

The debates on Santa Claus and the veil ban both illustrate how, in practice, human decision-making has a multidimensional grounding in terms of rationality. Basic support comes from expressive-rational arguments, but they can also receive sup-port by social-rational ones, as indicated by the left side of Table 6.4, first and second row, whereas the third row indicates critical evaluation. What can be observed here is an evaluation of the 'reasonableness' of emotions behind expressive rationality by applying norms and values that belong to a wider social context, as indicated by Scherer (2011: 333).

Expressive rationality supporting the pro case in the Santa Claus debate is based on emotions like sympathy, appreciation and admiration of the sculpture. These emotions are supported by social-rational judgments that frame the value of Santa Claus as positive due to its criticisms on extreme consumerism, capitalism, violence and hypocrisy, and for initiating debate. Similar supportive framing processes are visible in the veil-ban debate, as expressive rationality proves to be receptive for social-rational judgement again. Pro veil-ban emotions of Western people, like feeling uneasy and offended, are support by social-rational judgements framing the veil as a sign of discriminating women and as something prohibited in many (even Arab) countries where it is considered only suitable for private areas. Another social-rational judgement in support of the ban was disqualifying Muslim emotions as being oversensitive to a kind of criticism we are willing to take in a liberal and open Western society, even if it is painful.

However, social-rational judgements can also be challenging. They try to reframe Santa Claus as something obscene, not suitable for the eyes of children and for being

Table 6.4 Rationality evaluations by social rationality

Santa Claus debate	Veil-ban debate	Extension of Heathrow	Implementation of flex work
Expressive-rational opinions Pro Santa Claus (pro case): Appreciation, sympathy, want him close and admiration: McCarthy seen as leading artist.	**Expressive-rational opinions Pro veil ban (pro case):** British people feel uneasy, offended, not appreciated. Face veil is expressing rejection.	**Instrumental opinions Extension (pro case):** Growth of Heathrow is a means to create economic effects (economic growth, more employment, better infrastructure) with less environmental effects (noise, emissions) due to more air traffic efficiency.	**Instrumental opinions Flex work (pro case):** Flex work is a means to increase productivity, to save costs (office space), to reduce traffic and greenhouse gases, to attract employees and to improve their work–life balance.
Social-rational support: Santa Claus is good for criticizing consumerism, capitalism and violence, for inviting debate, for criticizing both hypocrisy and ignorance of (unwelcome) citizen participation.	**Social-rational support:** The veil is an undesirable barrier to communication, identification, integration and improper special treatment. Niqab is not obligatory in Islam, not allowed in many countries and only suitable for private areas. A ban from some places is not discriminatory. Niqab harms common sense. The veil-ban debate is healthy and Muslims' reactions are oversensitive.	**Social-rational support:** There is overall consensus among business-minded people that a third runway is needed. London's infrastructure needs improvement and Heathrow's extension is part of it. Extension can be realized within the limits of strict environmental regulations. Not extending at this moment is against earlier agreements and implicates legal claims.	**Social-rational support:** Flex work resonates well with ideals like autonomy and freedom for employees. It contributes to a greener economy.

(Continued)

Table 6.4 (continued)

Santa Claus debate	Veil-ban debate	Extension of Heathrow	Implementation of flex work
Social-rational objections: Santa Claus cannot be good when being criticized so much, is not suitable for children's eyes, is below standards (obscene, hermetic, elitist), is the result of a neutral government unwilling to give moral guidance.	**Social-rational objections:** The veil-ban debate is a non-issue, there is much religious diversity, wearing the veil is a human right, important as protection of the family unit and banning works less well than open discussion and understanding.	**Social-rational objections:** Environmental effects are unacceptable and require compensation. Drop in quality of life in London (noise, pollution). Strong opposition by environmentalists and local community. Political parties disagree. Many legal claims of people losing their village. Consultation process has been flawed and dishonest.	**Social-rational objections:** Flex-work ideology erodes to cost saving only. Unacceptable consequences of flex work are higher levels of burnout, permanent stress and sick leave. The level of social security for flex workers is not up to standards and managers lose too much control.

elitist art. Such critiques work negatively on positive feelings towards the statue. They were so forceful that they influenced public opinion for some time, and even caused a delay of the moment Santa Claus was made public, which helped to mitigate the negative emotions. The social-rational framing by the opposition in the veil-ban debate worked even stronger. By framing the veil as a sign of expressing religious identity and by considering religious expression fundamental to human rights, all objections, irritations and aversions became somewhat futile. These social-rational judgments challenged and subordinated the Western emotions of feeling offended or feeling uneasy as less relevant, and gave priority to freedom of expression. Table 6.2 summarizes these five patterns of interaction based on the social-rational evaluation of expressive motives in the middle-upper field. They are supporting, challenging, framing, prioritization or subordination and temporization or mitigating.

Social norms, principles and values influence subjective perceptions, feelings and their expressive rationality based on arguments from classification. They illustrate deductive reasoning. First, this appears for the social-rational support of certain likings, as is visible in the support of preferences of workers for flex work based on the general principle that autonomy is good for professionals. Likewise, the principle of freedom of expression supports the wish of some Muslim women to wear a niqab or hijab. Their wish fits the principle when applied in an argument from classification. Challenging is a second form of interplay working from social to expressive rationality. The Dutch integration debate illustrates how desires of gay or liberal Muslims are challenged by the conservative norms in their communities: they do not fit the rule. However, Western key values regarding gender equality challenge conservative Muslim preferences in turn; they also do not fit these standards, when applying an argument from classification. A third form of mutual interplay that starts from social rationality is framing certain individual likings and preferences as better or worse based on relevant norms, values or principles. In the veil-ban debate, many Western people share a dislike of the niqab. Still they subordinate these feelings to freedom of expression as the key value, and frame the niqab as an example of religious expression, more than as a sign of inequality. It makes them tolerate what they dislike. Subordinating certain feelings as a fourth form of interplay goes hand in hand with prioritizing freedom of expression as the guiding value, thus giving room for religious expression. In the Santa Claus debate, liking the sculpture also gets more room than dislike, because greater priority is attributed to criticizing over-consumption than to preventing obscenity in the Dutch society. The latter value is less applicable in an argument from classification. Finally, there are examples of mitigation and temporization in the Santa Claus debate based on deductive reasoning grounded in the social-rational principle that negative emotions and anger in society should not get too strong. To realize this, the sculpture is granted temporary asylum in a museum to give the strongest emotions time to ease out.

Instrumental-rational claims evaluated by social rationality

The debates on Heathrow's extension and the implementation of flex work are presented in the right-hand columns of Table 6.4. Both have an instrumental-rational orientation, but as the debates are embedded in a social context, the means, ends and consequences of these policies are evaluated against social and ethical norms and values. Effects in these debates are not only assessed instrumentally in terms of their size, or their contribution towards a predefined end. Bergset (2015: 277) argues that only doing so might result in long-term irrationalities. Colic-Peisker (2016: 3) also hints at economic 'irrationalities', evaluated against a social perspective.

On the positive side, Heathrow's growth is a means to improve London's infrastructure, air traffic efficiency and economic growth more generally, which are economic effects that receive a positive social evaluation as they contribute to our welfare. In addition, there is social-rational support in the Heathrow debate for meeting the legitimate expectations of business-minded people, for preventing legal claims of investors and for contributing to more employment. Similar positive framing is visible in the flex-work debate. Some effects are evaluated as positive from a social-rational perspective, like giving employees more autonomy, trusting them more and giving them more freedom in balancing work and life obligations. Also, the reduction of greenhouse gases due to flex work is supported from a social perspective.

The support indicates the social rationality of certain effects in both debates, but there are also negative evaluations. The growth of Heathrow implies an increase in noise and pollution. This does not matter in economic terms as the intended end of accommodating travel demands is realized, but from a social-rational perspective these unintended effects are negative – they harm the environment and the health of London's inhabitants, and so environmental organizations challenge these effects. Social rationality evaluates the means (growth) and the unintended effects as irrational against social-rational standards, in spite of their instrumental rationality. In addition, the demolition of a village with 700 inhabitants, forcing other sectors to compensate for Heathrow's extra pollution, and a flawed decision-making process are challenged and framed as negative from a social-rational perspective. These social-rational arguments try to subordinate Heathrow's growth under a condition of sufficiently green and social growth. The unintended effects that go along with flex-work implementation are, likewise, challenged and evaluated as socially irrational, these being higher burnout rates and long-term sick leave. Also challenged is that social security regulations and collective labour agreements lag behind the new developments. These institutions should develop first, to create the right conditions for the new flexible work practices. The conditions to better protect workers should be given priority from a social-rational perspective and be integrated into new public policies. These patterns of interaction are summarized in the middle field at the bottom of Table 6.2. They are the social evaluation of ends, means, (unintended) consequences and policies that can be supporting and challenging, include framing, subordination and setting priorities or redirecting policies.

Social rationality has the same potential as expressive rationality in evaluating the means, effects and more integrated policies based on instrumental-rational logics. The grounds for evaluation are now socially shared values and principles, that are deductively referred to in arguments from classification, instead of many similar individual motives as input for arguments from generalization in expressive evaluation. The social prioritization of ends is criticized in the Gurkha debate, and, as a consequence, cost saving is subsumed under the debt of honour. It is also seen as more legitimate than spending money for saving banks based on the principle that Gurkhas deserve it more. The social evaluation of means is illustrated in the flex-work debate where the concept undermines overtime restrictions. This disqualifies the means for saving the environment or for making more profit. Overtime restrictions have to be effective in protecting employees. Undermining the law can be classified as illegitimate. Effects like higher burnout and long-term sick leave are classified by social security principles as unintended and illegitimate, making an argument from classification that suggests to choose other socially more acceptable means to realize profits. These social evaluations create deductive arguments that push in the direction of reconsidering the flex-work policies, adding to the expressive-rational evaluations pointing in similar directions for large groups of employees.

Rationality evaluations by instrumental rationality

Instrumental-rational controversy: spotting inconsistencies and unintended consequences

All six debates refer to instrumental rationality, as it is supportive in realizing expressive-rational or social-rational goals. However, how the goals are realized can also be more or less rational. When there are unintended consequences, or when intended consequences are not realized, and when means are not efficient in realizing the ends, instrumental rationality gets low and can be criticized internally due to inconsistencies (Davidson 2004; Diesing 1976; Majone 1992; Mason 1969; Tinbergen 1956). In addition, even trying to optimize can be irrational, as satisficing and following heuristics can provide better results in our large, uncertain real-life worlds (Gigerenzer 2010: 534–6; Gigerenzer and Sturm 2012: 262; March and Simon 1958).

Internal instrumental irrationalities are discussed in the flex-work debate when flex work aims at increasing productivity but realizes lower labour productivity due to increasing long-term sick leave, concentration problems and problems with work discipline as several unintended consequences. Such internal inconsistencies between means and ends are also identified in the Heathrow debate regarding the aim to reduce greenhouse gases. It is criticized as being irrational to reduce them by extending an airport. However, the argument is countered by claiming air traffic jams do not help either. In the Gurkha debate the inconsistency between policy objectives is addressed. Why save only a small amount of money on Gurkha rights, while spending such large amounts of money on saving banks who deserved it much less? Multicultural integration policies are also criticized on instrumental grounds for using the wrong means to reach the intended end; but, likewise, are the more restrictive new Dutch integration policies. Neither are the perfect means. So the veil ban is discussed as a means to remove a barrier for integration and communication by proponents, but also more critically by Muslims as a mere means for winning votes, thus mainly promoting politicians' self-interest. The least controversial from an instrumental perspective is the Santa Claus debate about the question of how and where to present the critical message about Western overconsumption. McCarthy is willing to negotiate the means of expression and to adapt the expected effects of the sculpture to its social environment. Marginal critiques that his means of expression is too expensive are easily rebutted. Table 6.2 summarizes in the right-hand bottom field these two patterns: the evaluation of unintended consequences and the means–end inconsistencies.

Instrumental rationality is internally more coherent compared to the other two rationalities. Still, as human rationality is bounded we are often mistaken about what are the best means to realize the ends we have set, and we debate our mistakenly assumed cause–effect relations or the unintended effects. The debates offer several examples of such inconsistencies, like the decrease of short-term sick leave due to flex work followed by the increase in long-term sick leave where the latter is an unintended effect. Aiming at the reduction of greenhouse gases by not extending Heathrow has the unintended effect of causing more waiting time before airplanes can land. Comparing such intended effects with the realized effects requires analogical reasoning. You then discover that ends and effects do not overlap. The overlooked cause of the unintended effects can, subsequently, be interpreted based on an argument from sign. The unintended effect (long-term sick leave or extra greenhouse gas) might be the sign of the cause of increased work pressures for some workers, or the waiting time for airplanes due to congestion. Still, these arguments from sign need to be connected with the underlying causal argumentation suggesting instrumental rationality. The most critical interactions challenge irrationalities related to unintended consequences and means–end inconsistencies as a result of wishful thinking or ignoring evidence (Davidson 2004; Henderson 2010), as is best illustrated by the instrumental irrationalities of flex work with its many unintended consequences that were actually not too difficult to foresee.

Expressive- and social-rational opinions challenged and supported by instrumental rationality

In four cases there are crossover evaluations based on instrumental rationality judging the other main rationality perspectives. Excluded are the cases in which instrumental rationality dominates, as they are discussed above based on their internal rationality tensions. Table 6.5 summarizes for the other four cases how the main pro arguments in the debate (first row) are supported (second row) or challenged (third row) by instrumental-rational arguments, first in the expressive-rational cases (left) and second in the social cases (right). Interactions based on the pro case, again, give the best illustrations of the possible relations and influences between the rationalities.

Expressive-rational claims evaluated by instrumental rationality

Table 6.5 summarizes the main instrumental support and opposition for Santa Claus and the veil ban in the two left-hand columns. Decisions mainly motivated

Table 6.5 Rationality evaluations by instrumental rationality

Santa Claus debate	Veil-ban debate	Integration of Dutch immigrants	Gurkha rights extension
Expressive-rational opinions Pro Santa Claus (pro case): Appreciation, sympathy, want him close and admiration: McCarthy seen as leading artist.	**Expressive-rational opinions Pro veil ban (pro case):** British people feel uneasy, offended, not appreciated. Face veil is expressing rejection.	**Social-rational opinions Stricter integration policies (pro case):** Old multicultural policies demand too little. All immigrants need to internalize Western key values. Muslim intolerance to other sexual inclinations, rights for women, other beliefs and atheism, is unacceptable. Zero tolerance for criminal behaviours. New immigrants need to be sufficiently educated.	**Social-rational opinions Full rights extension (pro case):** Equal rights for Gurkha veterans compared to non-British Commonwealth soldiers are fair and just. Loyalty and bravery need to be rewarded. Government should not act treacherously and dishonestly towards Gurkhas. Gurkhas have many supporters in society. Britain has a debt of honour, whatever the costs.
Instrumental-rational support: Art is an effective means for inviting personal reflections, especially in a shopping area. City council considers this art-work an effective investment. Temporary location at museum court is a means to mitigate resistance.	**Instrumental-rational support:** A veil ban removes a barrier to good/pleasant communication, improves integration, especially in schools, and it protects the expressive effect of school uniforms. Without the ban, a niqab draws too much attention as nobody else wears it.	**Instrumental-rational support:** Old open-ended policies have failed and were costly. New integration policies will be better aligned with EU policies, which improves them. Allowing only immigrants with completed levels of education prevents lower-class problems.	**Instrumental-rational support:** Cost for Gurkhas pale in comparison to cost used to bail out banks and total costs of immigration.

(Continued)

Table 6.5 (continued)

Santa Claus debate	Veil-ban debate	Integration of Dutch immigrants	Gurkha rights extension
Instrumental-rational objections: Santa Claus is too expensive, is a waste of means.	**Instrumental-rational objections:** Face veil is no real barrier to communication. Prohibition is an improper tactic for politicians to gain desired votes.	**Instrumental-rational objections:** Hard policies undermine open debate and are counterproductive. Successes are mainly due to immigrants themselves (asylum seekers, second generation), not policies. Fundamentalist beliefs are deeply rooted and not easy to change by force.	**Instrumental-rational objections:** There are costs, and the Ministry of Defence is overstretched already. There are consequences for others in Britain and for the Nepalese economy. Before 1997, Gurkhas were stationed in Hong Kong, and never experienced British life.

on expressive grounds need a reality check. Is it feasible to execute them, can we do it more efficiently or more effectively? If not, we act irrationally on instrumental grounds, as also illustrated by an example of failure in Calabretta *et al.* (2016: 20) regarding a design innovation, where 'affective evaluation' was not 'cognitively evaluated' for questions of feasibility. Fisher and Freshwater (2014) argue, likewise, that aesthetic rationality is crucial, but is not likely to suffice in an organizational context.

Instrumental arguments support Santa Claus as an effective means of expression to criticize consumerism and invite critical reflection; however, instrumental-rational arguments also indicate it is not feasible to expose Santa Claus in a public space right away, due to initially strong emotional resistance. Instrumental considerations thus help to evaluate policies of reducing public resistance first. Second, they help evaluate how to effectively express a critical artistic message. The effect of instrumental rationality in the discussion about the most effective means of expression to reach the goals of the artist leads to temporary exposition in a museum. For McCarthy, provocation has never been an end in itself, so he has made the colour of the statue less provocative than initially planned. The means to express were selected based on the effectiveness of such means to reach intended expressive effects. Supportive instrumental-rational arguments in the veil-ban debate focus on the effects of banning the veil – it is an effective way of removing the niqab as an unpopular and often hated communication barrier. It would also protect the current effects of school uniforms in the UK, which are still liked by many for their effect of perceiving all pupils as equal without emphasizing class or religious differences. Both a niqab and hijab would undermine that effect. Such instrumental-rational arguments support the policy of banning the face veil, as it is evaluated as an effective means of removing the cause of many unpleasant emotions. Thus, people should not be allowed to wear the niqab whenever they like.

Instrumental opposition in both debates is secondary compared to social-rational opposition. There is the minor complaint that Santa Claus is too expensive, thus criticizing an inefficient use of means. Opponents in the veil-ban debate contradict the instrumental argument that the niqab is a communication barrier by claiming communication with a niqab is still feasible and effective, as in a telephone call. Integration also remains possible as it does not depend on religious identity. Therefore, a veil ban is not really worth the effort. It is very costly and, thus, inefficient, and maybe not be feasible due to higher legislation. These forms of interaction between expressive-rational motives evaluated by instrumental rationality are summarized in Table 6.2 in the right-hand side of the top row. They check for effectiveness, efficiency and feasibility of the means used for realizing expressive ends.

All such instrumental evaluations are based on arguments from cause. Realizing expressive ends can be assessed for effectiveness of the use of means first. Examples are the public exposition of Santa Claus compared to its exhibition in a museum court. The latter option was assessed as more effective for getting McCarthy's artistic message across for a period of three years. Public exposition in a shopping area, as planned, would raise too much anger and resistance, which were unintended effects. However, after this period, public opinion became more positive and so public exposition became more effective for getting the message across, as initially planned. The instrumental evaluations of expressive-rational ends assess if the intended effects are realized sufficiently, based on arguments from cause. Second, the efficiency of expressive means can be assessed. This implies personal goal realization at minimum costs, or by not wasting resources. Personal goal realization in the flex-work debate comes at a high cost for those who like the autonomy, but miss sufficient self-management skills. They are not able to switch off their phone, and they start working without breaks. Burnout is a high cost for them, and so it is for their employer who might have a personal liking for the concept as well. A more efficient form of personal goal realization would be to receive self-management training before having this freedom, or that employers better organize the monitoring of their workers. Again, the evaluation is based on means–end argumentation and causal logic. Third, the feasibility of realizing personal goals can be assessed. Given the resistance to Santa Claus initially, McCarthy's idea of public exposition might have resulted in damage to the sculpture, which has often happened to his sculptures. This made the option of public exposition questionable in terms of feasibility. The opposite happened in the Gurkha debate, were people wanted an extension of Gurkha rights so strongly, that feasibility considerations did not impress anymore. In the first case, conditions to realize the intended effects are not fulfilled, and in the second example, that kind of suggestion is criticized. Both arguments require cause-based logic.

Social-rational claims evaluated by instrumental rationality

Instrumental-rational evaluation can be supportive to social rationality by showing the possibilities to act on the values and principles suggested, and undermining by showing the opposite. Table 6.5 shows such supporting and critical arguments in the right-side of the second and third rows. In both social-rational debates, instrumental rationality offers the primary critical perspective, suggesting utopian or far too expensive idealism. Esposito (2011) criticizes such irrationalities by evaluating fashions against standards of instrumental logics: the irrationality of driving big cars in the city centre or wearing expensive but impractical clothes due to fashion. Weber (1972: 13) has also commented on the potential irrationality of value rationality due to the ignorance of consequences.

New Dutch integration policies need to include important, novel and social targets like cultural integration and the reduction of intolerance and criminality, with the intention to develop more effective policies seen from an instrumental-rational point of view. Proponents of stricter integration policies criticize the previous multicultural policies as being very expensive and inefficient. In addition, they have realized many unintended effects by only focusing on social-economic integration. By changing the means (only allowing immigrants with completed education and by aligning with EU policies), new integration policies can be more effective, thus creating instrumental-rational support for these policies. In the Gurkha debate, proponents present the rights extension as feasible, and even too important to consider the costs. Moreover, costs are negligible compared to the costs the government was willing to make for saving UK banks. This creates instrumental support for the rights extension.

-   Opponents in the Dutch integration debate claim most integration problems have been dealt with well, except, perhaps, those related to the radical Muslims. The proposed new policies are not a step in the right direction of better solving the integration problems. The new policy objectives might be noble and attractive in themselves, but they lose motivational impact if they are as utopian and infeasible as multicultural policies, and, on top of that, are also more counterproductive. Terrorism and fundamentalism cannot be reduced by stricter rules. These means are criticized as ineffective. Still, they are executed as the better alternative and something that needs to be tried. In the Gurkha debate, the government suggests the partial rights extension is more feasible. However, the government admits that pension and settlement rights have to be extended. As they also exaggerate costs, it makes their arguments quite feeble, as a full rights extension is feasible as well. The kinds of critical interaction based on critical instrumental evaluation of social-rational arguments is summarized in the middle field of the right-hand column in Table 6.2 as checking for the effectiveness, efficiency and feasibility of the means to realize the social values.

Realization of social-rational ends can be assessed on effectiveness, efficiency and feasibility by using causal arguments. First, a critical assessment of the effectiveness of the social-rational tolerance principle is visible in the Dutch integration debate when discussing multicultural integration policies. The effectiveness of the tolerance principle for causing better integration is questioned particularly for its tolerance of intolerance towards key Western values. This undermines gender equality, or tolerance for homosexual preferences. The tolerance principle is thus assessed as the wrong means for realizing integration. Second, the efficiency of the principle of autonomy that inspires flex work is criticized based on the one-size-fits-all application. The principle is nice, but too costly if applied to workers that miss the necessary self-management skills as 'means', thus turning a decrease in short-term sick leave into a costly increase in long-term sick leave. Third, the feasibility of realizing a social value is criticized in the Gurkha debate grounded in cause-based argumentation. The feasibility is doubted by the Ministry of Defence; they like the principle of equal rights for Gurkha veterans, but say they do not have the financial means to grant them such full rights. They also claim it is infeasible for them to spend this money. The argument proved to be flawed later, but if not it would have undermined the realization of this social ideal, suggesting it is utopian or unrealistic – a claim that better holds for the Dutch integration policies.

Concluding: rationality interplays and argumentation patterns

Acting rationally is acting on good reasons. As contexts of action differ fundamentally, so do good reasons to act on. If our actions relate to our subjectivity, the context is fundamentally different from a social context, in which we consider others in our decision-making, or if our decision-making mainly relates to the world of objects in which we want to realize effects. Rationality has a different appearance in these three argumentation fields, which implies that what is rational in one of these contexts is not necessarily so in another. As a consequence, good reasons given 'out of context' can appear as irrational.

The six public debates offer various examples of 'out of context' rationality, like deciding about the pension and settlement rights of Gurkha veterans based on financial means–end considerations. They suggest the costs are too high for realizing the objective. This 'rational' motivation is seen as irrational, since the guiding rationality should be social in this context. The higher objective here is taking responsibility for those who deserve it, a principle that is social rational. In the flex-work debate, instrumental rationality is challenged based on expressive-rational grounds. Flex work might seem more efficient than traditional work, suggesting it is a rational choice; but if people get sick, others do not like it or get concentration problems, then how rational is it? Accepting this aversion, the concentration problems or illness would not seem rational from an expressive perspective. These examples illustrate that instrumental-rational considerations do not always fit the context of a decision sufficiently, in spite of their popularity.

As humans, we do not only relate to the outside world of things, we also relate to others and we relate to ourselves, mostly at the same time. Some contexts for decisions are more subjective, like when we decide how to dress, what to eat or where we want to live. Other contexts may be more social, like when we decide how to raise our children, how to behave in traffic and why to pay our taxes. Only when we decide, for example, on a more solid construction for building a table, the quickest way from home to work or the best fit when hiring an employee for a job do we relate to a more objective or outside reality, where instrumental rationality fits quite well. In practice, most complex decisions require a balancing of these three rationalities.

To be able to balance or to change a balance, it is necessary to be able to criticize the relevance of rationalities, or to prioritize the more important ones, as illustrated in the six debates. Stakeholders do challenge, subordinate or tolerate perspectives put forward by using one type of rationality against the other, or by addressing internal inconsistencies within one rationality perspective to play it down. The previous sections have illustrated how internal inconsistencies are articulated with the help of arguments from analogy. Means–end inconsistencies can also be explored based on arguments from sign.

Cross-rationality evaluations based on standards of expressive rationality build on motivational arguments that gain force if combined with arguments from generalization. Cross-rationality evaluations based on standards of social rationality apply arguments from classification. Cross-rationality evaluations based on instrumental rationality apply arguments from cause. Figure 6.1 summarizes how the three rationalities can influence each other, and what types of reasoning appear.

Internal rationality critiques are sparked by analogical reasoning

Based on internal comparison and analogical reasoning, assessments are made if particular reasons to act on within one rationality perspective are stronger than

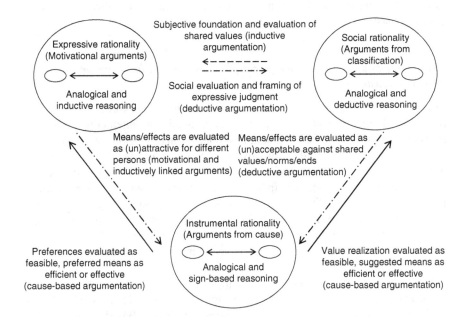

Figure 6.1 Persuasive interactions between and within types of rationality.

others, as visualized by the two small circles within each rationality field in Figure 6.1. The first internal assessment is based on how different people appreciate things differently while grounding their actions in expressive rationality, seen on the left-hand side of Figure 6.1. Internal assessments within social indicating value conflict are depicted on the right and instrumental-rationality assessments indicating means–end inconsistencies are shown at the bottom of Figure 6.1. The cases illustrate such debate on what is expressively, socially or instrumentally most rational, indicated by the many differences of opinion. This finding challenges the pretence of rationality as being universal, put forward by writers like Weber (1972) and Habermas (1988) regarding instrumental and value rationality. The findings from the cross-case analysis are more in line with MacIntyre's (1988) pluralistic view on rationality, although his argument applies to social rationality mainly. The controversies also illustrate the view of March and Simon (1958) regarding our boundedness, which can make it difficult to reach agreement on instrumental-rational arguments. Expressive rationality appears to be most pluralistic from the start. It is grounded in the motives, views and likings of different individuals (Engelen 2006; Greenspan 2004; Hargreaves Heap 2001; Scherer 2011).

All debates illustrate how analogical reasoning is the dominant form of argu-mentation in searching for greater rationality within each type of rationality, resulting in sharing and imitation or challenging and differentiation regarding personal motives and social values. In the case of instrumental rationality, we also find some arguments from sign that try to relate unintended effects to the underlying

causes when mismatches between intended effects and their realization are discovered based on analogical reasoning.

Expressive- and social-rationality interplays sparked by inductive or deductive reasoning

The upper half of Figure 6.1 illustrates the interplay between expressive and social
rationality. Expressive rationality and social rationality are interacting closely in
five out of the six public debates, both in supportive and critical ways. Expressive
rationality influences social rationality by supporting, challenging and shifting
priorities and values. Many social norms and values appear to be grounded in
shared subjectivity, based on inductive arguments based on generalization.
However, social rationality is able to influence back by supporting, challenging,
setting priorities, framing or mitigation and temporization of expressive judgments. What we experience subjectively can be socially influenced by applicable
norms, values and principles that are referred to in deductive arguments based on
classification.

The inductive influence of expressive rationality on social rationality appears in
the debates when individuals feel and recognize that their feelings related to a
decision and its implied values or principles are shared. Based on expressive
rationality, such values can be inductively grounded, developed and challenged
(Haidt 2001; Sedlacek 2011; Smith 1982). This observation supports what ten Bos
and Willmott (2001) claim, that our moral impulses (with a subjective origin) are a
condition of existence for moral principles with more general relevance.

The pattern of influence from social rationality towards expressive rationality is
deductive in its way of argumentation by using arguments from classification.
People align their feelings and expressions with the most relevant social standards.
Feelings that do not fit get repressed, like the wish for an individual work spot in
situations where flex work is the standard. Or feelings get protected by values, like
the wish for religious expression by means of a niqab in a fundamentalist Muslim
community. This deductive application of principles and values is quite in line with
the ideas of Weber (1972) or Habermas (1988), embedded in their definition of value
rationality, and it resembles how deontological ethics can legitimize our actions
(Hegel 1986; Kant 1990), even though the values and principles in the cases never
appear as universal (MacIntyre 1988).

Most importantly, the cases show a two-way interaction between expressive and
social rationality: principles guide individuals deductively, but individuals also
establish principles inductively. The most critical interactions address expressive
irrationalities like intolerable wishes, as tried in the Santa Claus debate and the veil-
ban debate. The whole idea of the veil ban was to make wearing the niqab an
illegitimate expressive act. And the reverse is illustrated as well, to frame norms,
rules, values and laws as frustrating, upsetting and not preferred from a personal
expressive perspective, which resulted in pushing back the veil ban and the Santa
Claus ban as irrational on expressive-rational grounds.

Instrumental rationality influenced by motivational and classification arguments

While expressive rationality and social rationality can mutually influence each other on the level of values, the interplay when social and expressive rationality influence instrumental rationality is more unidirectional regarding the content of personal and social values. These influences are illustrated by the two arrows that point downwards and to the middle in Figure 6.1. Expressive and social rationality can set personal or general objectives, while instrumental rationality then selects the best means to realize what is important to me or to us. Expressive and social rationality help setting objectives based on what motivates me or what is valuable to us, whereas instrumental rationality helps to make it feasible and do it efficiently or effectively.

Based on expressive and social rationalities, ends can be defined or given priority, and the qualities of the selected means can be evaluated. Some means can help to realize an attractive end, but in itself these means can be unattractive to me or to us, or not worth the end. Also, the realized, and sometimes unintended, effects can be evaluated against personal preferences or social values, and these evaluations can inspire the redirection of policies. Such assessments are based on motivational arguments in the case of expressive-rational evaluation, and on arguments from classification in the case of social-rational evaluation. Motivational arguments (expressive rational) and arguments from classification (social rational) can tell if these means, ends and realized effects sufficiently match our intentions, desires, principles and larger objectives.

The more critical interactions between expressive rationality when evaluating instrumental rationality can assess the means or effects as painful, irritating or upsetting from an expressive perspective. Such irrationalities against standards of expressive rationality appear when individuals experience concentration problems or burnout due to a flex-work setting which does not fit their nature. Social evaluations based on arguments from classification can addresses immoral or illegitimate effects or use of means. That is, for instance, when flex work undermines labour laws and Heathrow's extension undermines international environmental agreements. Both irrationalities are criticized from a social perspective.

Currently, the focus on instrumental rationality as grounded in economic reasoning dominates our understanding of rationality (Bergset 2015; Diesing 1976; Eisenhardt and Zbaracki 1992; Harrison 1993). The relations to other rationalities are under-explored. However, the focus on how we can best realize objectives and optimize the use of means should not blind us from the rationality of what we intend to achieve or what is important to us, as addressed by Diesing (1976), Habermas (1988), Peacock (1992) or Weber (1972). However, the single hierarchy assumed by Weber (1972) and Habermas (1988), where only value rationality guides instrumental rationality by setting objectives, needs to be nuanced by splitting the task between social and expressive rationality. Five out of six debates illustrate how many relevant objectives stem from more subjective, local, temporal and personal values and intentions originating from expressive rationality (Engelen 2006; Fisher and Freshwater 2014; Li *et al.* 2014; Scherer 2011). Also, social-rational arguments in the debates are mostly not referring to universal, but to contested values (MacIntyre 1988). Still, these local social and expressive rationalities are quite convincing and powerful in their evaluations, and they clearly make a difference in the studied debates.

Instrumental reality check of social- and expressive-rational arguments

Content-wise, instrumental-rational ends are influenced by social and expressive evaluations, but instrumental rationality can influence in return as well. Some ends or personal values might seem attractive, but when considering how difficult it is to realize them, their appeal can become weaker. The assessment to what extent values, principles or personal likings can be realized is based on causal argumentation, as shown in Figure 6.1, by arrows pointing upwards to the sides. The critical questions put forward are if the intended effects are realized sufficiently effective, efficient and feasible and, thus, if the personal or social objectives are set realistically.

The most critical interactions between social and expressive rationality when evaluated by instrumental rationality show the impracticality of wishes or desires: wearing the niqab is impractical in communication and for integration. The evaluation of social rationality against standards of instrumental rationality addresses irrationalities like utopian ideals or moral principles that are not feasible, like solving the problems of fundamentalism with integration policies. Such critiques can make ideals less attractive or their execution more effective.

The interplay between social or expressive rationality and instrumental rationality thus works in two directions, not only downwards as assumed by Habermas (1988) or Weber (1972), but also upwards, with instrumental rationality influencing the other two. Arguments from cause help to assess expressive- and social-rational reasoning regarding effectiveness, efficiency and feasibility. If they do not stand the test, they appear as unrealistic. Personal motives and social ideals can also influence in return by making constraints over time more flexible due to what we learn and invent (Majone 1992), or because we very strongly want something, as in the Gurkha debate. Such mutual interactions are rarely explored, and demand much more attention as pointed out by Gigerenzer and Selten (2001b: 9–10).

Discussion

Theoretical contributions

The cross-case analysis of six public debates on rationality interactions does add new insights to the economic, philosophical and sociological debates on rationality. The mere focus of economists on instrumental rationality with an emphasis on optimization (Bergset 2015; Klamer 1987; Klein 2001; McCloskey 2016; Weirich 2004) proves to be too limited for covering what we consider rational in the light of making complex strategic decisions in practice. Even the two predominantly economic decisions on Heathrow's extension and on flex-work implementation demonstrate multiple rationalities to argue for the decision. The counterbalancing influences of social or expressive rationality are of crucial importance, illustrating many ways to correct instrumental-rational logics in finding good reasons for action. This conceptualization enables a more inclusive view on what decision makers present as rational. It also resonates well with a rationality concept understood as the ability to give good reasons to act on (Davidson 2004: 169; Elbanna 2006: 3; Elbanna and Child 2007: 433; Elster 2009: 2; Engelen 2006: 427; Gigerenzer and Sturm 2012: 243–5; Green 2004: 655; Henderson 2010: 32). The three origins of rationality explain how decision makers prepare and defend their decisions, and why, at the same time, stakeholders can argue the opposite.

The criticism that instrumental rationality as understood by economists is a too-narrow perspective to account for rationality in general, is not new (Diesing 1976; Elster 2009; Gigerenzer and Selten 2001b; March and Simon 1958; Sen 1977; Weber 1972). However, previous studies have mainly investigated different rationalities next to each other, or have focused on particular types of rationality (Cabantous *et al.* 2010; Diesing 1976; Eisenhardt and Zbaracki 1992; Engelen 2006; Harrison 1993; MacIntyre 1988). There has been little attention for the interactions between different rationalities, evidenced by the call for research in Townley (2002: 177) to study interactions between different rationalities. My way of differentiating three rationalities and mapping their possible interactions further details the indicated interactions between disembedded (instrumental), embedded (social) and embodied (expressive) rationality in Townley (2008), as her differentiations are quite similar. For instance, instrumental-rational arguments pro and con appear to be quite able to integrate emotions, and refer to them as motives in labelling effects as attractive and unattractive. Likewise, Calabretta *et al.* (2016: 31) find that there are mutual interactions possible between instrumental rationality and affective evaluations, thus denying a one-way dominance of instrumental rationality where emotions can only interfere as suggested in Kahneman (2011). Also, the suggested opposition between moral post-hoc reasoning and emotional decision-making, as in Haidt (2001), appears to be somewhat artificial, because social and expressive rationality can develop in interaction over time – a mutual influence illustrated in several debates.

Starting from Bouwmeester's (2013) characterizations of expressive, social and instrumental rationality, the current study has detailed how expressive, social and instrumental rationality interact mutually, and generate softer and stronger pressures on each other by articulating tensions, challenging them or even letting one perspective dominate, next to mutual forms of support. These mutual pressures are grounded in different types of reasoning, which are mainly motivational and inductive for expressive-rational evaluation, deductive for social-rational evaluation and cause-based for instrumental-rational evaluation. The variety in discursive interactions makes rationality as a concept more dynamic, and challenges several taken-for-granted assumptions.

The first challenged assumption is that instrumental rationality is the least contested type of rationality, due to its foundation in causality (Habermas 1988; Weber 1972). The challenges not only originate from the perspective of bounded rationality

(March and Simon 1958), but are also due to ecological rationality (Gigerenzer and Selten 2001b: 9–10; Gigerenzer and Sturm 2012: 255) and context dependency (Bouwmeester 2013; Sandberg and Tsoukas 2011). Consequently, instrumental arguments can work as irrational in a context that also demands social or expressive rationality, as most clearly illustrated in the Gurkha and flex-work debates. Second, even though reasons for social-rational legitimization of action can be considered more general than those based on expressive rationality, in the context of decisions with mainly personal impact expressive rationality can also contest general social arguments as less rational or less relevant (Fisher and Freshwater 2014; Gaut 2012), instead of only the other way around, as assumed in studies that stress the irrational effects of emotions (Fessler 2001; Kahneman 2011). The Santa Claus and veil-ban cases give nice illustrations of the interaction where values are influenced and contested bottom-up. Third, the common rationality hierarchy inspired by Weber (1972), with value rationality setting the objectives and instrumental rationality helping realize them efficiently or effectively, also proves to be only one possibility to set objectives. Value rationality as understood by Colic-Peisker (2016), Gross *et al.* (2013) or Weber (1972) is a quite general form of social rationality. The veil-ban and Santa Claus debates both illustrate the greater importance of expressive rationality over social or value rationality in setting objectives for such public decisions with great personal impacts. It is a possibility also pointed out by Fisher and Freshwater (2014) in an organizational setting.

Studying the interactions between the three basic forms of rationality and giving them equal status in supporting and challenging each other is this study's first main contribution to the debate on rationality. The rationality concept developed here appears to be three-dimensional, and includes the dynamic possibility of three different perspectives of rationality assessment. It further proves the existence of what Boltanski and Thevenot (2006) consider 'orders of worth' that require their own argumentation rules, what Toulmin (1994) considers the field dependency of argumentation, and Bouwmeester (2013) the required fit between instrumental, social or expressive rationality and their fields of application. This conceptualization challenges the taken-for-granted assumption that instrumental-rational optimizing is the standard for being ultimately rational. Deviations from this ideal due to emotions are usually considered irrational (Elster 2009; Fessler 2001; Kahneman 2011; Sen 1977). It can, indeed, be a form of irrationality, but there are many more forms of irrationality (Gaut 2012).

Irrationalities are most often associated with internal inconsistencies. That is, realizing unintended effects (Davidson 2004; Henderson 2010; Majone 1992; Tinbergen 1956), realizing value conflict (Gross *et al.* 2013; MacIntyre 1988; Majone 1992; Townley 1999) or the lack of authenticity and forms of emotional self-deception (Davidson 2004; Habermas 1988). Such internal inconsistencies can appear as internal irrationalities within each of the three rationality perspectives indicated by means–end inconsistencies, conflicts in value application or emotional misfit. A three-dimensional rationality concept is not only able to address such irrationalities within the three perspectives, but also between the three perspectives, which is rather new.

The cross-case analysis adds to these new conceptualizations of irrationality by crossover-rationality evaluations. Instrumental-rational considerations can be constructed as irrational against expressive-rational standards (flex work does not make everyone a happy worker) or social-rational principles based on the law (flex work undermines labour laws). Arguments based on social rationality can also be constructed as irrational when evaluated by the two other rationalities: the veil ban upsets many Muslims, making a veil ban irrational against standards of expressive rationality, and the values of tolerance behind multicultural policies appear as unrealistic or utopian against standards of instrumental rationality. Evaluations can also socially construct expressive rationality as irrational by judging wishes or expressions as illegal, which is tried by banning both the niqab and Santa Claus, based on social-rational arguments. Wishes or desires can appear unrealistic or unpractical against standards of instrumental rationality, as was visible in critiques on communicating while wearing a niqab. Defining three sources for constructing irrationality in cross-rationality evaluations enriches the current views on irrationality discussed in Davidson (2004), Henderson (2010) and Kahneman (2011). The identification of multiple irrationalities resonates with the research agenda in Calabretta *et al.* (2016).

A second contribution adds to mapping existing conceptualizations of different rationalities like aesthetic, political, legal or value rationality and their conceptual relations with social and expressive rationality. The top of Figure 6.1 relates to (inter)subjective motivations, whereas the bottom relates more to physical and material realities that constrain our socially constructed human world. This human top has a left side that is more personal or subjective, and a right side that is more social or intersubjective. There are no strict lines between those two sides, because the subjective and intersubjective realities interact closely. Earlier characterizations of social and personal forms of rationality can be positioned between these extremes of purely subjective and purely intersubjective rationalities. Value rationality as conceptualized by Habermas (1988) and Weber (1972) is like deontological ethics based on universal social values and principles, which would give it an ultimate right-side position. However, in practice, these universal values are hard to find and if claimed to be so, are always quite contested (MacIntyre 1988). Human rights come close, but legal rationality (Diesing 1976) has a national reach, which is far from universal. Political rationality leans more towards the subjective side, and receives its force from stakeholder support in its more democratic appearance (Diesing 1976; Eisenhardt and Zbaracki 1992; van Houwelingen and Bouwmeester 2008). Aesthetic rationality (Habermas 1988; van Houwelingen and Bouwmeester 2008; Kant 1990; Schiller 1983) has even more subjective roots as it strongly originates from subjective inspirations. Still, it can create shared values as many people learn to like famous artworks, and these works set new standards or create fashions (Esposito 2011). As aesthetic rationality is still firmly rooted in subjective motives, it resonates most strongly with expressive rationality as based on one's personal wishes, intentions, impulses, inspiration and intuitions. Conceptualizing subjective and social rationality as two connected extremes helps to understand the human origin of such different rationalities that share social and subjective elements in a different mix. Likewise, we can rank rationalities as more or less material and objectified. Laws are more materialized than values, and some forms of expression are materialized as well, like McCarthy's Santa Claus, whereas emotional expression can also be spoken in words only, which is much less material when compared to debates expressed in written words, as studied here. This conceptualization of rationality on a continuum ranging from subjective to social and from human to more material is a contribution that adds to the debate on multiple rationalities, which has been somewhat fragmented due to many ad-hoc character-izations of different rationalities and their boundaries (Diesing 1976; Eisenhardt and Zbaracki 1992; Engelen 2006; Habermas 1988; Harrison 1993; van Houwelingen and Bouwmeester 2008; Weber 1972).

A third fundamental contribution of this study relates rationality back to its original meaning of having good reasons to act on, and by exploring empirically what decision makers and stakeholders consider good reasons when they discuss complex strategic decisions in practice. Different calls have suggested a more ecological and practice-based approach of studying rationality in context (Cabantous *et al.* 2010; Gigerenzer 2010; Gigerenzer and Selten 2001b; Sandberg and Tsoukas 2011). Current philo-sophical debates on rationality remain overly abstract and present, at best, theoretical and stylized examples on abortion or euthanasia without offering much guidance for real-life decisions (Davidson 2004; Habermas 1988; Haidt 2001; Henderson 2010; MacIntyre 1988). Rich descriptions of the actual reasons given when debating complex strategic decisions are hardly part of the rationality debate yet. These deliberations are mostly quite complex; they are about what the real problem is, including the purpose of the decision, they relate pros and cons, discuss conditions for executing a decision and assess decisions socially and emotionally. The current analysis adds the missing rich descriptions to an academic debate that still suffers from empirical poverty and lack of permeable disciplinary boundaries, as criticized in Calabretta *et al.* (2016), Gigerenzer (2010), Gigerenzer and Selten (2001b) and Mueller *et al.* (2007). By exploring the reasons that were considered worth acting on, the analysis further shows how different types of arguments like inductive generalizations, analogical arguments, deductive classifications, motivational and cause-based arguments fit to different rationality interactions and cross-rationality evaluations. These interactions help in arriving at a set of well-balanced reasons that can support or challenge decisions in practice better than any one-dimensional rationality could. By following this approach, the study substantially adds to earlier work on argumentation rationality and decision-making explored in Bouwmeester (2013), Fischer and Forester (1993), Majone 1992, Mason (1969), Rieke and Sillars (2001) and von Werder (1999).

Limitations and agenda for studying expressive and social rationality in more depth

A case study is always limited by the particular selection of cases. These limit-ations do also affect the current analysis of expressive, social and bounded instrumental rationality as practised by decision makers in the six debates. The many existing heuristics for being effectively bounded rational (Gigerenzer and Selten 2001a; Gigerenzer and Sturm 2012) are hardly visible in this study. For instance, the 'one-clever-cue heuristic' for making decisions (Gigerenzer and Gaissmaier 2011: 463) does not fit the context of complex decision-making, where many cues are at stake. Due to the ecology of the cases, which is characterized by controversy, and due to the focus of the study on complex argumentations, such shortcuts effective in other contexts (ecologies) have not been subject to investigation. There are also numerous social rationalities with a validity in bigger or smaller communities (MacIntyre 1988) and only some are illustrated in this study. Expressive rationalities can show as much variation due to the differences between decision makers and relevant stakeholders. These limitations call for further study. In particular, studying the variety in expressive rationalities hand in hand with the study of social rationalities needs to be focused on, as both rationalities appear to be independent but interrelated, and also mixed in different degrees, dependent on context.

As the current study is only based on written communication as published in newspapers, it is not be possible to assess the emotional truthfulness of words, or to question and probe expressions as possible in an interview study or by observation. However, we know people can behave socially based on instrumental or opportunistic grounds, thus only pretending to be social (Racko 2011: 782). The opposite can happen as well, using economic arguments to foster a social agenda (Townley 2002: 168). Similarly, expressive-rational motives based on anger or indignation can be hidden behind a social-rational argument judging some behaviour as unacceptable. Such processes can be suspected in the Heathrow debate as expressive rationality is absent. Still, the inhabitants of the village that would have to disappear must have been made unhappy by this perspective. Their emotions might have been translated into social-rational arguments against growth. In the veil-ban debate, expressive arguments come more to the forefront and stress the desire to express religious identity – a request which receives a warm welcome in a Western context, given its support of freedom of expression. However, as the real religious intentions and the social pressures behind the veil do not convince so well in a Western context, some rationality transfer seems to be possible here as well. Processes of rationality substitution seem to be quite interesting to study in more detail, as they appear to be examples of functional dishonesty. However, these questions cannot be studied with the methods practised for the current study. Anthropological and sociological research methods might be better suited to investigate such questions (Racko 2011; Townley 2002). Likewise, they might help to study particular social rationalities within cultures and traditions (Boyd and Richerson 2001; Fessler 2001). Deeper insights into expressive rationality, including sources of creativity, inspiration, moral intuitions and authentic expressions, might also benefit from research methods and thought experiments that belong to the domains of the arts and humanities (Gaut 2012).

In the rationality debate, feelings and subjectivity appear to be the most ignored sources of inspiration for giving and evaluating good reasons when making decisions. We know emotional judgments can become flawed, as convincingly studied by Kahneman (2011), due to overconfidence, self-deception, framing, priming and halo effects. Nevertheless, the cross-case analysis performed here shows how expressive rationality can also contribute positively to decision-making, as when you 'listen to your heart' when making a decision. Today, we know less about this positive contribution than about the negative side, but they both exist (Greenspan 2004; Kirman *et al.* 2010; Li *et al.* 2014; Scherer 2011). The study of emotions and decision-making is important. For instance, ten Bos and Willmott (2001: 770) argue that both emotion and reason is needed for moral judgment. Haidt (2001: 823) makes a similar argument when he claims that moral emotions better explain moral action than does moral reasoning. Haidt (2001: 825) argues: 'people are often motivated to help others and that the mechanisms involved in this helping are primarily affective'. Haidt (2001) and Sedlacek (2011) both refer to a classical debate in which Adam Smith and Hume participated, both of whom considered moral sentiments to be of greatest importance and were also supportive of moral reasoning. The current study finds similar patterns. It suggests a research agenda to study these positive influences in more depth and based on qualitative research designs (for a recent example, see Calabretta *et al.* 2016). A multiple case study, using argumentation analysis as a lens, can only be a first step in better understanding the richness of human rationality. As expressive rationality strongly interacts with our values, by helping us to assess the social and personal relevance of effects we realize, these interactions could be studied in more detail as well. Even though our subjectivity is quite receptive for social evaluations, it is also quite formative in creating, evaluating and recreating our private lives, our social lives, our bureaucracies, our technologies and our social constructions of rationality.

References

Bergset, L. (2015) The rationality and irrationality of financing green start-ups. *Administrative Sciences*, 5(4), 260–85.

Boltanski, L. and Thevenot, L. (2006) *On Justification: Economies of Worth*. Princeton, NJ: Princeton University Press.

Bos, R. ten and Willmott, H. (2001) Towards a post-dualistic business ethics: Interweaving reason and emotion in working life. *Journal of Management Studies*, 38(6), 769–93.

Bouwmeester, O. (2010) *Economic Advice and Rhetoric: Why Do Consultants Perform Better Than Academic Advisers?* Cheltenham: Edward Elgar.

Bouwmeester, O. (2013) Field dependency of argumentation rationality in decision-making debates. *Journal of Management Inquiry*, 22(4), 415–33.

Boyd, R. and Richerson, P. J. (2001) Norms and bounded rationality, in Gigerenzer, G. and Selten, R. (eds), *Bounded Rationality: The Adaptive Toolbox*. Cambridge, MA: MIT Press, pp. 281–96.

Brockriede, W. and Ehninger, D. (1960) Toulmin on argument: An interpretation and application. *Quarterly Journal of Speech*, 46(1), 44–53.

Cabantous, L., Gond, J. P. and Johnson-Cramer, M. (2010) Decision theory as practice: Crafting rationality in organizations. *Organization Studies*, 31(11), 1531–66.

Calabretta, G., Gemser, G. and Wijnberg, N. M. (2016) The interplay between intuition and rationality in strategic decision making: A paradox perspective. *Organization Studies*. DOI: 10.1177/0170840616655483.

Colic-Peisker, V. (2016) Ideology and utopia: Historic crisis of economic rationality and the role of public sociology. *Journal of Sociology.* DOI: 10.1177/1440783316630114.

Corvellec, H. (2007) Arguing for a license to operate: The case of the Swedish wind power industry. *Corporate Communications: An International Journal*, 12(2), 129–44.

Davidson, D. (2004) *Problems of Rationality.* Vol. 4. Oxford: Oxford University Press.

Diesing, P. (1976) *Reason in Society: Five Types of Decisions and Their Social Conditions.* Westport, CT: Greenwood Press.

Eisenhardt, K. M. and Zbaracki, M. J. (1992) Strategic decision making. *Strategic Management Journal*, 13(S2), 17–37.

Elbanna, S. (2006) Strategic decision-making: Process perspectives. *International Journal of Management Reviews*, 8(1), 1–20.

Elbanna, S. and Child, J. (2007) Influences on strategic decision effectiveness: Development and test of an integrative model. *Strategic Management Journal*, 28(4), 431–53.

Elster, J. (2009) *Reason and Rationality.* Princeton, NJ: Princeton University Press.

Engelen, B. (2006) Solving the paradox: The expressive rationality of the decision to vote. *Rationality and Society*, 18(4), 419–41.

Esposito, E. (2011) Originality through imitation: The rationality of fashion. *Organization Studies*, 32(5), 603–13.

Fessler, D. M. T. (2001) Emotions and cost-benefit assessment, in Gigerenzer, G. and Selten, R. (eds), *Bounded Rationality: The Adaptive Toolbox.* Cambridge, MA: MIT Press, pp. 191–214.

Fischer, F. and Forester, J. (eds) (1993) *The Argumentative Turn in Policy Analysis and Planning.* Durham, NC: Duke University Press.

Fisher, P. and Freshwater, D. (2014) Towards compassionate care through aesthetic rationality. *Scandinavian Journal of Caring Sciences*, 28(4), 767–74.

Gaut, B. (2012) Creativity and rationality. *The Journal of Aesthetics and Art Criticism*, 70(3), 259–70.

Gigerenzer, G. (2010) Moral satisficing: Rethinking moral behavior as bounded rationality. *Topics in Cognitive Science*, 2(3), 528–54.

Gigerenzer, G. and Selten, R. (eds) (2001a) *Bounded Rationality: The Adaptive Toolbox.* Cambridge, MA: MIT Press.

Gigerenzer, G. and Selten, R. (2001b) Rethinking rationality, in Gigerenzer, G. and Selten, R. (eds), *Bounded Rationality: The Adaptive Toolbox.* Cambridge, MA: MIT Press, pp. 1–12.

Gigerenzer, G. and Gaissmaier, W. (2011) Heuristic decision making. *Annual Review of Psychology*, 62, 451–82.

Gigerenzer, G. and Sturm, T. (2012) How (far) can rationality be naturalized? *Synthese*, 187(1), 243–68.

Green Jr, S. E. (2004) A rhetorical theory of diffusion. *The Academy of Management Review*, 29(4), 653–69.

Greenspan, P. (2004) Practical reasoning and emotion, in Mele, A. R. and Rawling, P. (eds), *The Oxford Handbook of Rationality.* New York: Oxford University Press, pp. 206–21.

Gross, M. A., Hogler, R. and Henle, C. A. (2013) Process, people, and conflict management in organizations: A viewpoint based on Weber's formal and substantive rationality. *International Journal of Conflict Management*, 24(1), 90–103.

Habermas, J. (1988) *Theorie des Kommunikativen Handelns, Band 1, 2.* Frankfurt: Suhrkamp.

Haidt, J. (2001) The emotional dog and its rational tail: A social intuitionist approach to moral judgment. *Psychological Review*, 108(4), 814–34.

Hargreaves Heap, S. (2001) Expressive rationality: Is self-worth just another kind of preference?, in Mäki, U. (ed), *The Economic World View: Studies in the Ontology of Economics*. Cambridge: Cambridge University Press, pp. 98–113.

Harrison, E. F. (1993) Interdisciplinary models of decision making. *Management Decision*, 31(8), 27–33.

Hegel, G. F. W. (1986) *Grundlinien der Philosophie des Rechts*. Frankfurt: Suhrkamp.

Henderson, D. (2010) Explanation and rationality naturalized. *Philosophy of the Social Sciences*, 40(1), 30–58.

Houwelingen, G. van and Bouwmeester, O. (2008) Situationele rationaliteit in publieke besluitvorming. *Filosofie in Bedrijf*, 18(2), 26–40.

Kahneman, D. (2011) *Thinking, Fast and Slow*. New York: FSG.

Kant, I. (1990) *Kritik der Praktischen Vernunft*. Hamburg: Felix Meiner.

Kim, N. (2016) Beyond rationality: The role of anger and information in deliberation. *Communication Research*, 43(1), 3–24.

Kirman, A., Livet, P. and Teschl, M. (2010) Rationality and emotions. *Philosophical Transactions of the Royal Society of London B: Biological Sciences*, 365(1538), 215–19.

Klamer, A. (1987) As if economists and their subjects were rational, in Nelson, J. S., Megill, A. and McCloskey, D. (eds), *The Rhetoric of the Human Sciences*. Madison, WI: The University of Wisconsin Press, pp. 163–83.

Klein, G. (2001) The fiction of optimization, in Gigerenzer, G. and Selten, R. (eds), *Bounded Rationality: The Adaptive Toolbox*. Cambridge, MA: MIT Press, pp. 103–14.

Li, Y., Ashkanasy, N. M. and Ahlstrom, D. (2014) The rationality of emotions: A hybrid process model of decision-making under uncertainty. *Asia Pacific Journal of Management*, 31(1), 293–308.

McCloskey, D. N. (2016) Max U versus Humanomics: A critique of neo-institutionalism. *Journal of Institutional Economics*, 12(01), 1–27.

MacIntyre, A. C. (1988) *Whose Justice? Which Rationality?* London: Duckworth.

Majone, G. (1992) *Evidence, Argument and Persuasion in the Policy Process*. New Haven, CT: Yale University Press.

March, J. G. and Simon, H. A. (1958) *Organizations*. New York: John Wiley.

Mason, R. O. (1969) A dialectical approach to strategic planning. *Management Science*, 15(8), B403–14.

Mellers, B. A., Erev, I., Fessler, D. M., Hemelrijk, C. K., Hertwig, R., Laland, K. N., Scherer, K. R., Seeley, T. D., Selten, R. and Tetlock, P. E. (2001) Effects of emotions and social processes on bounded rationality, in Gigerenzer, G. and Selten, R. (eds), *Bounded Rationality: The Adaptive Toolbox*. Cambridge, MA: MIT Press, pp. 263–79.

Mueller, G. C., Mone, M. A. and Barker, V. L. (2007) Formal strategic analyses and organizational performance: Decomposing the rational model. *Organization Studies*, 28(6), 853–83.

Peacock, A. (1992) The credibility of economic advice to government. *The Economic Journal*, 102(414), 1213–22.

Racko, G. (2011) On the normative consequences of economic rationality: A case study of a Swedish economics school in Latvia. *European Sociological Review*, 27(6), 772–89.

Rieke, R. D. and Sillars, M. O. (2001) *Argumentation and Critical Decision Making*. New York: Longman.

Sandberg, J. and Tsoukas, H. (2011) Grasping the logic of practice: Theorizing through practical rationality. *Academy of Management Review*, 36(2), 338–60.

Scherer, K. R. (2011) On the rationality of emotions: Or, when are emotions rational? *Social Science Information*, 50(3–4), 330–50.

Schiller, F. (1983) *Über die Ästhetische Erziehung des Menschen: In einer Reihe von Briefen*. Stuttgart: Reclam.

Schipper, F. (1996) Rationality and the philosophy of organization. *Organization*, 3(2), 267–89.

Sedlacek, T. (2011) *Economics of Good and Evil: The Quest for Economic Meaning from Gilgamesh to Wall Street*. Oxford: Oxford University Press.

Sen, A. K. (1977) Rational fools: A critique of the behavioral foundations of economic theory. *Philosophy & Public Affairs*, 6(4), 317–44.

Smith, A. (1982) *The Theory of Moral Sentiments*. Indianapolis, IN: Liberty Classics.

Tinbergen, J. (1956) *Economic Policy: Principles and Design*. Amsterdam: Noord Hollandsche Uitgeversmaatschappij.

Toulmin, S. E. (1994) *The Uses of Argument*. Cambridge: Cambridge University Press.

Townley, B. (1999) Practical reason and performance appraisal. *Journal of Management Studies*, 36(3), 287–306.

Townley, B. (2002) The role of competing rationalities in institutional change. *Academy of Management Journal*, 45(1), 163–79.

Townley, B. (2008) *Reason's Neglect: Rationality and Organizing*. Oxford: Oxford University Press.

Weber, M. (1972) *Wirtschaft und Gesellschaft: Grundriss der Verstehenden Soziologie*. 5th ed. Tubingen, Germany: JCB Mohr (Paul Siebeck).

Weirich, P. (2004) Economic rationality, in Mele, A. R. and Rawling, P. (eds), *The Oxford Handbook of Rationality*. Oxford: Oxford University Press, pp. 380–98.

Werder, A. von (1999) Argumentation rationality of management decisions. *Organization Science*, 10(5), 672–90.

7 Implications for practice
How to spot irrationalities

Introducing rationality evaluation

Most studies on rational decision-making start with the requirement of having good reason or arguments for a decision. Still, they often proceed quite theoretical or experimental without analysing such good reasons as given in a real-life context (Davidson 2004; Elster 2009; Kahneman 2011; MacIntyre 1988; Weber 1972). Also, studies on bounded rationality focus on heuristics, programmes or routines that improve decisions, without much attention given to the content of the reasons to act on (March and Simon 1958; Gigerenzer 2008; Gigerenzer and Selten 2001). Only a few studies analyse the given arguments to prepare complex decisions in practice (cf. Bouwmeester 2013; Mason 1969; von Werder 1999). Still, for better understanding practical decision-making, the study of decision-making debates seems a promising avenue. That so little studies have tried this research approach remains mysterious, especially given the definition of rationality as having good reasons to act on (Davidson 2004: 169; Elbanna 2006: 3; Elbanna and Child 2007: 433; Elster 2009: 2; Engelen 2006: 427; Gigerenzer and Sturm 2012: 243–5; Green 2004: 655; Henderson 2010: 32).

When consultants prepare actionable advice, they sort the relevant arguments supporting a decision in the most logical way. Doing so is applying what many consultants call the pyramid principle (Minto 1995, 1998). The pyramid is helpful in better grouping related pro arguments and checking their relation to the conclusion. The tool helps to evaluate whether the arguments give sufficient reasons to act on. It is limited though by only focusing on pro arguments, which seems most important for preparing a decision. Still, it is only one key element that can be identified in decision support.

Von Werder (1999) has developed a richer view on decision support. He adds balance as a criterion for argumentation rationality, as rational decisions need to pay attention to counterarguments as well. It prevents the bias of one-sidedness, which, if ignored, could create serious problems. He argues that at least four arguments need to be counterarguments. This is an important improvement compared to Minto's pyramid principle as it also allows a consultant or manager to argue as a devil's advocate (Mason 1969; Saxton 1995). However, compared to decision-making in practice, the requirement of four counterarguments is still insufficient. The six decision-making debates studied here have counterarguments that range from 20%

to almost 50% of all used arguments, and in absolute numbers they range from ten rebuttals in the Gurkha debate to 24 in the Dutch integration debate. As a consequence, these rebuttals tell almost half of the story of complex decision-making. The question to be answered is how these rebuttals contribute to decision rationality. That is by regarding what avenues to avoid, but also as a way to articulate the conditions that need to be satisfied, and how to develop policies for executing a decision successfully. These aspects of fine tuning (addressing conditions and developing implementation policies) point at two more key elements of decision preparation, not discussed by Minto or von Werder. On top of that, all studied decisions appear to have an implied purpose, which depends on what decision makers see as the problem that has to be solved, or as the opportunity that can be explored.

Next to overlooking these key elements in preparing and supporting a decision, theoretical and experimental studies on rationality hardly differentiate between fields of reasoning as addressed by Boltanski and Thevenot (2006), Bouwmeester (2013), Diesing (1976), Habermas (1988) or Toulmin (1994). Standards of rationality differ among such fields. Building on Bouwmeester (2013), the analysis of the six discussed debates differentiates good reasons for action along three fields. First, decisions that relate to our subjectivity – these demand expressive rationality by asking how the decision is relevant to me. Second, decisions being socially oriented – these demand social rationality and ask how the decision is relevant to us. Third, decisions aiming at realizing effects – these apply cause–effect or means–end argumentation, and demand instrumental rationality to influence the objective or material world as we experience it outside us.

Within each of these three rationality fields we can identify irrationalities. Means–end inconsistencies related to instrumental rationality are, for instance, discussed in Majone (1992), Mason (1969) or Tinbergen (1956). MacIntyre (1988) and Weber (1972) discuss oppositions and tensions within social rationality. Tensions within expressive rationality (Engelen 2006; Scherer 2011) are the least discussed, but they stem from a lack of authenticity, self-deception and misunderstanding one's own interests, wishes and motives (Davidson 2004; Habermas 1988). Thus, the three rationalities all show internal rationality tensions, undermining rationality of the decisions by such flaws. However, this is not the entire story about irrationalities. The six studied debates also illustrate cross-rationality tensions. For instance, a change from winter to summertime can be instrumental rational as it realizes better use of daylight which increases efficiency. However, it is irrational from an expressive point of view: most people and farm animals have difficulties in adapting their rhythms, and many do not like the change. Until now, studies have not looked at such cross-rationality evaluations, and at how decision makers and stakeholders can handle these tensions.

This chapter first inductively identifies five key elements that contribute to rational decision preparation, like giving the decision a purpose, and articulating the pros and cons of a decision, and, in addition, elaborating on the conditions to make the decision successful and designing policies to improve decision execution. While the first three elements discuss more the 'why' questions behind a decision based on expressive- and social-rational grounds, the last two focus more on the 'how' questions by using an instrumental-rational perspective. Second, the chapter discusses irrationalities. These are three internal irrationalities belonging to each of the three rationalities themselves due to emotional misfit, value conflict and means-end inconsistencies, and six rather under-explored irrationalities identified by cross-rationality assessments. Each irrationality section will start with the discussion of a question that helps to diagnose one of the nine irrationalities. With these diagnostic questions the chapter seeks to help policymakers, managers and consultants with examining their complex decision-making in practice.

From key arguments to key elements that contribute to decision rationality

An overview of the main arguments in the six studied debates indicates what key elements have helped to prepare these decisions. These key elements are relevant for politicians, policy analysts, managers, consultants or interested stakeholders alike, as they do not want to miss a key part in their preparation. They all want a decision without having to regret the outcome and they want to be able to explain to each other that they have sufficient reasons for doing what needs to be done. Decision makers want to be able to explain to those affected by the decisions why this decision is feasible, legitimate or beneficial, and to whom. Critical stakeholders can examine these elements as well. The five key elements visible in the debates on major decisions are the objectives of these decisions, the arguments pro, the arguments con, the conditions that need to be fulfilled and the policies that help to manage negative effects or to better realize the intended effects. Consultants with an interest in guiding decision makers are well advised to consider all of these elements.

To assess the degree of rationality for the key elements that provide the main reasons for an intended decision, stakeholders and decision makers can ask five questions, as listed in Table 7.1. These questions help to evaluate, per key element, if or how the intended (change) action should be executed.

The questions in Table 7.1 are guiding in discussing the rationality of the key elements of decision preparation. They help discuss the strength of the main arguments supporting strategic decision-making in each of the six cases as summarized in Table 7.2. The questions seek to include the three rationality perspectives where their presence is most demanded. Taking into account stakeholder interests enables the assessment of particularly expressive and social rationality from different stakeholder perspectives. The questions help preparing for the right decisions as manager, policymaker or adviser and they also help critical stakeholders to assess policy decisions that affect them.

There is variety in the types of rationality related to the key elements. For goals, supporting motives (pro) and countermotives (con), the good reasons for or against action are mainly versions of expressive and social rationality. Expressive rationality motivates by referring to personal interests, desires, wishes, ambitions, intuitions, etc. Social rationality motivates by reference to shared values, principles, norms, laws, shared majority views, etc. Conditions for the successful execution of

Table 7.1 Checklist for questioning the rationality of strategic decisions

Key elements in argumentation	Questions to assess the rationality of intended strategic decisions
Purpose/intended effects (ER/SR)	• Does the decision have an overarching purpose that is expressive or social rational for relevant stakeholders because they want, like or value it as important?
Pro: advantages, motives, forces, means–end arguments (ER/SR/IR)	• Which good reasons for action motivate the decision from the perspective of relevant stakeholders, given what they consider expressive, social and instrumental rational?
Con: disadvantages, countermotives, bad effects (ER/SR/IR)	• Which good reasons motivate relevant stakeholders to fight execution of the decision given the expressive, social and instrumental rationality behind the counterarguments?
Necessary or (un)fulfilled conditions (IR + SR/ER)	• Which necessary conditions for executing the decision are or can be fulfilled, and what necessary conditions cannot, thus undermining instrumental rationality of the decision?
Required or alternative policies or strategies (IR)	• How can alternative policies help to better reach intended effects, or supportive policies to better manage relevant conditions, thus strengthening a decision's instrumental rationality?

Note: IR: instrumental rationality; SR: social rationality; ER: expressive rationality.

the decision and supporting policies have predominantly an instrumental logic. They motivate by pointing out how a goal can be achieved more effectively, efficiently or how it becomes more feasible. Still, conditions can in themselves be of an expressive or social nature, for instance, when enthusiasm is a fulfilled condition that enables or even partly causes action, or when a law prohibits certain behaviour and thus also works as a countercause.

Table 7.2 summarizes in every row one key element, indicating for each debate the kind of arguments used in preparing the intended decisions. In every column, all key elements are summarized for every case, based on the main arguments in that debate.

Table 7.2 shows that the conclusions in each debate were only partly in line with the original intentions. Santa Claus, a controversial statue designed by McCarthy, was intended as public art for a shopping area in Rotterdam. The conclusion was to first put the statue in a museum, due to public resistance. The intended veil ban, prohibiting the niqab in certain public areas in the UK, got rejected. The idea of stricter integration policies in the Netherlands was gradually implemented, in spite of strong controversy. The intended decision to partially extend pension rights of Gurkhas got rejected; public opinion was in favour of a full rights extension, and forced the government to adapt policies. Heathrow's extension got a positive decision for further preparation, but only if growth would be sufficiently green,

Table 7.2 Key arguments for decision preparation or advice

Debated decision:	Santa Claus public?	Veil ban?	Stricter integration policies?	Gurkha rights extension?	Heathrow's extension?	Flex-work implementation?
Debate's conclusion:	Yes, but later	No	Yes	Full, not partial	Yes, if green	Yes, only for some
Implied purpose:	Criticizing overconsumption	Reducing women's repression/ inequality	Improve integration	Create more equality and fairness	Increase airport capacity	Better implement flex work
Pros: Advantages, motives, forces, means–end arguments	Santa designed for shopping district City support between 2000 and 2002 New city support around 2007 (due to growing support from general audience, shopkeepers)	Removes a means of women's suppression Removes a barrier to interaction Less separation Better integration Better identification Common sense should guide how we dress	There are too many social problems with immigrants (no political integration, radical Islam, underperformance in Islamic schools, etc.)	Gurkhas are loyal Gurkhas deserve full rights; not giving them this is treacherous Equal rights for Gurkhas is fair British care for the Gurkhas Gurkhas are no average immigrants Manageable costs	Expansion is vital for UK economy Heathrow works at max capacity: minor incidents have big effects London transport infrastructure needs updating	Facilitates workers' autonomy Benefits employees, companies, society and flex-work supporters (better work–life balance, cost saving, less traffic, etc.)

(Continued)

Table 7.2 (continued)

Debated decision:	Santa Claus public?	Veil ban?	Stricter integration policies?	Gurkha rights extension?	Heathrow's extension?	Flex-work implementation?
Cons: Disadvantages, counter-motives, unpleasant, immoral, bad effects	Strong resistance around 2003 due to obscenity, emptiness (Christian parties, liberals, local parties, general audience, art critics)	Loss of religious expression, which should be allowed No freedom of expression in choosing clothes, as should be allowed Legal claims	New Dutch attitude is problematic for immigrants (intolerant, crude, stereotyping, etc.) New policies ignore immigrants have achieved a lot	Nepal might veto recruitment by UK Gurkhas are mercenaries, not normal citizens	Local resistance Noise levels too high Environmental organizations resist Broad critical political coalition	Unpleasant effects for employees, companies, society (more burnout, distractions, lower productivity, more permanent stress, etc.)
Conditions: Necessary or (un)fulfilled	Implied unfulfilled condition: temporary resistance between 2003 and 2007	It is not obligatory to wear a face veil There are veil-ban precedents	Multicultural policies were insufficient (homosexual/women's repression, crime, intolerance, etc.)	Equal rights demand extra financial means Gurkhas knew what they signed up for	Extension causes environmental damage (beyond standards) Consultation process was flawed	Many unfulfilled conditions (tailored designs, coaching, management by objectives, etc.)
Policies for decision execution: Alternative and/or additional	Temporary exposition at museum court	Discuss religious differences more openly instead of banning the face veil	New policies, laws, regulations needed (demanding, for tolerance, etc.) Open debate is also a way to defend liberal values, etc.	Partial or full extension of pension and settlement rights	Good alternatives like more high-speed rail, better taxation, etc.	Additional policies needed for managing negative side effects

which was a compromise. Flex work was implemented more and more in the Netherlands, but was also more and more debated. During the debate, the conclusion developed that it is no one-size-fits-all solution, in spite of the attractiveness of the possible savings on office space. It is good for some companies but not for all, and good for some workers but not for all.

Constructing decision rationality by purpose or intended effects

Purpose can appeal to the values or interests of decision makers and stakeholders, and, as such, provide good reasons to act on. Objectives that are expressive rational may receive sympathy from people on personal grounds and those that are social rational may receive approval based on shared values or generally accepted principles. When assessing the rationality of the purpose behind an intended decision, decision makers and their advisers can use the first question from Table 7.2: *does the decision have an overarching purpose that is expressive or social rational for relevant stakeholders because they want, like or value it as important?*

We get positive and negative answers in the six debates, as visible in Table 7.2. The main stakeholders mostly have sympathy for the overall purpose behind the intended decisions, but in some debates this purpose does not represent the entire picture of what is relevant. Criticizing overconsumption with Santa Claus is sympathetic to most stakeholders; the butt plug as a means to criticize such impulses, much less. In the veil-ban debate, the objectives of integration and supporting equality between man and women are sympathetic, but in conflict with the value of giving room for the religious habits and religious expression of some Muslim women. Most stakeholders consider room for religious expression more important than the initial social-rational purpose behind the veil ban. The purpose of better integration is widely shared among Dutch politicians and citizens in the Netherlands. Discussion is mainly about the means. In the Gurkha debate, all stakeholders applaud the purpose of extending pension and settlement rights. However, many dislike the fact that it is meant to be a half-hearted, partial rights extension. That is not fair in comparison with other Commonwealth veterans, a judgment supported by strong feelings of sympathy towards Gurkhas.

The two instrumental debates have an implied purpose, as the suggested means only suit specific objectives: a greater Heathrow aims at economic growth and better airport facilities to enable more person and cargo flights, which is sympathetic to most stakeholders. Flex work as a means facilitates cost saving, but also more professional autonomy, which is a sympathetic purpose both on expressive- and social-rational grounds. However, in the flex-work debate, workers were the first who could not identify with the overall purpose that calls for more autonomy, as some workers felt they needed managerial guidance and more workplace stability. The purpose of Heathrow's extension is contested likewise, due to green values that become compromised.

The question on purpose can thus help decision makers and their advisers to evaluate the intended decisions by identifying stakeholders that might not applaud the implied expressive or social rationality behind their purpose. Thus, we need to ask if they resonate well with the expressive- and social-rational sympathies of the relevant stakeholders; to some extent they do in the cases, to some extent they ignore too much. Overall, purpose adds rationality to our decisions.

Arguments pro: reasons for action that strongly appeal to expressive or social rationality

Arguments pro are the most obvious, explicit and direct support for a decision. Pro arguments for a decision can be expressive or social rational when suggesting why the decision is a good one. Instrumental support is more indirect by suggesting how to execute the decision effectively and efficiently, given an already accepted social- or expressive-rational purpose. When assessing the rationality of pro arguments, decision makers need to ask the second question from Table 7.2: *which good reasons for action motivate the decision from the perspective of relevant stakeholders, given what they consider expressive, social and instrumental rational?*

The third row in Table 7.2 shows that all debates present pro arguments that can convince many relevant stakeholders, but never all of them; otherwise there would be no debate. Expressive-rational pro arguments stem, for instance, from the people who like Santa Claus. Still, many groups do not like the sculpture, so the decision needs to be changed fundamentally. A pro argument for the veil ban is to let our common sense rule and not an import culture, because the niqab is dysfunctional in having contact with others, in being open and in letting people recognize you. Also, other values of integration, interaction, identification and sexual equality are considered convincing, but less than the expressive-rational counterarguments referring to the wish for freedom of expression, also resulting in a change of plans: no veil ban. Public opinion in the Gurkha debate argues that the government should apply the fairness principle more generously. Based on social-rational logics, Gurkha veterans deserve the same rights as other Commonwealth soldiers. The integration debate has social- and expressive-rational pro arguments that argue for better integration. They refer to the many and widely acknowledged social problems with immigrants that need to be managed. Also, stakeholders involved in multicultural policies acknowledge the problems like higher criminality, unemployment, low school performance, etc.

The Heathrow debate is more instrumental in its main pro arguments, as growth is a means to vitalize the economy, for improving London's infrastructure and for preventing any small planning problems from causing major knock-on effects. The need to do so is based on economic demands that are widely acknowledged. Still, growth should not hurt others, which is the reason why the debate began. The main arguments for flex work are only partly instrumental by referring to cost savings in order to convince companies. To convince workers and society, the main arguments pro are expressive and social rational. They refer to what many workers and society prefer: a better work–life balance and less traffic. During the start of the debate, the pro arguments were quite convincing; that is, until people gained more experience with the downsides of flex work.

The cases indicate that decision makers have overlooked stakeholder groups, when choosing their pro arguments. Or they have misunderstood the values and interests most important to them. Santa Claus raised resistance, the veil ban got blocked and Gurkha policies got changed, to name the most controversial cases. Decision makers and their advisers can try to prevent the illustrated turnarounds of their policies by evaluating beforehand how stakeholders might respond to their pro arguments. The strongest pro arguments are social and expressive rational, but stakeholder differentiation related to them is huge as well. As a consequence, arguments that convince one group may not convince another. Mapping stakeholder interests related to the different types of pro arguments helps to improve the overall rationality of a decision.

Arguments con mostly present expressive- and social-rational grounds to adjust a decision

When preparing a decision, arguments con show decision makers where resistance might stem from. Arguments against a decision are mainly expressive or social rational. When assessing the rationality of con arguments, decision makers and their advisers need to ask the third question from Table 7.2: *which good reasons motivate relevant stakeholders to fight execution of the decision given the expressive, social and instrumental rationality behind the counterarguments?* The question mirrors the second one and helps to explain the force, time and locus of the resistance.

In all debates we see resistance, as indicated in the fourth row of Table 7.2. The Santa Claus and veil-ban debate both illustrate expressive-rational counter-arguments against the intended decision. In the Santa Claus debate, resistance and aversion ease out over the years, only causing a temporary adjustment of the decision: the exhibition of Santa Claus in a museum court for three years. In the veil-ban debate, arguments criticizing the implied lack of freedom of religious expression are able to fully reverse the intended decision of a ban. In the integration debate, the rude, intolerant and preoccupied Dutch attitude is criticized on social-rational grounds as unacceptable, without making a real difference. Decision makers in the Gurkha debate initially oppose the final conclusion of a full rights extension by referring to the interests of the Nepalese government as a stakeholder that might vote against full pension and settlement rights. Other stakeholders express fear for Gurkhas being mercenaries. However, these counterarguments appear to have little influence compared to the arguments of the pro camp.

The instrumental debates refer to unintended effects like climate change and high noise levels related to Heathrow. Critical local, environmental and political interest groups provide social-rational counterargumentation against Heathrow's extension. The unintended effects caused by flex work, such as more burnout, distractions, lower productivity and more permanent stress, negatively affect personal pre-ferences and shared social-rational values, making them something we really want to avoid. Even though pro argumentation in the two debates is instrumental by referring to environmental and social effects, the main force behind the counter-arguments is expressive and social rational – they motivate decision makers to adjust their decisions.

To conclude, resistance is strong and local (Christian parties) but temporal in the Santa Claus debate, and strong and local (Muslims, fewer autonomous workers) in the veil-ban and flex-work debates. Resistance is strong and more general (shared public opinion) in the Gurkha debate and general but more incremental in the integration and Heathrow debates. Local resistance uses more expressive-rational counterarguments, whereas the more generally shared resistance stems from widely shared social-rational counterarguments. Decision makers and their advisers can improve decision preparation by mapping the kind of resistance (local or general, temporal, incremental or more fundamental) and by analysing in what kind of rationality potential stakeholder resistance is grounded.

Necessary conditions that need to be fulfilled for executing decisions

There is hardly any decision we make that does not require conditions to be fulfilled. You can decide to eat easily, but it only works under the condition that you have access to food. However, decision makers often overlook necessary conditions (Argyris 1996; Majone 1992) due to the fact that we are bounded in our rationality. Unfulfilled conditions have the power to obstruct decision execution. Thus, decision makers must spot them in advance. Necessary conditions always relate to instrumental rationality, also if the condition is legal, social, political, aesthetic, etc. Their absence causes trouble, whereas their fulfilment is a means of enabling execution of the decision. When assessing the fulfilment of conditions in support of a decision, those who are involved need to ask the fourth question from Table 7.2: *which necessary conditions for executing the decision are or can be fulfilled, and what necessary conditions cannot, thus undermining instrumental rationality of the decision?*

In all debates, we see arguments pointing at fulfilled and unfulfilled conditions, as summarized on the fifth row in Table 7.2. The Santa Claus debate illustrates how decision makers have overlooked resistance. Sufficient support was an unfulfilled condition causing much trouble. The main arguments in the veil-ban debate point at two fulfilled conditions for the ban: there is no (religious) obligation to wear a face veil and there are legal precedents of a veil ban in other countries. However, acceptance was the unfulfilled condition. The Dutch integration debate refers in its main arguments to multicultural policies that have been ineffective in realizing cultural integration. They were, thus, insufficient as a condition for integration. In the Gurkha debate, politicians argue that one condition for a partial rights extension is fulfilled: the Gurkha veterans knew their contract when they signed it, which makes it fair policy. In addition, the financial means of the government were insufficient, which appears as an unfulfilled condition for a full rights extension. Both arguments were rebutted.

In the Heathrow debate, environmentalists argued that the legal conditions would be violated by Heathrow's extension, and also by ignoring consultation procedures. Both are unfulfilled conditions of social-rational signature. The flex-work debate refers to unfulfilled conditions on all three levels of rationality. From an instrumental perspective, workplace facilities are often insufficient: insufficient workplaces for accommodating peaks, too few concentration rooms, the wrong management style applied, etc. From a social-rational perspective, labour regulations were not ready for supporting employee health sufficiently. From an expressive-rational perspective, many workers lacked the required skills and autonomy to become happy flex workers.

Summing up, the unfulfilled conditions make very strong arguments for not executing a policy. This is the case in the Santa Claus and veil-ban debates due to unexpected strong resistance, and is tried in the Gurkha debate to fight a full rights extension based on budget restrictions. Other policies needed to be adapted due to unfulfilled conditions: multicultural policies needed to become stricter, Heathrow's growth needed to become greener and in the flex-work debate the concept needed to be tailored. It is only in the Gurkha-rights debate that the opposite is visible. Arguments about insufficient financial means are rebutted as treacherous, and a full rights extension is granted. Decision makers could have improved decision preparation by better mapping the necessary conditions for executing the decision, and assessing if conditions could be fulfilled. Together with their advisers, they could improve the instrumental rationality of their decisions.

Policies for better realizing intended effects

Sometimes decisions or policies need to be adapted when not all necessary conditions can be fulfilled. There are also situations in which relevant stakeholders suggest there are more effective ways to reach the intended purpose, or implement a decision. The debates illustrate a variety of additional and alternative policies. The main focus of such policies is instrumental, by improving on how a decision's purpose can be realized more effectively or with different means. When assessing the instrumental rationality of a decision's implementation policies, decision makers need to ask the last question from Table 7.2: *how can alternative policies help to better reach intended effects, or supportive policies to better manage relevant conditions, thus strengthening a decision's instrumental rationality?*

The last row of Table 7.2 indicates how the Santa Claus policies had to be adapted temporarily, due to massive resistance. Artistic expression became more effective by not exhibiting Santa Claus in public, but in a museum for the first three years. The city, together with other important stakeholders, decided for this alternative policy as a response to the unexpected condition of resistance. In the face-veil debate, an alternative for banning the veil is the suggestion to discuss religious preferences more publicly. Open debate is considered a more positive and effective approach for realizing integration than enforcement by law. A similar policy of open debate is suggested in the Dutch integration debate, as an alternative for stricter integration policies, including confrontation by naming the problems and by openly defending liberal values. In the Gurkha debate, public opinion suggests full rights extension as an alternative for the partial rights extension as suggested by the government.

In the Heathrow debate, alternative policy suggestions are high-speed rail and more efficient taxation, to better reconcile the interests of economic growth and protection of the environment. They are not executed but still have an influence by pushing Heathrow's extension more towards green growth. Additional policies for managing the negative side effects are also demanded in the flex-work debate. Lower-level arguments suggest, for instance, a server shutdown in the evening to prevent employees from working at night.

The discussed policy changes all help to increase instrumental rationality by seeking a better way to reach the intended effects. Changes and additions are often advised and implemented. Alternative policies mainly fuel the debate and indirectly provide decision makers and their advisers with suggestions to improve the initial strategy.

The role of third parties in improving key elements that support a decision

In all debates, we see a dialogue between decision makers and stakeholders about the decision, sometimes including advisers and experts that act as third parties. This is often the case when aspects of the implementation of the decision are complex or demand specialist knowledge. Of the six cases, the flex-work debate is the most influenced by advisers, as they invented the flex-work concept. The debate is quite outspoken regarding the management of conditions and negative effects, by focusing strongly on how-questions during implementation. Advisers in the debate urge decision makers to reflect on the necessary approaches that could make flex work more successful, like management by objectives, sufficient coaching and more trust in employees, next to managing the more physical conditions like flex offices and good information technology infrastructure. The Dutch integration debate is second in being influenced by experts like consultants, researchers and opinion leaders, as this debate is also quite complex and long term. Heathrow's extension also comprises the active involvement of many parties including experts, and it also discusses the implementation question. The other debates are more between decision makers in direct contact with stakeholders: Rotterdam deciding on Santa Claus and the UK government deciding on the veil ban. These are complex decisions given the conflicting stakeholder interests, but their technical implementation is not so complex. This also applies to the Gurkha debate, where not consultants or experts, but a public movement acts as third party, to defend Gurkha interests.

Irrationality checks on main policy arguments

The key elements of decision support found in the six debates are: first, decision purpose, based on ambitions, ideals or a defined problem in need of a solution; second, the arguments pro; third, the counterarguments; fourth, the necessary conditions; and fifth, the implementation policies. These key elements all relate to the conclusion directly. However, the main arguments can be rebutted or supported themselves by lower-level arguments that relate to the conclusion only indirectly via the main arguments. The lower-level rebuttals can criticize an expressive-rational argument based on a personal wish as being illegitimate on social-rational grounds, thus framing the wish as irrational. Or the wish can be criticized as impractical, making it irrational on instrumental grounds.

The main arguments supporting and opposing a decision are often expressive and social rational. Instrumental argumentation is more dominant in the discussion of conditions and alternative policies that suggest new or additional means to reach the intended ends. This does not mean that we like all means only because they help to realize our ends. And we do not like all intended ends if we discover the means to realize them can be questioned. The means that are rational from an instrumental perspective can be evaluated as irrational (immoral, emotionally upsetting) from a social or expressive perspective, while policy objectives with strong expressive or social rationality can be deemed irrational (impractical, utopian) from an instrumental perspective. The six debates illustrate these cross-rationality evaluations with many examples. Acting on these irrationalities helps to improve the overall rationality of a decision. These checks are important, especially when decisions are complex and affect many stakeholders. Internal and external advisers can help decision makers by making rationality cross-checks.

Table 7.3 gives an overview of how the rationality of main arguments can be evaluated by lower-level arguments of the same rationality (in the diagonal fields of the table, which are shaded grey) or by using a different rationality perspective (all other fields). The debates offer diverse illustrations for the six possible combinations of cross-rationality evaluation (see bullet points in Table 7.3), leading to six types of irrationality based on cross-rationality evaluation next to three internal irrationalities. Sometimes these irrationalities are already acknowledged by rationality scholars. The following sections include an occasional reference that relates to these earlier ideas.

In the following sections, each question preparing an irrationality check will be discussed per column, starting with the first column of Table 7.3. For every column, the internal irrationality check will be discussed first, as indicated by the numbers before each question. This rationality sets the standard in each column, and the stronger this rationality is, the more powerfully it works in the cross-rationality evaluation. The first column evaluates the main arguments based on standards of expressive rationality. The second column applies standards of social rationality and the third one standards of instrumental rationality.

Expressive-irrationality cross-checks: unmasking frustrating norms and upsetting effects

Internal emotional misfits

When discussing expressive-rationality cross-checks by following the first column of Table 7.3, decision makers and their advisers can assess the degree to which expressive rationality is internally contested in a decision-making debate by asking first: *is there sufficient alignment between decision makers and relevant stakeholders in how they feel about the decision and its consequences, also over time?* Preferences or desires can be conflicting over time, when the search for short-

Table 7.3 Irrationality checks on the main arguments for a decision

Check on:	Expressive-rationality (ER) check	Social-rationality (SR) check	Instrumental-rationality (IR) check
Expressive rationality	**ER/ER RATIONALITY CHECK** (emotional misfit) 1. Is there sufficient alignment between decision makers and relevant stakeholders in how they feel about the decision and its consequences, also over time? • Pro/con divide Santa Claus • Pro/con divide veil ban	**SR → ER IRRATIONALITY CHECK** (intolerable desires) 5. Are expressive-rational arguments for a decision sufficiently aligned with the social norms, values and principles shared in our society? • Initial motives veil ban • Early Santa Claus critiques	**IR → ER IRRATIONALITY CHECK** (unrealistic desires) 8. Are expressive-rational arguments for a decision, as based on subjective motives, sufficiently feasible, effective and efficient in their consequences? • Face-veil impracticalities
Social rationality	**ER → SR IRRATIONALITY CHECK** (frustrating norms) 2. Are social-rational arguments based on values or principles sufficiently aligned with what is important to decision makers and relevant to stakeholders personally? • Santa Claus revival • Veil ban stopped	**SR/SR RATIONALITY CHECK** (value conflicts) 4. Is there sufficient consistency between the values and principles shared by decision makers, relevant stakeholders and society, when applied to the decision and its consequences? • Degree conflict Gurkhas • Old/new values integration • Value conflict veil ban	**IR → SR IRRATIONALITY CHECK** (utopian ideals) 9. Are social-rational arguments for a decision, as based on shared values and principles, sufficiently feasible, effective and efficient in their consequences? • Low feasibility integration policies • Autonomy condition flex work not met

(Continued)

Table 7.3 (continued)

Check on:	Expressive-rationality (ER) check	Social-rationality (SR) check	Instrumental-rationality (IR) check
Instrumental rationality	ER →IR IRRATIONALITY CHECK (upsetting effects)	SR →IR IRRATIONALITY CHECK (immoral effects)	IR/IR RATIONALITY CHECK (means–end tensions)
	3. Are arguments suggesting means to realize ends sufficiently aligned with what decision makers and relevant stakeholders desire, or care about? • Flex work: is no one-size-fits-all solution	6. Are arguments suggesting means to realize ends sufficiently aligned with social norms, values and principles as shared in our society? • Legal critique flex work • Critique: Heathrow effects • Critique: Gurkha 'costs'	7. Is there sufficient consistency between the higher-level ends related to the decision, its lower-level ends and their means? Are there unintended effects? • Unintended consequences Heathrow • Productivity and health issues flex work

term benefits leads to long-term regrets (Boyd and Richerson 2001: 282; Elster 2009: 40–5). Likings can also be in conflict between stakeholders. Other forms of emotional misfit are self-deception (Davidson 2004), lack of authenticity (Habermas 1988) or feelings disconnected to a certain event like moods. They are irrational compared to immediate or anticipated feelings (Li *et al.* 2014; Scherer 2011). They can create internal expressive irrationalities. The more ambiguous and different the subjective motives and interests of stakeholders, the less clear it is what side will dominate in evaluating social- and instrumental-rational arguments.

In two debates, expressive rationality dominates due to the debated question. The Santa Claus debate shows growing expressive-rationality consensus towards the end. However, at the start of the debate, proponents and opponents are fighting each other on expressive-rational grounds, thus creating internal rationality tensions. Some people like the sculpture, while many hate it. Only towards the end does an expressive-rational consensus develop into a supportive counterforce, strong enough to neutralize social-rational criticisms. Likewise, expressive rationality is divided in the veil-ban debate. The intended ban opens the debate based on a social-rational logic, so first the perspective needs to change towards expressive rationality as the dominant perspective. The face veil does not meet much sympathy in the UK and other Western countries, so expressive rationality is divided on the niqab: some Muslims want to wear it, but many liberal Muslims and Western people dislike it. When looking at the first question in Table 7.3, the answer is initially negative in the discussed examples, making it difficult to decide based on expressive-rational motives in these instances. When alignment gets stronger over time, as in the Santa Claus debate, expressive rationality increases and provides the kind of reasons to act on that convince more and more people.

Expressive evaluation of social rationality

When expressive rationality is strong, it is able to evaluate social-rational views as irrational. Norms, bans, principles, ideals or values can be fundamentally at odds with what many people like or prefer. Sometimes, norms and principles are wrong, or applied wrongly. To prepare for the expressive-rational evaluation of social-rational arguments, decision makers and their advisers could ask the second question: *are social-rational arguments based on values or principles sufficiently aligned with what is important to decision makers and relevant to stakeholders personally?* Social-rational arguments suggest that Santa Claus is obscene in its expression due to the suggestion of a butt plug, and, therefore, the sculpture is not suited for children's eyes, so the public exposure of Santa Claus cannot be accepted. Towards the end of the debate, the argument is countered by the accounts of more and more people that like the sculpture, and who do not see the problem for children at all. Support comes from many sides: from visitors of the museum, including families, that come to see Santa Claus, but also from shopkeepers who want Santa Claus close and who paint his footsteps from the museum to their shopping street, imagining Santa Claus walks out of the museum court. Political parties and decision makers get more positive again, due to the progressive shift after the elections in

2006, while opponents reduce their resistance. Obscenity appears in the eyes of some beholders, while children do not recognize the intended reference to a butt plug, which is not part of the toys they play with. And there is also some resemblance with a Christmas tree. Therefore, applying the norm to not expose this form of obscene art in public is judged irrational here on expressive grounds, and quite frustrating for those who appreciate the sculpture. A similar frustration is visible in the veil-ban debate, as a ban is quite frustrating for those who want to wear their niqab. Towards the end of the debate, banning the niqab is seen as an irrational measure on expressive-rational grounds. The dislike of a face veil is fine, but it does not feel like a sufficient ground for a general ban when some do like it, without really hurting anybody, except for themselves maybe. The same expressive-rational force is visible in the Gurkha debate, suggesting the irrationality of a partial rights extension due to the feeling that it is unfair, and changing the intended policy towards a full rights extension. Expressive-rational resistance shows an inductive, democratic pattern here, by mobilizing enough voices to counter and invalidate the suggested pension and settlement rights by motivational counterarguments, thus revealing a misalignment that can be assessed by answering the second question of Table 7.3. Similar forms of expressive-rational resistance regarding social norms have appeared when fighting for the rights of homosexuals, for allowing premarital sex or against gender inequality. What we like or dislike is, when we share it, an important ground for what we tolerate as a society. As a consequence, old fashioned or outdated norms or laws can be challenged in this way, as they no longer align with how we feel.

Expressive evaluation of instrumental rationality

Expressive rationality is also able to correct instrumental logics. We can dislike effects, or the means to realize them, in spite of the validity of their instrumental logic. To check for such tensions, decision makers and their advisers can ask question three from Table 7.3: *are arguments suggesting means to realize ends sufficiently aligned with what decision makers and relevant stakeholders desire, or care about?* For many stakeholders, this appears not to be the case in the flex-work debate. Consultants have introduced flex work as a solution to problems like greenhouse gases, traffic, office costs, employee motivation, labour market issues and productivity. For many employees in professional service industries, the concept is attractive, which explains its early successes. However, not all promises work out well, as the flex-work solution does not fit all workers, all sectors and all companies. Based on expressive-rational logics, flex work is criticized for being applied as a one-size-fits-all solution. Still, it does not fit workers that cannot self-manage their workload, as too many become overworked, and it does not fit workers that get easily distracted. It also does not fit companies that need people to meet frequently to foster innovation and creativity. For these workers their jobs become less fun, less inspirational, less rewarding and more frustrating and upsetting. Such expressive irrationalities temper enthusiasm for flex-work arrangements, and they call for adjustments. Again, expressive-rational resistance is built up inductively and bottom-up in the flex-work debate, by proving that the general instrumental logic does not apply in too many cases. Flex work can be fun and efficient for some, or for one day a week. As a general model, it upsets and disturbs too many workers, which creates a motivational argument against flex work. Similar examples of resisting instrumental logics due to their unpleasant side effects are visible in the slow food movement when people became upset and disappointed by tasteless mass-produced fast food. Such forms of misalignment between expressive rationality and instrumental logics indicate a negative answer towards question three in Table 7.3. The negative evaluation indicates the need to search for different means or better policies to realize intended effects, in order to increase alignment.

The force of expressive-rational arguments in public debates depends partly on how many people want to oppose effects that result from instrumental-rational decisions due to their inconvenient, frustrating or upsetting nature, as illustrated for flex work. This force also depends on how strong the frustration is. When more people express a stronger dislike for norms, rules and legislation, or used means and realized effects, their combined motivational arguments have more force to stop or change these norms or effects bottom-up. Expressive rationality has great impact on social rationality in the Santa Claus and veil-ban debates, and on instrumental rationality in the flex-work debate. It creates an inductive argument that gains power by the numbers of those who feel upset or frustrated. It is this shared expressive rationality that can initiate the creation of new rules, new norms and new values, thus having an effect on social rationality. It is by this inductive argument that people discarded the obscenity judgment in the Santa Claus case. It is how others learned to appreciate Santa Claus. Together, people can make the power of expressive-rational opposition strong enough to change everything, and to start revolutions, as in the Gurkha debate.

Social-rationality cross-checks: against offensive wishes and immoral effects

Internal value conflicts

When discussing social-rationality cross-checks by following the middle column of Table 7.3, decision makers and their advisers first assess to what degree social rationality is internally divided regarding the decision they prepare. To identify the strength of the social-rational perspective they could ask question four, presented in the centre field of Table 7.3: *is there sufficient consistency between the values and principles shared by decision makers, relevant stakeholders and society, when applied to the decision and its consequences?* Value conflicts can lead to internal social irrationalities, grounded in tensions between community interests, in tensions between being honest and being kind, or when balancing tolerance for other cultures is in conflict with commitment to one's own values (MacIntyre 1988; Majone 1992; Sandel 2010). However, the more ambiguous and contested the shared norms, values and principles are, the less clear whose values will dominate in evaluating expressive- and instrumental-rational arguments, or what values are considered applicable to a situation.

In two of the studied debates, social rationality dominates due to the debated question. In the Gurkha debate, consensus about social values appears rather strong. All stakeholders are convinced that a rights extension is fair. The issue is the degree to which the rights can be extended. Here public opinion and government ideas initially diverge. But they reach full consensus during the debate. Values in the Dutch integration debate are more divided, where previous multicultural policies stress tolerance as a core value, while new integration policies advocate a more demanding and restrictive approach. This also becomes a debate about degree: how tolerant or how demanding should the new integration policy be? And how much room should there be for value systems accepted in the immigrant cultures, but in conflict with Western values supporting gender equality, freedom of expression or tolerance of homosexuality? Some traditions of especially Muslim immigrants are considered quite problematic, like honour killings or female circumcision, which sometimes happens over holidays during a visit to a home country. Western standards are more energetically set as the norm, and multiculturalist policies get criticized for having to be tolerant towards migrant views that actually need to be challenged. The third debate with a social-rational start is the veil-ban debate, which concludes as an expressive-rational one. Given that it is about a personal question on clothing, that start is contested. The idea of a veil ban is challenged due to a conflict with the principle of freedom of expression, which is considered better applicable. It is a strong supporter of expressive-rational autonomy in decision-making on personal questions. In the veil-ban debate, we thus find a weak basis for the social-rational evaluation of other rationalities due to internal tensions. In the Dutch integration debate, this basis is stronger, and the Gurkha debate shows the strongest value alignment, which enables a positive answer to question four in Table 7.3. As a consequence, evaluation based on social rationality is well supported in the Gurkha debate and can overrule instrumental-rational objections, whereas social-rational evaluations in the veil-ban and Santa Claus debates are not strong enough to overrule expressive-rational arguments.

Social evaluation of expressive rationality

When decision makers and their advisers want to evaluate the social rationality of their expressive-rational arguments supporting a decision, they can ask the fifth question in Table 7.3: *are expressive-rational arguments for a decision sufficiently aligned with the social norms, values, and principles shared in our society?* Answering this question can help to find out if some preferences may be illegitimate or socially unacceptable, like a preference to use hard drugs, a wish to hunt protected animals or smoking in a car while having children in it. Social rationality requires impartiality (Elster 2009: 13); thus, no dominance of self-interests at the cost of others. The veil-ban debate in the UK and the Dutch Santa Claus controversy both discuss banning a somewhat offensive or extreme form of human expression. The niqab is seen as undermining integration. It makes open communication more difficult and it implies a strong statement against the equality of men and women. However, later, a veil ban is seen as an inappropriate way to tell Muslims they have to treat their women differently. To complicate matters even more, some Muslim women defend the choice to wear a face veil as their own, and they claim their right of freedom of religious expression. This expressive argument resonates with a key value in Western societies. The value conflict between gender equality and freedom of expression makes it difficult to frame the niqab only as irrational on social grounds. Values point in two directions. Still, some countries have a veil ban, and there are other examples where social rationality can overrule subjective desires by using deductive logics. For instance, it has become an accepted rule not to smoke in offices, cafes and restaurants, in spite of the likings of smokers. A general principle or value is applied to such desires or wishes, which are then classified as illegitimate or unacceptable. Situations abound where we can appreciate the guidance by socially accepted norms, to prevent that we, or others, suffer from our somewhat irrational wishes and impulses, judged from a social perspective. If there is such misalignment between social principles and personal wishes, the answer to question five has to be negative. When social rationality is strong enough to set the standards for evaluation, we are inclined to adapt our behaviour and make it more rational from a social perspective, in spite of our private desires.

Social evaluation of instrumental rationality

When decision makers and their advisers want to evaluate instrumental-rational arguments supporting a decision by using a social-rationality perspective, they can ask question six from Table 7.3: *are arguments suggesting means to realize ends sufficiently aligned with social norms, values and principles as shared in our society?* If not, effects or used means can be considered illegal, immoral or socially unacceptable. Both debates dominated by instrumental-rational argumentation illustrate critical social-rational evaluations. In the Heathrow debate, the environmental effects of extension are severely criticized on social-rational grounds by many stakeholder groups. The narrow economic focus on traveller demands and capacity problems is forced into a stronger green growth objective, to mitigate the negative environmental effects. They would have been irrational against green standards. Flex work also has irrational consequences from a social perspective. Flex workers need to be protected against themselves, as some cannot stop working, get too stressed and suffer from burnout more often than normal office workers. This leads to a call for improving labour regulations and collective labour agreements. Simultaneously, several other measures on the company level are tried to handle these health problems, like server shutdown in the evenings to stop emails. Higher stress and burnout levels are unintended effects that need to be avoided from a social-rational perspective. The impact of social rationality in the Gurkha debate is quite forceful, with its high degree of value alignment across all stakeholders. Equal rights for Gurkha veterans is the result, despite the financial consequences. These costs are framed as insignificant in light of the values that are at stake. Stressing that costs are too high is considered irrational and immoral from a social-rational perspective, when considering the courageous role Gurkhas have played in the British army. Stakeholders consider the partial rights extension half-hearted and they call it betrayal. The modest financial consequences are put under a general moral rule or principle thus applying a deductive argument. In general, social policies and laws can protect us from the instrumental logics that dominate our economy today: environmental regulations, labour regulations, market regulations, safety regulations, privacy laws, etc. They all try to prevent the unintended and immoral effects of instrumental-rational logics by both marking them and judging them irrational against standards of social rationality. Here, question six in Table 7.3 has to be answered negatively. As a consequence, we should better align realized effects or used means with our social norms and values.

The impact of social-rational evaluations depends on the motivational force of values and principles, and on how convincingly they can be applied to a specific context. The type of argumentation is deductive by forcing particulars like unintended effects or unacceptable wishes under a rule or principle that renders them irrational or unjustified. When values are strong and well applicable, this confrontation usually works well, as in the Gurkha case. However, when expressive-rational arguments are evaluated from a social-rational perspective, they can push back inductively based on motivational grounds. This is best illustrated in the Santa Claus debate, where the social-rational principle not to expose obscene art in public is objected, and framed as irrational by expressive arguments based on sympathy for the sculpture. The evaluation process can, thus, work both ways. In the disputes with expressive-rational opposition, social rationality loses when expressive-rational arguments are strongly motivational and widely shared by substantial groups of people, thus making the social principles more contested. The push-back possibilities of instrumental-rational arguments appeared as weaker in the discussed cases, especially in the Gurkha case. Still, not everything is feasible, and instrumental rationality can push back as well, and provide its own evaluations of the other rationalities.

Instrumental-rationality cross-checks: avoid impractical wishes and utopian ideals

Internal means–end inconsistencies

When discussing instrumental-rationality cross-checks from the right-hand column of Table 7.3, decision makers and their advisers first assess the degree to which instrumental-rational arguments are contested from within. Question seven at the bottom of the column helps with this evaluation: *is there sufficient consistency between the higher-level ends related to the decision, its lower-level ends and their means?* Internal instrumental irrationality is visible in unintended consequences caused by means–end inconsistencies. Such inconsistencies can result from our boundedness by considering a too-narrow perspective, from wishful thinking or from overconfidence (Davidson 2004: 179; Kahneman 2011: 85–8; Tinbergen 1956: 1).

In two debates, instrumental rationality is the central perspective: Heathrow's extension and flex-work implementation. Initially, there are few means–end inconsistencies in the flex-work debate, but when experiences increase, the concept becomes contested due to many unintended and unforeseen effects. Upon its introduction, flex-work consultants make attractive promises, like higher labour productivity due to lower sick leave, but after a while it appears only short-term sick leave decreases, while long-term sick leave starts to increase. Other unintended consequences are less knowledge sharing, lower innovation speed and lower quality of work. Increasingly, the question is asked whether the benefits still outweigh these unexpected drawbacks. It makes the initial optimism rather irrational on instrumental grounds. In the Heathrow debate, similar instrumental inconsistencies are debated. Extending the airport has negative environmental effects, but so does *not* extending, due to increasing inefficiencies. Alternative policies are suggested to better reach the same objective of more transport capacity. Only focusing on Heathrow's extension as a means to reach that end is seen as less rational on instrumental grounds. Such inconsistencies weaken instrumental rationality, and suggest for such cases a negative answer to question seven in Table 7.3. As a consequence, cross-rationality evaluations based on standards of instrumental rationality also lose force if the underlying internal instrumental logics get weaker.

Instrumental evaluation of expressive rationality

When instrumental rationality is used to evaluate expressive rationality, decision makers and their advisers can try to answer the eighth question in Table 7.3: *are expressive-rational arguments for a decision, as based on subjective motives, sufficiently feasible, effective and efficient in their consequences?* The question helps to find out if some preferences or wishes are impractical, unfeasible or very difficult to realize, like wishes such as to become rich, strong or beautiful might be. The niqab, as a subject of one of the expressive debates for instance, is criticized as impractical and at odds with common sense. It makes communication less open and effective, and establishing good relationships in a Western society becomes less feasible. This form of religious expression is irrational from an instrumental perspective, as there are many alternative ways to express Muslim identity. However, the criticism is partly rebutted on instrumental grounds, as we can communicate by phone as well, so the problem of not seeing each other is argued to be less absolute than suggested. Instrumental evaluation of Santa Claus results in criticism that the statue is too costly and thus requires too many financial means. However, that argument had little impact on those willing to spend the money. Still, in general, costs do matter when we want to realize our wishes. We do not want to pay everything to realize them. Based on cause–effect arguments we can map the consequences of our wishes, and it can happen that we do not wish to accept these consequences. Current debates showing instrumental evaluations of our desires and wishes are, for instance, the fast food debate, criticizing the effects on obese children and adults. Their strong wish is to eat such unhealthy food, but it has severe practical consequences for people themselves, and for society. Following up on such desires is irrational from an instrumental perspective. Also, the wish to break up a marriage out of expressive-rational motives can have irrational consequences from an instrumental point of view, as life gets more expensive and it becomes more difficult to see your children. The misalignment between such personal wishes and their practical consequences indicates a negative answer to question eight in Table 7.3. The reconsideration of such wishes due to their irrationality is advisable in such cases.

Instrumental evaluation of social rationality

Social rationality supporting a decision can also be cross-checked for irrationalities against standards of instrumental rationality. Decision makers and their advisers can do so by asking question nine in Table 7.3: *are social-rational arguments for a decision, as based on values and principles, sufficiently feasible, effective and efficient in their consequences?* Our principles can be noble or idealistic, but, as with our wishes, they often come at a price. This can make them utopian, unrealistic or less effective. Hence, the social rationality of multicultural policies in the Dutch integration debate is evaluated as utopian on instrumental grounds. Multicultural policies have achieved some economic integration, but mainly due to the immigrants themselves and not the policies, which are increasingly disqualified as unrealistic in achieving cultural integration. All over Europe, multicultural approaches are considered a failure, in spite of their idealistic and quite positive underlying social values of tolerance and respect. Still, these policies hardly serve the purpose of helping immigrants to integrate, as multiculturalism has encouraged them to stick to their own culture, habits and circles. The criticism is forceful, and changes integration policies into more demanding ones. Similar criticisms do apply to the somewhat utopian flex-work ideals that assume autonomous workers are ready to use their freedom. Flex work appeals to many professionals, but not all workers can handle this autonomy, making the model infeasible for the more average worker. In such cases, question nine in Table 7.3 has to be answered negatively. This, instrumental-rational critique helps to uncover the less effective or feasible aspects of these social ideals.

The argumentation to address these irrationalities, evaluated against standards of instrumental rationality, is cause-based – by identifying causes for failure in realizing social values. Debates criticizing feasibility abound in Europe. Many countries feel that asylum seekers from Syria need a safe place, as long as the Islamic State (IS) rules over large parts of Syria, but when millions come to Europe there is a feasibility issue. Sometimes we have to tone down our ideals; for example, we sometimes need to be more modest in our personal wishes. At other times we need to be more courageous and willing to sacrifice, as argued in the Gurkha case. And over time, some constraints can become more flexible due to learning or innovation, but they rarely do in the short run.

Balancing rationalities

Of the three rationalities, instrumental rationality seems to be the most dependent one, as the goals, values and problem definitions always start with expressive- and social-rational considerations. However, its critical force towards these two other rationalities still remains quite strong when assessing the realism, practicability and feasibility of our intended actions by using means–end argumentation. The underlying causalities can produce strong arguments to reconsider idealism or personal ambitions as utopian or impractical. Beautiful values and acknowledged interests sometimes lose their shine when costs are considered, or the other necessary means to realize them. Discussions about the consequences of implementation are most detailed and complex in the integration, the Heathrow and the flex-work debates, which are also the debates in which consultants are the most involved. When implementation is less complex, decision makers are almost ready to go, the moment they know what they want to do.

All in all, the cross-rationality evaluations help to keep the right balance between the rationalities. They all have their means to criticize each other, and there is criticism possible from within, pointing at internal tensions. These criticisms help to keep the balance, or to counter imbalance. Imbalance means important rationality aspects are ignored, so stakeholder opposition can be expected or technical implementation will fail. The cases all indicate that in real-life decision-making, the three rationalities need each other as a cure against the irrationalities of their one-sidedness.

References

Argyris, C. (1996) Actionable knowledge: Design causality in the service of consequential theory. *The Journal of Applied Behavioral Science*, 32(4), 390–406.

Boltanski, L. and Thevenot, L. (2006) *On Justification: Economies of Worth*. Princeton, NJ: Princeton University Press.

Bouwmeester, O. (2013) Field dependency of argumentation rationality in decision-making debates. *Journal of Management Inquiry*, 22(4), 415–33.

Boyd, R. and Richerson, P. J. (2001) Norms and bounded rationality, in Gigerenzer, G. and Selten, R. (eds), *Bounded Rationality: The Adaptive Toolbox*. Cambridge, MA: MIT Press, pp. 281–96.

Davidson, D. (2004) *Problems of Rationality*. Vol. 4. Oxford: Oxford University Press.

Diesing, P. (1976) *Reason in Society: Five Types of Decisions and Their Social Conditions*. Westport, CT: Greenwood Press.

Elbanna, S. (2006) Strategic decision-making: Process perspectives. *International Journal of Management Reviews*, 8(1), 1–20.

Elbanna, S. and Child, J. (2007) Influences on strategic decision effectiveness: Development and test of an integrative model. *Strategic Management Journal*, 28(4), 431–53.

Elster, J. (2009) *Reason and Rationality*. Princeton, NJ: Princeton University Press.

Engelen, B. (2006) Solving the paradox: The expressive rationality of the decision to vote. *Rationality and Society*, 18(4), 419–41.

Gigerenzer, G. (2008) *Rationality for Mortals: How People Cope with Uncertainty*. Oxford: Oxford University Press.

Gigerenzer, G. and Selten, R. (eds) (2001) *Bounded Rationality: The Adaptive Toolbox*. Cambridge, MA: MIT Press.

Gigerenzer, G. and Sturm, T. (2012) How (far) can rationality be naturalized? *Synthese*, 187(1), 243–68.

Green Jr, S. E. (2004) A rhetorical theory of diffusion. *The Academy of Management Review*, 29(4), 653–69.

Habermas, J. (1988) *Theorie des Kommunikativen Handelns, Band 1, 2*. Frankfurt: Suhrkamp.

Henderson, D. (2010) Explanation and rationality naturalized. *Philosophy of the Social Sciences*, 40(1), 30–58.

Kahneman, D. (2011) *Thinking, Fast and Slow*. New York: FSG.

Li, Y., Ashkanasy, N. M. and Ahlstrom, D. (2014) The rationality of emotions: A hybrid process model of decision-making under uncertainty. *Asia Pacific Journal of Management*, 31(1), 293–308.

MacIntyre, A. C. (1988) *Whose Justice? Which Rationality?* London: Duckworth.

Majone, G. (1992) *Evidence, Argument and Persuasion in the Policy Process*. New Haven, CT: Yale University Press.

March, J. G. and Simon, H. A. (1958) *Organizations*. New York: John Wiley.

Mason, R. O. (1969) A dialectical approach to strategic planning. *Management Science*, 15(8), B403–14.

Minto, B. (1995) *The Pyramid Principle: Logic in Writing and Thinking*. London: Pitman Publishing.

Minto, B. (1998) Think your way to clear writing. *Journal of Management Consulting*, 10(1), 33–40.

Sandel, M. J. (2010) *Justice: What's the Right Thing to Do?* New York: FSG.

Saxton, T. (1995) The impact of third parties on strategic decision making: Roles, timing and organizational outcomes. *Journal of Organizational Change Management*, 8(3), 47–62.

Scherer, K. R. (2011) On the rationality of emotions: Or, when are emotions rational? *Social Science Information*, 50(3–4), 330–50.

Tinbergen, J. (1956) *Economic Policy: Principles and Design*. Amsterdam: Noord Hollandsche Uitgeversmaatschappij.

Toulmin, S. E. (1994) *The Uses of Argument*. Cambridge: Cambridge University Press.

Weber, M. (1972) *Wirtschaft und Gesellschaft: Grundriss der Verstehenden Soziologie*. 5th ed. Tubingen, Germany: JCB Mohr (Paul Siebeck).

Werder, A. von (1999) Argumentation rationality of management decisions. *Organization Science*, 10(5), 672–90.

Index

Locators in **bold** refer to tables and those in *italics* refer to figures.

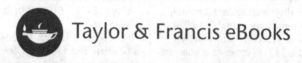